SO-AHF-685

16⁵⁰

Child Custody

CHILD CUSTODY

James C. Black
Donald J. Cantor

Columbia University Press
New York

Columbia University Press
New York • Oxford

Copyright © 1989 by James C. Black and Donald J. Cantor

All rights reserved
Printed in the United States of America

Library of Congress Cataloging-in-Publication Data

Black, James C.
Child custody / James C. Black and Donald J. Cantor.
p. cm.
Includes index.
ISBN 0-231-06248-6
1. Custody of children—United States. 2. Divorce suits—United
States. 3. Forensic psychiatry—United States. I. Cantor, Donald
J., 1931– . II. Title.
KF547.B59 1989
346.7301′7—dc20   89-33748
[347.30617]   CIP

Casebound editions of Columbia University Press books are
Smyth-sewn and printed on permanent and durable acid-free paper

∞

10 9 8 7 6 5 4 3 2 1

Book design by Ken Venezio

This book is dedicated to Laura and Coke Black and Lillian and Albert Cantor whose continuous and loving parenting spared us the pain and dislocation visited so often upon children of divorce for the future benefit of whom this book was conceived.

Contents

Two/Clinical Applications   77

FOREWORD

As sociologists in hindsight, one of the perhaps most remarkable societal phenomena of the last half of the twentieth century is the in-
credible rate at which we have dissolved our marriages. Nationally,
we are furnished with statistics as to the failure of 1 marriage in 3,
or 1 marriage in 4 depending upon the decade you are considering,
while regionally there are areas where the dissolution rate has approached 100%, i.e. for each marriage license issued during a given
period in a given region, an equal number of dissolutions are re-
corded. Numerically, in Connecticut (an area with which I am familiar), this has translated into 15,000 to 16,000 dissolutions of marriage per year for the last decade.

One of the least understood byproducts of this wholesale family
fracturing has been its effect upon the children of these shattered
relationships. While we in the judicial community in addressing issues of custody have conscientiously sought after the holy grail of
"the best interests of the child," the social and psychological implications of our efforts are just now beginning to emerge as social, legal
and scientific attention begins to truly focus on children, children's
rights and children as people.

This work, the collaboration of two scholars from different disciplines, one in law and the other in medicine, represents a comprehensive and insightful examination into this difficult and often tragically misunderstood subject. Hopefully, it will serve others in illuminating this intricate field of study.

Alfred V. Covello
Justice, Supreme Court
Presiding Judge, Family Relations Div.
Hartford Judicial District 1984–1987

Preface

There has been a fundamental change in the past twenty years in the American law of divorce and child custody. Most custody determinations are poorly made. This is not a new phenomenon. If anything, decisions are most sophisticated now than they once were. Today's custodial dispositions need not be part of the price one spouse has to pay to become unmarried. Divorce now is almost a right. The harshness of earlier divorce law, particulary for the spouse who committed moral offenses against the marriage, like adultery, might once have resulted in that parent's disqualification for the custody of chilren. Social change in relation to the maternal presumption and the tender years doctrine, while hardly dead, is giving fathers nearly equal legal consideration as child custodians. But the fact that the laws are better does not, and should not, hide the knowledge they are still flawed.

True sophistication is still missing from custody decisions. Too often merely satisfactory arrangements are decreed when better ones might have been available. Alternatives are not fully explored or understood by those who make custody decisions.

Arrangements for a child's custody can be a straggeringly complex task. Some investigators make custody decisions badly, too many others fall back on convenient presumptions to avoid making decisions at all. The legal standard for child custody—the best interests of the child—gives no guidance or definition.

In this book we provide a set of guidelines for use by custody evaluators that can be of assistance especially in cases where either claimant is clearly inadequate. These guidelines help to identify the aspiring custodian whose personality structure is more likely to promote the healthy development of the child. We do *not* presume to provide the answer to each future custody situation. We are too aware of the complications involved, of the fallibility of any evaluator, of the elusiveness of good parenting traits. But we point to the right direction.

This book begins with a history of the law of custody, necessary to highlighting the errors of the past. The divorce context must be understood, for custody cases seldom exist in a vacuum. We consider joint custody worthy of special attention. It has become fashionable and is thus in great danger of being misunderstood and inappropriately applied. The chapter on subsidiary custodial issues gives readers a familiarity with the process of custodial placement.

The overall survey of the many issues raised by child custody is not exhaustive in this book, but those who wish more detail are referred to sources cited throughout.

The problem of child custody, though arising in a legal context, looks to psychology for help and instruction. Thus the two disciplines of law and child psychiatry are combined here. To theory we have added our experiences in actually formulating our views and recommendations. All of these recommendations are made by us jointly, some reached easily, some after extensive debate and reflection.

Acknowledgement

The authors wish to acknowledge their gratitude for the special and important contributions of Rachel Cantor and Timothy Black and to acknowledge also with gratitude the assistance provided them by Paul N. Graffagnino, M.D., Alan Gurwitt, M.D., Kenneth S. Robson, M.D., The Honorable Francis X. Hennessy, Eva Klinger, Attorney Judith Leahy, and Laurye Stohr.

ONE

LEGAL ASPECTS

1
Perspective

He sat in his chambers, the trial in recess, feeling the need to be as wise as he thought his judicial robes made him. The talk turned to custody of children. "I never give custody to men," he said. Having thus synthesized his philosophy on that subject he spoke of others until the recess ended.[1]

On another occasion another judge talked of custody. "You don't milk bulls," he offered, "and matadors don't fight cows." Translated this meant that women raise children and men work. That was, to him, the natural way of things.[2]

In the late 1960s a Connecticut divorce occurred in which a judge took a week before his conscience would allow him to grant custody of two minors to the father where the mother was proved to have consistently left the children unattended; where she was at least a part-time prostitute; where the father was a devoted, attentive parent; where the mother had deserted the family months before; and where the mother had not even appeared to contest custody.[3]

These anecdotes are not offered to prove that judges think imperfectly whether or not the subject is custody. Judicial incompetence is not so extraordinary as to justify a cry of "Eureka" when one discovers it. What is noteworthy is that these three judges were not anomalies; they were rather representatives of a body of thought only recently subject to attack, still dominant, a body of thought that holds that for various reasons mothers are naturally better parents than fathers and that therefore mothers should generally obtain sole or primary custody of children of divorce unless unusual facts exist.

But it was not always so. At common law the father was the natural guardian of children, the one presumptively entitled to their custody. Though that right was presumptive, not absolute, the presumption was a strong one.

> . . . he (the father) is the person entitled by law to the custody of his child. If he abuses that right to the detriment of the child, the Court will protect the child. But there is no pretence that the child has been injured for want of nurture, or in any other respect. Then he having a legal right to the custody of his child, and not having abused that right, is entitled to have it restored to him.[4]

This presumption was not defeated nor threatened in the above case by the child in question being "an infant (8 months) at the breast of his mother."[5]

The presumption was one that only some form of abuse could overcome. According to some English authorities, moreover, the abuse had to be of large degree:

> With respect to the children I do not feel at liberty to take them out of the custody of the father. He is the natural guardian, invested by God and the law of the country with reasonable power over them. Unless, therefore, his parental power has been *cruelly* (emphasis added) abused, this Court would be very cautious of interfering with the exercise of it."[6]

> There is, in the first place, no doubt that, when a father has the custody of his children, he is not to be deprived of it except under particular circumstances; . . . The only question then is, what is to be considered the proper custody; and that undoubtedly is the custody of the father. The Court has, it is true, intimated that the right of the father would not be acted upon where the enforcement of it would be attended with danger to the child; as where there was an apprehension of cruelty, or of contamination by some exhibition of gross profligacy.[7]

In the latter case the father's custodial right was upheld despite his open and admitted "illicit connection" with a certain Mrs. Graham, the Court finding that Mrs. Graham would not keep the house the children were to live in. No specific conclusion was articulated by the Court indicating whether or not Mrs. Graham's illicit relationship with father would have constituted "gross profligacy" had it been father's intent to house Mrs. Graham and his children at the same address.

The common law was not, however, the only body of precepts in England that affected the custody of children. There were ecclesiastical or bishop's courts, which were never, of course, adopted here. These courts administered canon law and granted divorces *a mensa et thoro* (from bed and board, or legal separations) and thus often passed on custodial issues. Also, and more importantly, the principles of equity grew alongside the common law, some would say to ameliorate and improve it, others would say merely to supplement it,[8] but nonetheless with the power to alter its rigidity considerably. The intrusion of these principles of equity derived from "the Crown's prerogative as *parens patriae* (father of his country—in the sense of the sovereign power of guardianship over disabled persons such as minors and incompetents) to protect those of the Crown's subjects who were unable to protect themselves."[9]

This power to act on behalf of the defenseless was vested in the Court of Chancery, that Court being deemed to have delegated to it by the Crown the Crown's *parens patriae* responsibilities. Pursuant to this authority the Lord Chancellor (Eldon) did remove a child from its father where "the father was a person in constant habits of drunkenness and blasphemy poisoning the mind of the infant."[10]

Perhaps the most famous child custody case that arose in England was that involving the great poet Percy Bysshe Shelley.[11] Shelley had deserted his wife and children and, upon the death of his wife, sought to collect his children from their mother's family and raise them. The Lord Chancellor denied this request and issued an order restraining him from taking possession of the children. He so ordered not only because had Shelley written a work "in which he blasphemously derided the truth of the Christian revelation and denied the existence of a God as creator of the universe"[12] but also because he felt it clear that Shelley would so educate the children in question. Only because his life had been found to be *so* immoral and his beliefs such a great threat to the proper education of his children was Shelley denied their custody, but of major importance was the residual fact that a father *was* denied because he was found unfit.

The Courts also denied custody to fathers:

1. Where a twenty-one-month old infant was being nurtured by the mother.[13]
2. Where the father previously and voluntarily had relinquished custody to the mother.[14]

Moreover, there were also situations where the Court would not affirm the father's custodial right even if no unfitness in regard to his custodial capacity was proved. These occurred when the child in question was not of "helpless age."

> When an infant is brought before the Court by the habeas corpus, if he be of an age to exercise a choice, the Court leaves him to elect where he will go.[15]

Thus the English law that the United States inherited was not unitary. It had in it two strains of thought that were at core harmonious—both the common law and equity favored the father as custodian—but that in practice were often at odds. Equity was less impressed with the father's natural right to custody and was prepared to take it away or leave the choice to the child where these alternatives were deemed appropriate.

In terms of effect on American law the father presumption was to have a relatively limited life and, in the history of custody law, is to be seen as one extreme position of the pendulum. Of more lasting consequence was the Chancery principle of the child's choice, which is still today the ruling principle in custody cases where children are in their teens, often even younger, and where they articulate a firm parental preference.

Of all of the states that comprised the American Union by 1825, only Alabama, Illinois, Louisiana, Massachusetts, Mississippi, New Jersey, New York, and Ohio had statutes that specifically conferred upon the courts the power to enter orders respecting custody in the event of divorce.[16] The statutory language conferring this power was characteristically broad, typically allowing the court to "make such further order and decree, as to them may appear expedient, concerning the care, custody and support of such minor children, or any or either of them, and to determine, with which of the parents the said children, or any or either of them, shall remain."[17]

Atypical of the statutes existent in 1827 were those of Louisiana and New York. The Louisiana statute, derived not from the English but the French experience, provided as follows:

LAW 3

Whether the children ought to be in the care of the father or mother, in order that they may be nourished and reared up.

The mother ought to nourish and rear her children who are under three years of age, and the father, those who are above that age. But if the mother be so poor that she cannot take care of them, then the father is bound to furnish her, with whatever is necessary for that purpose. And if the spouses happen to separate for any just cause, the party through whose fault the separation took place, will be bound to furnish, out of his own estate, if he be rich, whatever is necessary to rear the children, whether they be above or below three years of age: and the other who is not in fault, ought to take them under his or her care, and maintain them. But if the other should have them under care for the reasons above mentioned, and she get married again, then she ought not to retain them: nor will the father be obliged to furnish her, with anything for their support; but ought on the contrary, to take them under his care, and rear and nourish them, if he have wherewith to do it.[18]

The New York statute empowered the court to make custody orders only in suits brought by a married woman for divorce or separation. Curiously, though only a wife could trigger the process, nothing in the statutory language favored her as the custodial parent.[19]

Because of the general language employed by most of the custody statutes in force by the end of the first quarter of the nineteenth century and because roughly half the states by that time had no statutes governing custody at all, it is to the case law of the period that one must refer to gauge what the attitudes were toward custody of children in divorce cases.

The Supreme Court of Pennsylvania in 1813 enunciated clearly the "tender age" doctrine, which was explicitly ordained by statute in Louisiana, though not decreeing as did Louisiana that "tender age" stopped at three. Deciding that two children (female) aged ten and six should stay with the mother who had without dispute treated them well, the Court stated:

> . . . it appears to us, that considering their tender age, they stand in need of that kind of assistance, which can be afforded by none so well as a mother.[20]

By 1816, however, when the father brought this matter again to Court, and the children were thirteen and nine, the Court returned them to the father's custody, determining that the adultress mother was no longer to be entrusted with the rearing and moral education of the children. Though the Court did not define the end of the "tender age" period, it was clear that thirteen was beyond it, and though the second child of nine must have been within this period since the older child was ten when the first case was heard, nonetheless the Court averred that "the sisters should not be separated" and thus found the older sister's need for correct moral guidance more compelling than the younger child's need for "tender age" mothering.[21] These Addicks cases do not so much stand for the presumption of paternal preference that existed at common law as for a maternal preference during the undefined "tender age," for a preference against the parent who has been guilty of moral wrongdoing (here adultery) even where all the evidence indicated a high quality of mothering, and a strong feeling that children should not be separated.

In 1819 the Supreme Court of Ilinois reaffirmed in principle the legal right of the father to the custody of his children, "unless he has forfeited, waived or lost it, either by misconduct, misfortune, or some peculiar circumstances, sufficient in the opinion of an enlightened chancellor to deprive him of it."[22] The Court in dicta blessed the "tender age" or "tender years" doctrine, saying "an infant of tender years is generally left with the mother, (if no objection to her is shown to exist) even when the father is without blame, merely because of his inability to bestow upon it that tender care which nature requires and which it is the peculiar province of a mother to supply."[23]

The Court went on to express its major sentiment relative to the custodial rights of fathers, saying:

> In no case do I find this legal right of the father asserted, where a divorce has been granted for his fault or misconduct. If such right ever did exist, so as to abridge or control the exercise of the equitable dis-

cretion of the Court of Chancery, it has been entirely removed by our statute.[24]

After commenting with obvious distaste on the "irascible temper and violent resentments" of the father, and pointing out that the father's occupation would give him far less time to superintend a growing daughter than the mother would have, the Court granted custody to the mother.

As the nineteenth century moved into its second quarter, custody cases still gave weight to the paternal presumption, to be sure in varying measure, but never without simultaneously stressing the Court's power and obligation to defeat this presumption where the welfare of the children so required.

> As to the question of the right of the father to have the custody of his infant child, in a general sense it is true. But this is not on account of any absolute right of the father, but for the benefit of the infant, the law presuming it to be for its interest to be under the nurture and care of its natural protector both for maintenance and education. When, therefore, the Court is asked to lend its aid to put the infant into the custody of the father, and to withdraw him from other persons, it will look into all the circumstances, and ascertain whether it will be for the real, permanent interest of the infant; and if the infant be of sufficient discretion, it will also consult its personal wishes. It will free it from all undue restraint, and endeavor, as far as possible, to administer a conscientious, parental duty with reference to its welfare. It is an entire mistake to suppose that the Court is at all events bound to deliver over the infant to his father, or that the latter has an absolute vested right in the custody."[25]

Similarly in general philosophy, but dissimilarly in result, a New York Court six years later, in 1836 granted custody to a father, citing the general preference to be accorded to paternal custody and finding no fault in the father to overcome it.

> In relation to the general question, it can hardly be doubted that the father is entitled to the custody of his infant children; and . . . The right of the father is preferred to that of the mother.[26]

In the ensuing decade the general presumption of paternal custody remained the starting point of American custody deliberations. In the following three cases this precept was further defined and refined by the Supreme Courts of Tennessee, Louisiana, and New Jersey.

On March 1, 1841, William Paine alleged in a Tennessee Court that his wife, Eliza, had abandoned him and taken his three minor children away. He sought by habeas corpus the return of these children to his custody. The children were "about seven," "about three," and five years old. Though "preponderance of the testimony" was that Mr. Paine was "hypochondriacal, peevish and capricious, and instances of coldness and neglect toward his wife were proved," nonetheless Mr. Paine and Mrs. Paine were "competent and fit to have the custody and control of the children in most respects." The Tennessee Supreme Court, in a review of authorities, reaffirmed the father's superior right of custody but, though also reaffirming that a habeas corpus proceeding could not be used to take children from a father's custody without proof of abuse, the Court also stressed that habeas corpus was an invocation of the Court's discretion and the proper exercise of that discretion required the Court to ascertain the "interest and welfare" of the children. The Court returned to the custody of the father the oldest boy (by the time of the appeal in 1843 he was "near eight years") but also ruled that "the other two are of too tender an age to be removed at present from the fostering care of the mother." The Court added, in apparent anticipation of an eventual change of custody, "that the daughter and youngest son remain with the mother until upon a change of circumstances it may be otherwise directed."[27]

In the same year Paine was decided, the highest court of Louisiana, in reversing a lower court decision, granted a divorce to the husband, the wife having committed adultery, and gave custody of the child to the father. The case neither reaffirmed nor created law, for which we may all be thankful, but it is of note because, though the court found that the husband murdered his wife's paramour "in cold blood, and in a manner both cruel and unmanly," not in a rush of passion when he discovered them but afterward, the Court did not allow this behavior to influence its thinking when called upon to choose that parent more able to raise the child.[28]

The concept of "tender age" or "tender years," which had arisen to play a prominent though varying role in the law of custody, was not defined by all courts in the same way. New Jersey, in 1849, put the matter into a state of further confusion. In the case of The State v. Stigall and Tumley once again a father sought by habeas corpus to compel his wife to return to him their three children aged five, three, and thirteen months whom the mother had taken with her to the home of her father. The New Jersey Supreme Court reviewed the common law authorities and made the ritualistic bow to the presumption of paternal custody and the exceptions to it. The court also reviewed the "tender years" theory and then held that she should have custody of the two younger children because they "are too young to be removed" and should therefore "for the present remain with her," but the oldest child, all of five years of age, was restored to the father.

The age of five, "tender" in Tennessee, was considered tough in New Jersey.[29]

By the end of the nineteenth century all of our states had divorce statutes that included provisions concerning the awarding of custody, except South Carolina, where divorce was constitutionally forbidden.[30] Thus in every state public policy had created custodial legislation, which thus replaced the common law heritage as the legal basis for custody decisions. The majority of these statutes were simple grants of power to the judiciary to vest custody in whichever parent would, in the court's discretion, better serve the interests of the child or children. This type of statute was the law of Arkansas, Colorado, Connecticut, Delaware, Florida, Idaho, Illinois, Indiana, Iowa, Kansas, Kentucky, Maine, Maryland, Michigan, Mississippi, Missouri, Montana, Nebraska, Nevada, New Hampshire, North Carolina, North Dakota, Pennsylvania, Rhode Island, Vermont, Virginia, Washington, West Virginia, and Wyoming.[31]

In Ohio and Utah there were similar statutes, but in each of these two states there was additionally specific statutory language giving children who were ten or more "the privilege of selecting to which of the parents they will attach themselves."[32]

In several states the parent who was found to be at fault for the disruption of the family unit was considered to be by definition less qualified to act as the custodial parent than the injured parent. In Tennessee a special statute favored the mother as custodian if abandoned by her husband "without a lawful cause" or if "she is entitled to the divorce."[33] In South Dakota a statute mandated that custody must go to the "innocent parent" in the event of an annulment on the ground of fraud or force, though the statute respecting custody decisions in divorce cases was a general grant of authority only without any words of presumption.[34] New York had a statute akin to the one in South Dakota relating to custody in the event of an annulment by force, fraud, or duress, but in New York it was a strong presumption, not an absolute imperative. Again no presumptions, similar or otherwise, infected the divorce custody statute.[35] In Massachusetts the concept of fault was contained in statutory language different from the other statutes cited but with the same basic intent. Massachusetts stated that in custody matters "the rights of the parents shall, *in the absence of misconduct,* be held to be equal (emphasis added)."[36] New Jersey's statute was identical.[37] In Louisiana custody was to go to the party without fault presumptively unless the judge ordered otherwise "for the greater advantage of the children."[38] Georgia, too, statutorily mandated the same presumption but allowed the court to overcome it "in the exercise of a sound discretion."[39]

The fault of a party did not, however, exist in a vacuum. Material though it was, definitive though it often was, there were occasions when the fault of a party in the divorce had to wrestle with other principles for ascendancy. Fault did not always prevail. In a Montana divorce action, for example, the court awarded custody of four children, ages thirteen, ten, eight, and one and a half, to the father even though the mother had been awarded a divorce on the ground of extreme cruelty.[40] The court appears to have been motivated, not primarily by the apparent fitness of the father as custodian—there was no discussion of the mother's fitness or lack of it in the decision—but by the articulated desire of the oldest three children to live with the father and the correlative principle that all four children should be raised together. A Maryland court left custody in a father who divorced his wife for her adultery although the child was a five-year-old girl and although the father's work required that he travel often and for extended periods. The court turned down the plea of the mother who, by the time the custody issue was heard, had married her paramour, not so much it seems because of her adulterous sin against the first marriage as because the father ". . . having lost his wife through her misconduct, he ought not to be deprived of the custody of his daughter and subjected to the humiliation of surrendering her to the support and control of the author of his marital misfortune."[41]

This doctrine of not punishing the cuckold further did not, of course, have its roots in any legal precept or decision, but it is instructive as an indication of how persuasive nonlegal factors can sometimes be. The case is unique because the court's consideration of nonlegal factors is admitted.

In several states the statutes gave a special status to the "tender years doctrine." In California that status was conferred explicitly:

. . . but other things being equal, if the child is of tender years, it should be given to the mother;

The statute went on, however, to enunciate a counterpresumption for older children:

. . . if it is of an age to require education and preparation for labor or business, then to the father.[42]

In the other states that had enshrined the "tender years doctrine" statutorily, the wording was less direct but carried the same message. In Alabama, Minnesota, Oregon, Texas, and Wisconsin the statutes required courts to pay heed in custody matters to "the age and sex" of the children.[43] This was not the nonpreferential language it appears to be; it was rather the embodiment of the increasingly influential philosophy that found males genetically unsuited to be tender to infants and understanding of the maturation problems of young females. This skepticism about the parenting qualities of fathers, created by males, was evidenced not only statutorily but in case law, not only in states with statutes incorporating the "tender years doctrine," but also in states with statutes silent about the doctrine.[44]

The history of child custody law, and that of the social mores that fathered the law, was, during the first six decades of this century, the story of the growth of the tender years doctrine and the general maternal preference it bred. An examination of our states' statutes and case law shows that by 1950, forty of our jurisdictions had formally announced the doctrine to be legally presumptive.[45] Indeed the principle was so accepted and dominant that in its 1959 edition Corpus Juris Secundum could summarize the status of the doctrine thus:

Unless a mother is shown to be unfit to assume such responsibilities, or unable to provide a suitable home, the courts are loath to deny her the custody of a very young child; and the rule generally applied, which has been recognized by statute in some jurisdictions, is that all things being equal, preference is to be given to the mother in awarding custody of a child of tender years. . . . Likewise, it is generally held that the mother is entitled to preference in the award of custody of a female child, or of a child who is not in good health.[46]

The "tender years doctrine" was notable for more philosophical content than the mere words of the doctrine bespoke. It gave rise to a general preference for the mother in all custody cases regardless of age. After all, if her love was purer, more needed, more healthful for the child of five, why would it not also be the same for the child of nine or twelve? Or sixteen? And if it were at the same time true that father could give more efficient guidance to a child in career choice or business knowledge was it not also true that he could be replaced in this by schools or guidance counselors while no one could replace the singular love capacity imputed to mothers? Could not father, if he cared as much as he claimed, give the kinds of guidance he was equipped for during visitation periods without wrenching the child from the needfully continuous succor of mother love? And if the child had gone to mother because of divorce during the child's tender years would not the trauma of separating mother and child at nine or twelve or fourteen be too disruptive to be overcome by the advantages father offered?

The general maternal preference not only arose from the tender years doctrine, it became the superior principle. Mothers were not generally superior custodians because they were better with infants; they were better custodians for all children and, a fortiori, they were better with children of tender years. Thus a legal treatise could summarize our law as of 1950 as follows:

And if, during the first half of the twentieth century the courts continued to pay lip service to the doctrine that the welfare of the child was the paramount and controlling factor in awarding custody, the preference for the mother was nevertheless evaluated into something approaching an independent principle by the numerous courts which held that a mother's love is so important to a child that the child should be given to the mother in preference to the father, even though the latter may have been without fault and may have been awarded the divorce.[47]

The maternal preference continued into and through the third quarter of this century to dominate utterly divorce custodial decisions. As of 1976, thirty-one states had by case law enunciated support of the maternal preference by decisions reached, in all but one instance, after *1960*.[48] The tender years doctrine had, as we have seen, received even wider judicial approval. (See note 45.) This maternal preference was not in all instances similarly described. Some courts declared that mothers should have custody unless proved unfit[49]; some said she should have custody presumptively unless father could overcome the presumption by showing the best interests of the child required otherwise[50]; some said the preference could be rebutted by "compelling evidence";[51] and some said the preference applied only if all the evidence was equal.[52] These differences were, of course, of no real importance; the message that came through with total clarity to lawyers everywhere in the United States and to all others who cared was that mother would get custody unless father had very powerful evidence that mother was too neglectful or uncaring or disturbed to be entrusted with the care of children. The tender years doctrine also expanded in some states to practically merge with the maternal preference by including within its scope children through twelve years of age.[53]

The history of the law of custody is not well perceived in vacuo. It is reflective of the greater social and economic forces that shaped values and thus the law these values created. This history begins when women were subject to a feudal order that, owing to its vertical system of guardianship and protection, placed man as the protector of woman and woman as the servitor or vassal of man. This system was reinforced by the common law property precepts, which gave the husband control of the wife's property and thus control over the family finances. It followed that men were the preferred sex to have the care, control, and educational guidance of children, and the law so stated, absent, of course, the kind of unfitness deemed to afflict such a depraved soul as Percy Shelley.

The family life of the colonial period was father-dominated, a fact of Americana that was not to change materially until after the War of Independence. Father was teacher, benefactor, and moral counselor to his children; mother was clearly subordinate and far less visible.[54] The male-female relationship of this time was described by Demos thus:

> Our forbearers of two and three centuries ago maintained some characteristic attitudes toward gender considerably at variance with our own. Man, they believed, must "overrule" woman, in domestic affairs no less than in other spheres of activity. For men had received from their maker a generally superior endowment of reason. Both sexes were liable to be misled by the "passions" and the "affections," but women were more liable since their rational powers were so weak.[55]

The subordinate status of women was in other legal areas consistent—they could not sue for damages or execute contracts. Their property rights were greatly limited.[56] Punishment for the crime of adultery was primarily directed at the female offender.[57]

During this period the most important family relationship was between father and son; next was father and daughter. Father and mother, and mother and children, were of lesser import. Father, as leader of the family and source of moral guidance, was the parent who provided the value system children were to emulate. Because the society then was predominantly one of agriculture and home crafts, fathers did not generally go off to work during the days but instead stayed in proximity to their growing children and thus strengthened bonds between them.[58] With these social patterns dominating, of course, father was the presumptive custodian when father and mother separated.

Subsequent to the American Revolution, America industrialized and urbanized. Change was rapid and profound and the nature of the family altered as well. The marital choices were increasingly based on love and respect rather than on parental choice and economic considerations as had previously been true. As the ties became more emotionally close, women's role perceptibly grew in importance. As father spent increasingly more time working away from the home, mother's role expanded and her ties to the children deepened. As womanhood and motherhood became newly defined and became armed with greater responsibilities and capacities, there was inevitably a concomitant lessening of responsibilities and capacities imputed to fatherhood. This increased allotment to mother and father of specific, different functions within, and for the benefit of, the family was known as the doctrine of "two spheres" or "separate spheres."[59] Though it was really just a division of labor theory, it became romanticized by some as "the cult of true womanhood."[60] It portrayed men as workers, supporters of the family unit, while women were to tend the home and care for the children. Men still performed what male-dominated society deemed the higher functions, but, for the history of the law of custody, women were becoming viewed as the primary custodial figures. This trend was to intensify and broaden and would in time give eminence to the "tender years doctrine" and the "maternal preference." Curiously, as women became more than chattels but less than equals, they acquired some supposed superiorities that were corollary to their general inferiority. It has ever been the irony of bias that it is not total in its arrogance but rather that it imputes to its victims virtues, though these virtues are of less moment than the imputed vices. Like the oafish black with the superior sense of rhythm, women were deemed unfit for affairs of state but better with children. And thus would man and woman basically view each other until very recently.

Perhaps equally dramatic as the changes in the relationship of husband and wife have been the changes in how children are perceived. In colonial America children were viewed as miniature adults.[61] After weaning, repressive discipline was common.[62] John Robinson wrote:

> And surely there is in all children . . . a stubbornness, and stoutness of mind, arising from natural pride, which must, in the first place be broken and beaten down; that so the foundation of their education being laid down in humility and tractableness, other virtues may, in their time, be built thereon.[63]

By age six or seven, the child was serving as apprentice to his parents. The boy worked at farming tasks with his father, whereas the girl undertook household responsibilities with her mother. This essentially served as formal education, which was not conducted in a classroom until at least 1671.[64] It was not uncommon for children at ten or eleven to be apprentices to other families. Certainly feelings of loss and abandonment were experienced by the children, and the practice suggested a lesser degree of investment in children as family members and people.[65]

The relative unimportance of children within the family can be affirmed by turning to the divorce laws of eighteenth-century Massachusetts. Only a third of the petitions mentioned children, and the comments were not occasioned by any concern about the impact of family dissolution on the children.[66]

A society does not concern itself with the rights of a minority group as long as that group is considered the property of the society's majority segment. As it was with women and blacks, so it was with children, who were the largest minority group in American society.

By the nineteenth century, the notion of children as depraved, marred from birth by original sin, was yielding to a view of children as pristine and innocent. Carl Degler discussed the impact of Wordsworth's "Ode: Intimations of Immortality" on nineteenth-century America. In Degler's words, "The poem portrayed children as recently arrived from heaven, and thus closest to God and virtue."[67]

The nineteenth century brought with it change in parental roles, concurrent changes in parental relationships to children. During the seventeenth and eighteenth centuries severe whippings offered in the interest of breaking the child's will disappeared from parents' disciplinary repertoires. Substituted early in the child's life were greater love and affection accompanied by parental permissiveness and the introduction of educational goals, moral and secular.[68]

It would appear then, in the evolving nuclear family of the nineteenth century, the child as a possession, object of obligatory training, and target for the administration of God's will became a conceptual memory of the past. The evolution of the child as a person opened the door to new and different family relationships that would previously have been impossible. Over the span of the next one hundred years, the child would often become a parental companion and the object of uncomplicated parental affection. Sometimes, the child would be the object of frustrated parental love, and not infrequently, the aim of unsatisfied parental ambition. The elevation to person status enabled the child to serve as a love object and source of satisfaction in a way that was formerly possible only for adults. The birth of the modern American family during the first quarter of the nineteenth century made possible the evolution of the complex psychological system we know today as the family. The intricacies of the interconnected ties, loyalties, and jealousies found in this system make child custody decisions so painfully difficult.

The nineteenth century also brought with it other social and economic changes that were to affect the roles of men and women and affect as well their perceived custodial capabilities. Beginning with the late 1840s American states enacted *Married Women's Property Acts,* which replaced the common law rules and allowed wives to own and retain their separate property and thus deprive husbands of total family economic dominance. Moreover, in this century, more women became educated than before, receiving the formal education previously available only to women from families of means. Thus the husband's prior claim to superior education was undergoing a process of erosion.

Although it is impossible to ever identify one event or time as the start of great social movements, it is reasonable to identify the publication of Betty Friedan's book *The Feminine Mystique* in 1963 as the onset of the current demand by women for full equality.[69] This book exposed the extent to which the culturally defined concept of womanhood had limited the growth and opportunities of women. Womanhood had become almost synonymous with motherhood, an identification that had made it impossible for a woman to disavow motherhood without defining herself as anomalous. The acceptance of society as a whole of this "mystique" had the second effect, of course, of making motherhood, the sole possession of women, synonymous with nurturing and thus not appropriately within the competence of males.

But as woman moves toward full equality she endangers the specific superiorities this mystique granted her. Thus her monopoly on nurturance has weakened and grows looser every day. The trend is clear. This trend, in turn, influences and is reflected by current changes in the law of custody. The maternal preference is under siege. Judges are not all presuming it. Statutes are decreeing equality, shedding maternal presumptions even for children of tender years. Joint custody is the new battle cry and legislatures are hearing it. Courts are responding also.[70] On December 20, 1979, the Supreme Court of Nevada specifically overruled Peavey v. Peavey[71] and thus terminated in Nevada not only the general maternal preference but also the tender years doctrine. The Court stated:

> Upon careful re-examination of Peavey, it is clear to us that the "tender years" doctrine, whether in its pristine form or as it has been reinterpreted in Nichols,[72] runs afoul of the standards this court and the legislature have announced[73] with respect to child custody determinations, and that it is nothing more than an expression of a culturally enforced bias favoring rigidly and unrealistically defined societal sex roles. The touchstone of all custody determinations is the best interests of the child; the foundation of these determinations is the particular facts and circumstances of each case. A preference for one parent over the other, solely on the basis of the parent's sex, has no place in this scheme. We, therefore, expressly overrule Peavey v. Peavey.

The unmistakable tide of change has not yet, however, overcome the maternal preference. Even where statutes change and Supreme Courts enunciate sexless rules, many of the trial judges who have lived under the maternal preference philosophy still sit and their preconceptions still live. Such notions do not die easily. But as women ascend toward equality in economics and descend to it in custody matters, the maternal preference diminishes. The question facing the law of custody today is not so much where it is going but when it will arrive and how sensibly will it solve custody problems when it gets there. Are we finally to determine custody on a rational, informed basis, or will we merely substitute new false presumptions for the old ones? Presumptions are the camouflage of the tired mind; we should never, therefore, underestimate the number of people attracted to them.

2

Joint Custody

To a member of the Divorced Men's Association of Connecticut, an order of joint custody is "finally, the promise of justice to fathers."[1] To the authors of *Beyond the Best Interests,* a joint custody order would be anathema.[2] To two of our most authoritative commentators on the law of the family, joint custody is simply another custodial alternative, whose propriety depends on the facts of each situation.[3] Are joint custody orders messianic, inappropriate, or occasionally best but often not? To answer this question we must first define joint custody, a process generally ignored by those who both laud and condemn the concept.

Custody of a minor means first the authority to make the decisions that affect the life and rearing of that minor. Parents naturally have that power, not half to each, but fully by both. This status of full authority by each continues until the minor becomes of age, is emancipated, or, if still a minor, sole custody is vested in one of the parents, or in a third party, owing to death of one or both parents or owing to the order of a court. Court orders of this nature may issue where one or both parents have been proved to be incompetent or where, as most often occurs, the parents divorce.

Second, custody implies, but does not necessarily have to include, the physical possession of the minor. It is a term "seldom explicitly defined" by case or statutory law "and has been characterized as a slippery word." Basically, however, it distills down to the right "to supervise, care for and educate the child."[4]

Because, therefore, the concept of custody involves legal authority over a child *and* the physical placement of that child, orders of custody must embrace both of these aspects. Consequently, there are five basic types of custody orders that must be distinguished:

1. Where one parent has sole custody and the other parent has rights of visitation. Here the custodial parent is the *only* parent legally vested with the authority to make the most important child-rearing decisions such as whether or not a medical procedure is appropriate, what school the child shall attend, or what religion the child shall embrace. The child's time is divided between the custodial and the noncustodial parent[5] with the latter having generally only a small portion of the child's time. Visitation orders may, however, vary greatly in regard to the amount of time involved.

2. Where the child spends one-half of the time with each parent and where the parent the child is with has the sole legal custody of the child during the period of possession. Here the rights of both legal authority and possession are equally divided. This "divided"[6] custody may not, however, be divided equally. Thus a variant of it is stated in type 3.

3. Where the child's time is divided unequally between the parents, but the parent the child is with has the sole legal custody of the child during the period of possession.

4. Where the child's time is divided equally between the parents but *both* parents retain full rights of custody all the time. Since each parent has a continuous, full legal right of custody, they are "joint" custodians, their "joint custody" being a legal concept that derives, not from the time of possession, but rather from their equal, continuous right to make the basic decisions of child rearing. It is still appropriate to label as "joint custody" an order like that in type 5.

5. Where the child's time is divided unequally but where both par-

ents retain, nonetheless, the equal, full, and continuous right to make the basic decisions of child rearing.

Although the primary custodial order in the history of American custody law has been that which bestowed sole custody and visitation rights, both divided custody and joint custody orders have their own history. In 1905 Pennsylvania upheld the legal power of a court to divide physical custody.[7] The practice was known in Mississippi at least by 1908, in South Dakota by 1910, and in Kentucky by 1917.[8] Apparently, prior to the twentieth century, many trial courts divided custody when each parent desired custody and, presumably, when the fitness of each parent and the quality of the residence each could provide were found to be suitable.[9] With the advent of the twentieth century, however, the practice of divided custody became one that appellate courts generally condemned and allowed only "under very exceptional circumstances."[10] Often the reason courts disallowed divided custody was if this necessitated a change of schools during a school year.[11] Kentucky divided custody equally in one case *until* the children were of school age, at which time a new order was contemplated.[12] In Kansas the same philosophy prevailed where the court divided custody of a four-year-old boy on a six-month basis until he entered school, at which time he was to be in his mother's custody during the school term and his father's during vacations.[13] This latter form of divided custody—school time to one parent, vacation time to the other—has often been approved by appellate courts.[14] But other appellate courts have unequivocally disapproved divided custody, opining that the "shifting" or "shunting" of a child back and forth between homes is not conductive to stability.[15] Divided custody is "an evil fruitful in the destruction of discipline, in the creation of distrust, and in the production of mental distress in the child" said the highest court of Maryland.[16] Some courts have felt that divided custody was especially inappropriate for children of tender years,[17] whereas other courts have allowed it.[18] The proximity of the homes of the parents has been an effective argument in favor of divided custody where courts have been most concerned with the possibly disruptive effects of radical changes in a child's environment.[19] But, curiously, other courts have found divided custody appropriate *be-*

cause the parents lived far apart, on the theory that normal, frequent visitation was difficult and the children should spend time with both parents.[20]

The history of case law on the subject of custody orders other than orders vesting sole custody to one parent is one that adds nothing of importance to our present evaluation of such orders. Courts did not distinguish generally between divided custody and joint custody. Neither have many of our present or past commentators.[21] But even more basic, one can examine the literature that propagandizes for joint custody without finding any real examination of the differences between, on the one hand, joint or divided custody, and on the other, rights of visitation.[22] What one confronts, is, in bald form, a set of generally irrational responses whether one reads old strictures against joint or divided custody or new polemics in favor of them. This is the biggest problem posed by the question of joint custody—it is a concept bristling with emotionality. A large group of males see it at once as both guarantee of future fairness and revenge for past wrongs. A sizable number of men were in the past robbed by the maternal presumption of the right to contest custody, and now, more in reaction than reason, they have elevated the concept of joint custody orders to the level of panacea.

What would a dispassionate, comparative examination of these concepts show?

1. Rights of visitation are not in any way restricted as a matter of law. Nothing prohibits the noncustodial parent from having a child's physical possession for *any* percentage of that child's time. Nothing prohibits the noncustodial parent from a child's physical possession at any *place* of that parent's choosing.
2. No legal principle gives a parent with joint custody more time with a child if that parent has joint custody rather than divided custody or visitation rights. This is especially so if the parent with joint custody has a child less than one half the time. There is also no principle of law that provides that a parent with joint undivided legal custody *must* have the children for any specific or minimum amount of time or for any period of time which presumably would exceed the time that an order of visitation of rights would confer.

3. The reason a healthy parent normally wishes joint or divided custody of a child after divorce is that the parent wants quantitatively and qualitatively sufficient time with that chid to maintain and improve the relationship, i.e., to love, be loved, and be with and influence that growing child. Yet nothing at all distinguishes possessory time under a joint or divided custody order from possessory time under a visitation order.

The possessory parent under a visitation order does *not* have the authority that joint or divided custody bestows. This is true, but how important is it?

The possessory parent pursuant to an order of visitation has all the normal authority of daily living. That parent determines bedtime, mealtimes, and the day's activities and runs the show. That parent exerts all the authority an adult would exert over a child under care respecting the ordinary decisions that would have to be made under such circumstances. The only areas closed to the authority of the possessory parent during visitation periods are more general, continuing decisions, such as the child's religious affiliation or schooling, which are reserved to the legal custodian.

Does this lack constitute a major deprivation?

Let us deal first with schooling. This is not an appropriate area for joint decision-making usually for children under the age of five. As a matter of logical necessity the school a child attends will generally be the neighborhood school which serves the primary residence. Thus the parent with joint or divided legal custody who has the child's possession less than half the time will normally have no logical alternative to that neighborhood school. That parent's legal authority actually confers no practical authority, and that parent is not, therefore, really any more authoritative than the parent with only rights of visitation.

The same holds true for choice of religion and choice of medical personnel. Where there is a primary residence it is expected that the child will be part of that unit, sharing that unit's religious preference. It also follows that the parent with primary possession will choose the medical personnel for the child since that parent will most likely have to take the child to the physician, apply medicines, obtain prescriptions, etc. It must be remembered also that whether custody is joint or divided, while the child is with the primary possessory parent, that parent is vested with the full authority to make these decisions without any mandatory obligation to discuss them with the other parent. Again, being practical, the parent who has joint custody or divided custody but is not the primary possessory parent really has nothing of importance except the possessory rights. This puts that parent in the same real position as the parent with visitation rights only.

But how about the situation where joint or divided custody exists with equal possessory rights? Here there is no parent logically endowed with a presumptively superior power of decision. How likely, however, is equality of custody? And, if it is ordered, how long can it be expected to last?

Equality of possessory custody for school-age children logically presupposes that the parents will reside in the same school district. It is possible, of course, to imagine situations in which there may be equality of possession without geographic proximity, but the logistics of the matter will preclude this occurring except rarely. (Percentagewise few children attend private school; fewer yet do so after divorces; and unless a child boards at private school, *some* geographical proximity is still necessary.) Equal possession will not require geographic proximity for children too young for school, but if there is no geographic proximity when they come of school age, the order for equal possession will have to be changed so that primary possession rests in the parent who lives in the school district the child will use. Some parents will manage to live in the same school district but for how long? We are a mobile society of transient habits. We move often and for varied reasons. We move because of reassignment by an employer, because of voluntary employment changes, for a better house, for a less expensive house, for a change of climate, because of a new spouse's wish or requirement, or because of a desire sometimes to just get away from the past—to name only a few reasons. In all those situations, therefore, where equal possession requires geographic proximity—the great majority of cases—orders of equal possession will usually terminate before the child's majority or, if they are legally unchanged, become empty phrases unfulfilled and unfulfillable.

Other foreseeable factors threaten orders of equal possession. The greatest of these is the new spouse. Or the new spouses. One has to start with the realization that *few* people will survive a divorce with the desire and capacity to work constructively with a former spouse for *any* reason. To do so respecting a child, and to do so with shared authority and equal time, requires not only desire and capacity; it requires that there be no divisive influences. The relationship between former spouses, however seemingly effective and apparently friendly, is going to be fragile. They have, after all, disappointed each other in a major way and therefore destructive resentments must be presumed to lie in each of them, ready to obtrude at any time that each perceives the other to be the author of a new disappointment.

Given these tender sensitivities the advent of a new spouse will usually be most divisive. If left out of the authority complex that governs this equally governed and possessed child, the new spouse will generally feel slighted, posing a threat to the new marriage. To avoid this problem, the parent will want the new spouse to be part of the decision-making process. The other spouse *may* not object to this, but what if the other spouse feels jealous, or sees this new stepmother or stepfather as a threat to the parenting role, or perceives this new spouse as a reason or *the* reason why the parents were divorced? It must be presumed that for equal authority and possession to be constructive for a child, the parents must substantially harmonize on matters of values, ethics, and life-style. But what if the new spouse actually differs materially in these areas or is perceived to differ? What if the new spouse does differ and becomes the dominant influence in the household? What if the new spouse brings children to the new marriage, reared on different principles than the parents had heretofore adopted, clearly threatening by this example the enforcement of those shared principles in the future? The ways in which one new spouse can cripple the cooperation of two sharing parents are numerous and lethal, but they increase geometrically if both parents remarry. Then not only do the relations between the new spouse of each parent and the other parent pose a danger but they are joined by the potential discord of the new spouses to each other.

There is another major problem with joint custody orders—whether possession be equal or not. Custody orders, whatsoever their nature, are modifiable, which means that upon proper motion filed with a court of competent jurisdiction, these orders may be changed if the court determines that it is in the best interests of the child to do so.[23] Thus the parties who share joint custody know they have something that may be taken away. It is also true that most courts consider joint custody to be feasible *only* where the parties both wish it. Therefore if one party should petition for a modification of a custody order to obtain sole custody rather than joint custody, it is to be presumed that one or the other party will end up with sole custody, the fact that there is a dispute over joint custody being at least prima facie proof that joint custody has not worked. Thus the party most likely, or thought to be most likely, to end up with sole custody has an enormous power advantage over the other. The presumed winner can impart to the other parent the message that if things are not handled the winner's way, they will end up back in court and then the loser will be without joint custody. Where the joint or divided custody order provides for unequal possession, as is usual, and thus a primary parent can be distinguished, the parent with the lesser possession is quite correct in presuming that shared custodial authority will be lost if a custody battle ensues. Thus what such a parent really has is the power to agree or the power to persuade—exactly what that parent has in actuality with rights of visitation.

This ability to bully will not so readily exist where possession is equal, for then the eventual winner of sole custody cannot be so easily presumed. But the respective wills of the parents, their readiness to litigate, their financial ability to litigate, may all create an atmosphere in which one parent is loath to precipitate litigation and thus submits when custodial decision-making disputes arise. Such a power play may also, of course, exist where visitation rights have been ordered whether the visitation rights are equal in time or minimal.

One can thus conclude as follows respecting orders of joint and/ or divided custody:

1. Without equal time, shared custody orders really convey nothing of legal substance to the parent with the lesser possession of the child.
2. Such shared authority orders really convey per se nothing more than is obtained by the right to visitation.
3. Joint and/or divided custody orders with equal rights of posses-

sion may in fact make true custodial partners of the parents, but since they cannot work without a cooperative predisposition, a basic similarity in approach to the questions of child-rearing, an absence of postdivorce bitterness, and probably, geographic proximity, they are not likely to be appropriate often.

4. Even where it is appropriate as an original custody order, it must be doubted that it will often last long, because one or two new spouses become involved, or because one or both of the parties move away, or because they simply with time find that they need a divorce from custodial partnership just as they previously needed one from their marital partnership.

But though we believe these conclusions to be an accurate reflection of legal reality, there is much more to consider in assessing the worth of orders of joint or divided custody.

We are strongly committed to the idea of joint custody if it is effectively used. We define joint custody for our purposes as an arrangement that allows and fosters the continuous, shared, and substantial involvement of each parent in the healthy development of their children. We describe here the problems inherent in joint custody orders, not because we oppose such orders, but because we feel it necessary to warn that such orders do not ipso facto create in fact what they order in law, i.e., true joint custodial involvement of both parents. However, even though such orders may not deliver what they promise, they may have great value.

Parents of divorce are not simply parents; they are people. They have, therefore, feelings, perceptions, and belief systems. They have insecurities and anxieties, weaknesses, and vulnerabilities. They are affected by their culture and its values. They know that if they divorce and retain court-sanctioned roles in the custody of their children they are more estimable in the eyes of others. It is probable that such a designation will also make many parents of divorce more estimable in their own eyes whether they begin with secure or insecure perceptions of their worth as parents. As they progress through their divorce and custody process they will be exposed to cultural influences, perhaps including their own counsel, that will reinforce the value system so prevalent today, which praises the custodial parent. They will learn or presume that their children's attitudes may be, if not shaped by, at least influenced by whether or not the court orders give them a custodial, as opposed to a mere visitational, role in their children's lives.

Thus can the ramifications of a joint custody order provide beneficent attitudes and a degree of involvement not inherent in the order itself. A parent with joint custody but lesser possession may not actually have more than visitation rights, but that parent may have, as the children may, so completely different a sense of role that the role will be materially altered for the better. If the label "joint custodian" makes it socially acceptable and avoids peer or family disdain or disappointment, the result is a happier, healthier person and parent. More importantly, if the order of joint custody gives to even the secure parent a greater degree of self-respect because it enhances that parent's perception of self as an equal parent, then the parental performance level will rise. It is reasonable for a parent to so react since this perception has been implanted and fortified often by peers, often by counsel, and sometimes by the court. This is likely to increase substantially the motivation to cooperate and work hard to co-parent. If the label "joint custodian" imbues the nonresidential parent with a greater feeling of responsibility for, and involvement in, the children's lives, the chances of that parent's contributing constructively to the children's development must be presumed to increase.

Further, this has an impact not only on the nonresidential parent but also on the residential parent, who may perceive joint custody as a way to cooperate and participate in future co-parenting and, by so doing, expiate the guilt caused by past failures. The main benefit may, however, inure to the children, who may for the first time have parents able to interact effectively. Thus the children obtain the next best thing to an intact, happy family. Also, the children will have the opportunity to salvage a major advantage of the intact family, i.e., the chance to identify to a substantial degree with the personalities and interpersonal functioning of two adult models.

It is not baseless conjecture to suppose that many child snatchings are directly traceable to the feeling that the snatcher had only the choices of snatching or noninvolvement or that many parents guilty of nonsupport would have made their payments if they had felt that they had a role in their child's upbringing, especially one sanctified and recognized by court order. Any experienced lawyer in the field of family law knows that the offer of joint custody can be an enormously helpful way to settle custody and divorce litigation.[24] Joint or divided custody may well be more valuable for what it does extralegally than for what it does legally.

An order of joint custody, called that or called divided, shared, or alternating custody, can be an extremely useful tool in resolving custodial disputes and in subsequently providing a healthy atmosphere for the development of children of divorce. But such orders are not panaceas; they do not per se accomplish what they are intended to accomplish. They must not become so idealized that they are deemed the new presumptive remedies to the problems of postdivorce child-rearing. Only hard, sophisticated, insightful work will have a chance to produce such remedies. Because this field has historically been victimized by presumptions (paternal, then tender years, then maternal); and because the existence of presumptions offers easy ways out for the investigator, lawyer, and judge; and because we feel that each case must be thoroughly examined on its merits, we oppose making joint custody orders presumptive.[25] We accept joint custody orders as a logical alternative, preferable, we hope, in most cases, but urge against the adoption of any presumptions in the area of child custody. Presumptions stifle inquiry; children of divorce deserve inquiry.

3

The Divorce Context

In studying the history and dynamics of the custodial process, it is easy to forget that this process has never existed alone in a vacuum. The great majority of custodial decisions are necessitated because parents divorce, and when this occurs, many other issues must be determined along with the allocation of custody. These issues coexist in time and are interdependent, in the minds both of the parties and of those others involved in the judicial context. For the divorce to be resolved by negotiation, *all* matters, including custody, must be resolved. Limited agreements are the rarity; package deals are the rule. Thus alimony, support, custody, visitation, division of assets, and insurance protection all become interdependent areas of bargaining, with the price for concessions in one area being the giving of concessions in another area.

It is not often that one party, assured of winning custody in court, will surrender it for financial considerations, but it does occur. What more often occurs is the trading of incidents of custody for either financial gain or a rapid divorce. Joint custody may be conceded to acquire a favorable disposition of the residence, or more visitation time may be surrendered for a higher support order. The list is endless. The point is, however, simple: custody of children in divorce has ever been and will ever be a bargained-for item, occasioned by the multiplicity of matters at stake in divorce and also by the understandable impulse of most divorcing persons to end the torturous stress of an unresolved divorce by negotiation rather than submit their lives, their property, and their children to the unknowable decision of a judge.

Most of the divorce decisions made about all the relevant issues that arise, including custody of children, are made by the parties and their counsel. With all the imperfections this may occasion, we are surely the better for it. But obviously a great many cases involving custody of children are not resolved without trial, and many others are not resolved without preliminary intervention by court personnel, psychiatrists, or psychologists into the area of custody and the rendering by such personnel of advisory opinions regarding custodial arrangements.

In today's American courts, custody disputes are an everyday occurrence, for although most custody dispositions are agreed upon by the parties, the sheer quantity of custody-divorce litigation that goes through trial or requires experts to render advisory opinions before settlement is possible is very large.

The presumed primary causes of the great quantum leap in child custody litigation in the past decade are attitudinal. The attitudes of men have changed. They do not now accept as they used to the notion that they are as a gender innately incapable of nurturing children, and consequently, men now seek and fight for custody as never before. The attitudes of women have changed. As a group they do not presume as they used to that fathers cannot be primary parents and thus now may surrender custody without presuming that so doing will condemn their children to inefficient if not dangerous rearing. More important, however, many women have come to understand that the act of giving primary custody to a father does not mean that they must be anomalies, that they are intrinsically flawed as women. Social attitudes have changed. A man can nurture today without necessarily being deemed effeminate and a woman can seek a career in business rather than at home without her relatives feeling shame.

We are, in regard to these attitudes, in transition. The new attitudes have arrived and become influential, but the old ones have not yet been fully displaced. One can only generalize; in any given case either the new or the old attitudes may dominate, and this is true not only of the parties but also of the lawyers, judges, and investigative personnel who may be involved. The trend is, however, clear and the recent changes in our law of custody reflect it. (See chapter 1.)

Strangely, however, the change over the past decade that has probably had the greatest effect on American custody is the change in the law of divorce. To grasp fully the nature and effect of this change we must perforce understand what the nature of marriage was up to and as of the advent of the 1970s.

Marriage was often referred to as a contract. One New York court defined it with these glorious words:

> Marriage is a mutual and voluntary compact springing from sentiment, emotion, affection and the desire for sacrifice and surrender each for the other, properly based on mutual regard and love, suitably ratified, to live together as husband and wife until death, with the object of constituting a family for the perservation of moral and social purity, the continuance of the race, the propagation of children and their nurture, training and preparation for family welfare and the general good of society.[1]

This definition was not legally apt, even though marriage must be a "mutual and voluntary" decision. But no legal concept of marriage ever required the elements contained in the rest of the definition. A marriage of convenience for the crassest of reasons between two persons who despised each other, intended to live apart, loathed children, preferred society sullied, and hoped for humankind's early extinction would have been as lawful as the one this court described.

Although this court, other courts, and commentators liked to discuss the marriage "compact" or "contract," it was truer to say that marriage had contractual aspects to it than to say it was a contract. For though spouses had legally imposed duties and rights, defined under the title *corsortium*, nonetheless, the basic characteristics of a contract were absent. A marriage could not just be created by decision of the parties. Legal requirements existed regarding qualifications and ceremony, without which no "marriage" could exist.[2]

Most importantly, the marriage could not be terminated by the mutual and voluntary decision of the parties. Under normal contract law the parties may terminate their arrangement at will. This fully terminates the relationship. Moreover, if one of the parties unilaterally wishes to end a contractual relationship, that party may do so. The other party may have the right to money damages, but with a few exceptions not relevant here, cannot compel the continuation of the contractual arrangement, and this is especially so where the nub of the contract was the exchange of personal services. Of course, the marriage "contract" is the preeminent example of an arrangement for the exchange of personal services.

The fact was that, despite the aspects of marriage that seemed contractual, marriage was not truly a contract but was instead a legally constructed status. The law determined how it must start, what it should consist of, and how it could be ended. The law in regard to the creation of marriage by and large made sense. Blood tests served a social purpose; licenses provided community income and kept a socially desirable record. Nonage, bigamy, incompetence, and fraud were sensible proscriptions. The theory of consortium was rather idealistic, but it was benign, and so the legal definition of marital rights and duties did no harm. But the law describing termination of marriage, the law of divorce, was a supreme example of law run amok causing a degree of social harm beyond calculation.

Divorce was a lawsuit. The one wanting out—the plaintiff—had to commence a civil action seeking the termination of the marriage, and secondarily, such other orders relative to custody, alimony, support, division of assets, etc., as were desired. In order to obtain this divorce the complainant had to satisfy the legal requirement that he or she had been injured by the defendant. Not *any* form of injury sufficed. It had to be one of the specially prescribed types of injuries that the law in its wisdom deemed adequate to end a marriage. As of 1971 the grounds for divorce most widely recognized by American courts were adultery (49 states); desertion or abandonment (47 states); cruelty, physical or mental (45 states); conviction of crime or imprisonment (44 states); alcoholism (41 states); nonsupport (32 states); and insanity (29 states).[3] All of these were grounds descriptive of a form of gross offense against the marriage, though insanity and alcoholism were arguably not intentionally offensive. But insanity and alcoholism were seldom used, as were the few statutes then in force allowing divorce because the parties were incompatible or because they had been separated for lengthy periods. The great bulk of American divorces proceeded upon the ground of "cruelty" (physical or mental), not because more spouses were cruel than adulterous necessarily, but because mental cruelty was a very elastic concept, capable of broader definition than the other grounds and not requiring proof as precisely defined. It was not, however, easy to establish in the absence of severe physical beatings. And, like all the other divorce grounds, it was subject to special defenses.

The law of divorce recognized four special defenses: condonation, collusion, connivance, and recrimination. These were simply legally recognized reasons why a plaintiff would not be entitled to a divorce even if the plaintiff proved that the defendant had been cruel, adulterous, deserting, nonsupportive, or guilty of other behavior covered by the grounds for divorce.

Let us look at these special defenses:

1. Condonation was the foregiveness of a prior marital offense. It was generally held that it was a forgiveness conditioned upon nonrepetition of the offense, but if offenses were repeated after being forgiven, they could again be forgiven. Forgiveness was generally inferred from continued cohabitation, especially if that cohabitation involved sexual intercourse. Our law curiously presumed to the point of near certainty that sex must mean love and that love implied forgiveness. Lust was somehow not considered a likely cause of sexual activity between spouses. Thus, what could happen, and did happen, was that one spouse could have many affairs, or brutalize the other, or be an incessant drunk, but the other could not get a divorce by proving such if the other had consented to sexual activity with the offending spouse after the offenses had occurred and the victim-spouse had knowledge of them.

2. Collusion occurred when the acts that constituted the grounds for divorce were committed with the agreement of the other spouse, or when no acts constituting a ground were committed but both spouses agreed to claim otherwise, or when both parties by agreement withheld evidence that, if known, would have defeated the claim for divorce. Collusion was the law's prohibition against spouses working together to end their marriage when, without this cooperation, no legal basis for divorce existed. Collusion meant agreement, and divorce was not available by agreement. Being an adversary pro-

ceeding, it was deemed available only to one who wrenched it away from another because of that other's misconduct. The law gaveth and the law tooketh away.

3. Connivance was the consent to, or the active participation in, the marital misconduct of the defendant by the plaintiff. Though connivance and collusion could overlap where plaintiff passively consented, say, to defendant's having an affair, it would have been clearly connivance if the plaintiff engineered the tryst in addition to assuring the defendant that it was all right.

4. Recrimination was the most often used of these four special defenses, probably more often than the first three combined. It was simply the charge that the plaintiff had performed acts that constituted a ground for divorce. The effect of proving that this was so was to deny the plaintiff a divorce even if the defendant had been proved to have done what the plaintiff charged. The theory was that since a divorce was relief given only to the innocent, no relief could be given where both spouses were guilty. No matter, either, if the degree of guilt was disproportionate. One affair by the plaintiff could equal in legal effect long, continuous adultery by the defendant. There was no savior called comparative rectitude. Only pure innocence could prevail, but total innocence was, and is, a rare commodity, and thus a defendant who raised cruelty as a recriminatory special defense, and who did not balk at perjury, had an excellent chance of being sufficiently believed to thwart plaintiff's divorce.

These special defenses, powerful as they were, were only a few of the weapons in the arsenal of a defendant bent upon defeating a divorce. They did not have to be raised or, if raised, be successful for a defendant to prevail. The plaintiff had to bear the burden of proving the allegations of misconduct by the defendant. If he alleged adultery, it was not enough that witnesses saw her kissing another man and arriving home late at night. Adultery was not easily inferred, precisely because it was deemed such a major transgression. There were judges who would not believe adultery occurred simply because the detective watching defendant could not testify that when the defendant and paramour were alone in paramour's apartment from 8:00 P.M. to 1:00 A.M. all the lights were out. Cruelty was also very hard to prove without evidence of unforgiven and unreciprocated physical abuse. The other grounds were also difficult to prove besides being rarely applicable.

The result, therefore, of all these factors was that a divorce was very difficult to obtain when one of the parties opposed it.

The key was, however, the element of opposition. For although a suit for divorce over opposition was generally unsuccessful, a suit for divorce where the other party did *not* contest it was easy. To be sure there was a general aversion to the idea of divorce itself both in the law and in much of the judiciary, but despite this, an uncontested divorce was usually obtainable. Sometimes it required intelligent judge-shopping; sometimes it required waiting for judges to change assignments; sometimes it required trips to Nevada or Mexico; but almost always it was available with patience, ingenuity, or mobility. There were by the onset of the 1970s many judges who had become philosophically attuned to the propriety of divorce when both parties had agreed to it or, to put it in the terms then required, when one party wanted to divorce and the other party chose not to contest it. Thus very often the degree of proof needed to get an uncontested divorce granted was minimal. This was generally accomplished by the court's granting the divorce on the ground of cruelty and not demanding much evidence to do so. The uncontested divorce became often more of a ritual than a trial, more a joke than a legal proceeding.

Because a contested divorce was, at best, hard to obtain, and because an uncontested divorce was, generally, easy to obtain, it naturally followed that the spouse who wanted a divorce most usually paid to get it. That spouse might have to agree to an unfair alimony or support order, or agree to receive an unjust share of the assets, or agree to a custody arrangement ultimately deleterious or even destructive, but this was done because it was the price of freedom. This was, therefore, the nature of the context in which custody used to be decided when an American couple divorced: it was more often given to the parent who wanted a divorce less than to the parent who had more to give to the child.[4]

The rigor of this body of divorce law was ameliorated in several ways. First, most divorces, probably 90 percent or so, ended up as uncontested matters. Whereas this was a blatant evasion of the prohibition against collusive divorces, it was, however, possible only with spousal agreement and this agreement was too often paid for with too high prices and at the expenses of children. Second, with agreements, divorces could be obtained in such places as Mexico and Nevada. But these migratory divorces were dangerous.[5] Third, many states moved away from the traditional divorce grounds of adultery, cruelty (mental and physical), desertion, nonsupport, and intemperance to separations (for varying periods) and, occasionally, incompatibility.[6] But though these additions were an amelioration, they did not effect fundamental change. The separation statutes, which required mutual consent, still made an agreement necessary, and all the separation statutes necessitated a waiting period before divorce that was onerous. The incompatibility grounds, though they read like no-fault grounds, were not always interpreted that way and thus clearly incompatible spouses were denied divorces.[7] Fourth, the restrictive laws, in particular the defenses, were not always honored by judges of liberal persuasion who felt in a given case that spouses so contesting should not remain married. Kansas, for example, was reputedly a jurisdiction where this often occurred.[8] But whether or not this was so, and to whatever extent this sometime judicial view softened the basic law, it was still true that it was not a certainty anywhere. Thus the basic problem always existed even where it was least prevalent.

The law, however, changed radically. A revolution in mores occurred that the law both fomented and reflected. Beginning in California in 1972,[9] "no-fault" divorce statutes swept the United States until today every state has rejected the old concepts.[10] These "no-fault" statutes did not change marriage conceptually; it is still a legal status, not a contract, still with entrance requirements, still terminable only when a court finds the necesary allegation proved. But now a court need not find that one party has committed an offense against the marriage before the marriage can be ended; now it is the marriage itself, not the behavior of one or more parties, that is placed under the judicial microscope. Thus the marriage will be dissolved upon the court's conclusion that the marriage has broken down irretrievably. No longer is it relevant to the issuance of a divorce how badly the plaintiff behaved during the marriage. All a court needs to do is conclude that these two people are not going to reconcile and the plaintiff will be maritally free no matter what he or she may have done.

The odious special defenses are no longer germane because individual misconduct is not of itself relevant to the issue of divorce.

Although it is true that individual judges have occasionally not been willing to find that a marriage has broken down and thus should be dissolved even though both parties have so claimed, nonetheless, these are scattered and nonrepresentative bits of judicial aberration. It is a safe generalization today that where only one of the spouses requests a divorce and stays constant in this attitude through trial, that marriage will be dissolved and that reaches near-certainty if the parties live separately while the divorce is pending.

Therefore, any divorce plaintiff knows today that the marriage will be dissolved if one does not tire in pursuit of it. Divorce no longer has to be purchased. Custody no longer may have to be conceded as part of the marital freedom price. Nothing else has to be given away either. Parties can proceed to litigate every contested aspect of their divorce and know that whether or not they prevail in this litigation they will still end up divorced.

No one can know that children will be better off for having their custody open for litigation rather than traded off for freedom. Maybe the mere fact that one was prepared to make such a trade said something crucial about parenting. But we prefer free marital choice to arranged marriages because we accept freedom of choice as the better way to live and decide. Surely we can accordingly presume that children's custody will be best allotted if any parent who wants it has a chance to prove why.

4

The Custody Trial

We like to believe, and generally presume, that the greater the decision the greater will be the ability of the one who must make it.
Having been exposed to many years of mediocre capacity and rip-
ened venality in high political office, the likelihood of Americans so
presuming has markedly diminished in the last two decades. We believe, however, that this presumption still attaches to the judiciary
and still, on the whole, describes the attitude with which American
parents regard those charged with the terrible responsibility of deciding the custody of children.

That this presumtion is not warranted is a shame, if not a tragedy.
But the absolute truth of the matter is that judges are not specially
equipped to determine child custody. This is not because judges are
venal, subject to bribes, or some other form of unethical suasion.
This is also not because they are as a group too unintelligent to grasp
the issues raised or too uncaring to give the issue the concern it merits. Indeed, on the whole, it is our experience and belief that judges
as a group are honest, competent, and diligent persons well aware of
the importance and difficulty of custody decisions.

If this is so, why would we claim that judges are "not equipped"
to make custody decisions?

The reason is that nothing in the training of judges, from law school through courses for new judges, instructs them how to do it. Nothing in our statutes or case law is of assistance. Of course, they have a standard to follow—the best interests of the child[1]—but this standard provides no clues to how it is to be satisfied. Judges could just as easily have no standard at all. It would be as helpful to them to be simply told before trial, "Do your best."

Leaving judges with an ultimate standard but with no real guidance on how to satisfy it puts them in a position of having only two ways to do their job: either they follow their own instincts or they rely on the expertise of others. Following their own instincts is simply another way of saying that they act in a vacuum, a philosophical vacuum, in which their particular experience, upbringing, biases, and, perhaps, irrationalities lead them to a concusion. This form of decision-making is not only personal, bearing no necessary relation to what another judge might decide on the facts, but also utterly without any necessary relation to what is best for the child in question.

It might here be intelligently argued that it is not the judge's place to rely on *unguided* discretion but rather on discretion guided by the evidence adduced at trial. The problem with this is that all participants in a custody trial suffer from the same lack of an accepted standard to determine custody. So the judge who tries to diligently perform by ingesting the evidence at trial not only has no means of knowing what is a given child's "best interest" but also will receive that evidence either from those who also have no real standards or from those who all have different standards. In custody trials where one parent is blatantly unfit or where the child has a pronounced preference and is near majority, this absence of a generally accepted means of determining a child's best interests will not matter. But custody trials do not normally occur in such cases; these situations usually settle without trial. The lack of such a means of determination means a great deal, on the other hand, where the child is too young to articulate a dispositive preference and where each of the contending parents is of roughly equal competence.

In the past the absence of real child custody standards was deplorable, but the void was filled by easily usable presumptions in favor of father, then in favor of mother (see chapter 1). These presumptions so dominated the law of custody that only where the presumably better parent was really incompetent did the other parent have a chance; thus the custodial inquiry distilled down to answering the question whether or not the presumptive custodial parent was really *that* bad. This was a much simpler intellectual exercise than deciding which of two competent parents would be the better custodian.

It is unfortunately human to look for easy ways to solve hard problems. Hard ways, after all, mean hard work and imply a high risk of mistake. Thus do judges and others in the field of child custody (as in all other fields) search for and create simplistic ways to make their decisions.

Let us look at one of them. Call it the possession presumption. It can come into being in several ways. One hypothetical but oft-repeated way is as follows:

Mr. and Mrs. Smith, parents of two children, ages ten and eight, live together amid increasing tension. They have become, through no fault of either, incompatible and each faces the imminent and necessary collapse of their marriage with insecurity and fear. Their arguments grow daily in both virulence and volume. The children, who used to hear these battles only by distant echoes after bedtime, now have orchestra seats for each performance. The parents realize what is happening and, although unable to stop the fighting, still feel deeply regretful of what they are putting their children through. Finally, the husband, because of traditional chivalry, leaves the house alone for the sake of the children. Soon after he leaves, either husband or wife initiates a divorce. Both want custody. The father, having moved out, stays out during the pendency of the divorce. When the professionals attached to the court whose job it is to make custodial recommendations commence their investigation the children are at home with mother, and father is living elsewhere, usually alone, usually in a smaller, less appealing abode, and usually in another school district if not in a different town.

Let us make some observations on this hypothetical case before completing it. First of all, it is irrelevant whether it is father or mother who leaves the house. Second, the reason for leaving may not indicate special sensitivity and concern. It may be spousal hatred or fear or an inability to handle stress or whatever. The point is that neither who leaves nor why the leaver leaves has any necessary connection with the relative parenting abilities of *these* parents to have custody of *these* children.

The investigating officer determines that both are caring, nurturing parents who love their children. The officer cannot get an articulated preference from either child for either parent. The children obviously love both parents and seem to miss the parent they are not with at any given moment. The officer has to make a recommendation; that is in the job description. But how to do it? Let us further presume that this investigator is too good to rely on the facile maternal presumption. Without the tools to ascertain which parent will best foster the healthful development of these particular children at this particular stage in that development what does the officer rely on as a basis for the recommendation that must be made?

The tendency is to find an easy way out. And in fact the situation we have hypothesized offers one. The question under investigation changes from "Who will be the better parent?" to "How have the children done while living with their mother alone?"

What now happens is the investigating officer checks with the children's teacher and gauges school progress, academically and attitudinally. Are they getting good grades? Are they better or worse than before the parental separation? How is their socialization? The officer also checks with coaches and choir masters and band teachers and all others who may see the children's peer interactions. If the chidren appear to have made a succesful adjustment to the family dissolution, as measured by these superficial indicia, then the officer will recommend custody to the mother (or perhaps joint custody with the children residing with the mother, which is essentially the same thing). These questions will never be recognized, let alone answered:

1. Would these children have made a more successful adjustment living with the other parent?
2. Was the adjustment truly successful or are these superficial indicia really masking an interior distress or a parenting lack?
3. In the long run, which parent would provide better care?

This inertial response, this choice of the superficial, justifies itself by identification with the adage "let well enough alone" as though "well enough" rather than "best" were the end to be sought. The saying "possession is eleven points in the law"[2] applies as much in custody as anywhere. Little wonder that an experienced custody lawyer has written:

> And it is this fundamental concept which determines custody—*the children, don't leave home without them.*[3]

This "possession presumption" is not the only easy way out utilized in custody decision-making. There is also the children's choice presumption. This is exactly what it sounds like—the investigating officer ascertains or guesses at what the child (children) wants and then recommends it so long as the fact situation does not provide any strong apparent reason conflicting with that choice. This will not occur, of course, at least normally, with very young children, but one case, observed by one of the authors, involved such a recommendation based upon the voiced choice of an eight-year-old child. It is not that this presumption is used for very young children or that it is used to vest custody in blatantly incompetent parents that makes it improperly utilized. It is that it is used when the investigator lacks the perception and training necessary to distinguish between two seemingly good parents. It is used *instead* of *knowledge*. It is used when the wisdom of the child's choice is unknown to the investigator; indeed when even the real reasons for the child's choice are unknown to the investigator. It is far from seldom that chidren will not give their true choice, because they fear a parent's retribution, because they fear losing utterly a parent whom they *don't* prefer, because they desire to be with the parent of greater means, because they sympathize with the distraught parent, because "daddy (mommy) needs me more," because one parent gives more freedom, or does not spank, or whatever. Our custodial process, afflicted by its lack of expertise, too often lets children determine their custody when those same children would not be allowed to decide what they should have for supper.

Judith Wallerstein's research led her to state:

> Although the wishes of children always merit careful consideration, our work suggests that children below adolescence are not reliable judges

of their own best interests. Their attitudes at the time of a divorce may derive from the crises itself and may be very much at odds with their usual feelings and inclinations.

Many nine to thirteen years olds were angry at the parent they believed was responsible for the divorce. Some were eager to be co-opted into the parental battling: they eagerly took sides, often against a parent to whom they were tenderly attached during the intact marriage. Alternatively, and equally disconcerting, was the passionate commitment of some of the youngsters in that age group to rescue a depressed or suicidal parent. Their loyalty, while commendable, was sometimes to their own detriment. . . . Furthermore, their propensity to split the parents into "good parent" and "bad parent" often in contradiction with the parents' respective roles over the years, caused us to doubt the children's ability to make informed judgments about their own best interests.[4]

Another approach to custodial decision-making enjoying some present vogue is the concept of the psychological parent. In the context of divorce the psychological parent would be, according to Goldstein, Freud, and Solnit,[5] that parent whom the child (or children) perceives, consciously or unconsciously, as the better parent. Although this standard has not been accepted, to the best of our knowledge, by the highest court of any jurisdiction as the appropriate means of determining divorce custody and has in fact been specifically rejected by some trial courts,[6] nonetheless, it has strongly influenced many custodial evaluators and thus appears frequently in custodial evaluations as a focal point. This concept is a great step forward in that it identifies an extremely important component of any sound custodial recommendation. We reject the concept of the psychological parent if used exclusively, not because it lacks value, but because it does not measure many other factors crucial to a custodial placement.[7]

There are, of course, inappropriate bases for custody decisions other than those we have listed. There are cases that have hinged on a judge's bias against a particular life-style or on predilections of many descriptions. It is not necessary, indeed it would be impossible, to attempt to describe them all. It is sufficient, we feel, to state that the law of custody badly needs a uniform set of criteria to be used for custodial decision-making and that trying to meet that need is the primary reason for this work. (See chapters 5, 6, and 7.)

If the need for this set of criteria is recognized, or even if it is not the question remains: How and by whom should custody decisions be made?

Because custody decisions are so uninformed, so painful, and so momentous, it is to be expected that there would be enormous dissatisfaction with how they are now rendered. It is thus not at all surprising that demands are made to change the process entirely by removing it from the courts and vesting others than judges with the power of decision. These demands are, however, invariably based more on outrage than on thought, more destructive than constructive. The present method of dealing with custody disputes will never be perfect; no complex determination by mere human beings can be other than flawed. But it is the best means available and its worst flaws can be remedied by the adoption of the custodial criteria recommended herein. We take this position for the following reasons:

1. The divorce trial and the custody hearing should be one proceeding. If custodial issues are to be decided other than by a judge, then necessarily the divorcing parents will be obliged to spend the time and money and suffer the effects of two procedures rather than one. In divorces where children are called for testimony relevant to issues other than custody, the children will also face the need to be embroiled twice rather than once. Duplication of effort and anguish are very much to be avoided; thus the forum in which the divorce is to be heard should also be the forum for the custody hearing and the hearings should be simultaneous. Since divorces are and must be a legal proceeding, custody hearings must be the same.

2. The custody hearing should be a legal proceeding even if heard separately from a divorce, as in postdivorce motions to change custody.[8] It is, after all, a dispute between persons that requires the taking of evidence. Rules must be established, therefore, for the method of receiving, compelling, and determining the admissibility of evidence. This is what the law of evidence does. Judges should know that law; laypersons do not and cannot be expected to learn it. Also, who is to amass, collate, and present the relevant evidence if lawyers do not? Who is to compel its presentation by subpoena in situations where the holders of the evidence will not

voluntarily come forth? Lawyers have this authority because they are schooled in the proper use of it. Laypersons are not. If testimony is given, who is to examine and cross-examine the witness? Lawyers do this from experience and training; laypersons could not be expected to do it with the same skill. On the assumption that the new process were to use the law of evidence and use lawyers to collect and present evidence, would it be better to substitute a psychiatrist or other behavioral specialist or group of specialists for the judge? The answer to this must also be "no." Again, the person running the hearing must know the law of evidence and the other legal principles that could apply such as physician-patient confidentiality and privileges against incrimination. Laypersons would lack this crucial knowledge. Moreover, a judge, being a generalist, a nonexpert in child psychology or any other discipline besides law, is the precise person best able to reach ultimate conclusions free of bias, especially when the experts disagree. Psychiatry itself has made it explicit that the proper role of the psychiatrist is to "do psychiatry, i.e., to present medical information and opinion . . . and to explain in detail the reason for his medical-psychiatric conclusions" but not to attempt to make ultimate conclusions "about which they (judges), and only they, are expert."[9]

Moreover, the psychiatrist, psychologist, or other behavioral specialist who investigates should not make the ultimate decision, because the very process of investigation will awaken biases that affect the decision. Thus the prudent specialist will *want* another to make that ultimate decision; thus also should the investigator be obligated by the procedure to defend and explain the recommendation. If done to a judge, by examination and cross-examination, the specialist's views will then be subjected to proper scrutiny and challenge and then weighed by one less likely to be biased.

3. Custody differences are not just "issues," they are disputes. One commentator has written that "child custody does not belong in court. It is a social issue, not a legal one." He recommends that a panel of arbitrators decide custody matters, the staff thereof to consist of "qualified representatives from psychiatry and pediatrics as well as psychologists, sociologists, marriage-counselors and juvenile-guidance advisors as well as teachers and administrative

personnel from private and public schools." He opines that these professionals would be able to give a sound decision about custody free of "judicial impedimenta" and without even having to ask the child for a parental preference.[10]

This proposal is not sufficiently described or thought out to merit being specifically discussed, but its underlying fallacy is, i.e., that custody "issues are not disputes and thus not appropriately to be heard in a court." In fact, custody disputes are disputes of the highest importance and intensity to the disputants. The fact that the dispute concerns a person rather than a thing, and the fact that it should be resolved by determining what is best for the person rather than who owns the thing, do not make it any the less a dispute. Moreover it is a dispute over an interest exalted enough to have constitutional protection.[11] The United States Supreme Court has declared the "right of an individual . . . to marry, establish a home and bring up children" to be a right protected from governmental abridgment by the Fourteenth Amendment.[12] It follows ineluctably from this right that no parent could be divested of it without due process of law, which means the opportunity to have counsel, produce evidence, cross-examine witnesses, and otherwise be able to present a case in conformity with proper procedures. It would not, in our opinion, be constitutionally possible to take away or limit a parent's involvement with a child without all of the rights and safeguards accorded litigants. To suggest, therefore, that child custody is an "issue" rather than a dispute is to mislead. It cannot be extracted from the judicial process.

4. Pain is not a result to be expected only from the judicial procedure. Pain will result as much from any decision-making apparatus that excluded a court as it does now from judicial processes. Pain here derives from the real and anticipated loss of a child, conditions that would exist in any procedure used. A loss of custody would be no less painful if decreed by a pediatrician; neither would the anticipatory anxiety be less in such a case. We believe also that a judge's decision would tend to be better accepted by the parties, partially because judges have traditionally been accorded great respect, but also because there is no logical reason to think that pediatricians, sociologists, psychologists, juvenile-

guidence advisors, marriage counselors, teachers, or school administrators have any expertise at all in the field of custodial placement. What each has is knowledge in one or some aspects of child behavior, but none have by virtue of their disciplinary training enough knowledge to make judgments alone. And to suppose that a group of all of them can through discussion come to a common recommendation is often fatuous thinking; more likely such a group will either be riven with contrary views or will come to a consensus conclusion that is a compromise position truly espoused by none of them.

It should also be borne in mind that none of these disciplines, including psychiatry, is so mathematically precise that practitioners in any of them will necessarily come to similar conclusions in identical fact situations. Quite to the contrary, different practitioners will proceed often on different theories contained within the same discipline and end up with contrary conclusions; even practitioners who accept the same theories will often interpret them differently, as a result of different skill levels and emotional biases. Custody trials are replete with psychologists and psychiatrists, all with impressive credentials, who oppose each other's conclusions, not always politely.

Of course, some persons in these disciplines could, through additional training and experience, become conversant with sufficient knowledge to make a sound recommendation for custodial placement, but the point is they should make recommendations, not ultimate decisions. If psychiatrists, who surely begin with the best training to offer custodial views, feel it inappropriate to make these ultimate custodial decisions, why should others of lesser training make them alone or in concert with others? The true functions of all these disciplines in the custody context is to offer to the unbiased judge the aspects of child behavior and parental behavior they have been trained to evaluate and leave to the judge, hopefully without predilections, the burden of deciding who makes more sense and what should therefore be done. What is here essential is that judges have before them sufficient guidelines to tell them what to look for and how to weigh it against other evidence. This is precisely what we hope to provide in this work, or more accurately, what we hope in this work to begin the process of providing.

We believe further that it is crucial that any custody proceeding not only be fair but also be so perceived by the contestants. This is especially necessary in matters of custody, not just because future parenting by the "loser" may depend upon it, but also because violence and/or child snatching may well ensue without it. For any such perception of fairness to result, the arbitor *must* be seen as utterly impartial. For this reason we believe strongly that the ultimate issue of custody should be made by one who is a judge *only*, not one who is a psychologist most of the time and a judge of custody matters occasionally. We fear the actual and perceived impartiality of one who has intertwined professional relationships with those offering evidence and then, when not judging, with those to whom one may offer testimony. We fear the bias that competition between these professionals in their practices could infuse into a proceeding or be erroneously deemed to so infuse.

We believe further that for this perception of fairness to prevail, one seeking custody must have full access to a lawyer in order to produce all the evidence one thinks advances the cause. A contestant must not lose with the feeling that the system itself has not provided a full opportunity to be heard. No one but an attorney is possessed of the training and experience to do this properly. We reject the notion that a full exposition of relevant evidence is as likely to result from impartial investigators retained by the judging authority as it is from the efforts of partial counsel retained by each of the contestants. Here the partiality of each lawyer is balanced by the partiality of the other, and the expertise of each in attacking, especially by cross-examination, the evidence of the other and is checked by the total impartiality of the professional judge. We have seen too often the excesses of zeal produced by the adversary system, but we have also seen much more often how thoroughly this system produces all the evidence needed for a sound judgment. Unlike lawyers, whose job is often the seeking out of evidence, mental health professionals have traditionally been those who simply reacted to what evidence was placed before them. Moreover, the intended impartiality of the mental health professionals makes them a more likely victim of bias since they have no check or balance system that by intent attacks their conclusions. This is so because groups of mental health professionals, working together on a problem, are more likely to defer to each other than challenge each other, resulting usually in consensus decisions. The adversary process, however, primarily through cross-examination, challenges conclusions and places them under close scrutiny. It is no wonder that so many mental health professionals (and others) dislike taking the witness stand. We prefer a process that places custodial evidence of all types under this kind of challenge and scrutiny, with the challenge mounted by trained and partial advocates and the scrutiny that of a detached, full-time generalist.

5

Other Custodial Issues

We have attempted in this volume to present a comprehensive picture of the status of child custody law and practice as it arises in the context of American divorce—what it has been, what it is, and what we would like it to become. We have made certain value judgments in so doing. To those aspects we deemed most important we have devoted full chapters. In this chapter we attempt to present those aspects of lesser import, not meriting full chapters each with examination in depth, but still of significance to mention.

Interstate Custody Disputes

Justice Brandeis once described the States of the United States as "laboratories" wherein social experiments, codified by law, could be made for the benefit of the rest of the nation. If such experiments proved successful the results were available for the future adoption by the other states; if they were not successful, the other states would have learned this lesson without having to pay the price. Clearly the ability to have a multiplicity of "laboratories" has been a great advantage to us, an advantage derived from the peculiar history of this nation of unified sovereignties, but just as our special brand of federalism has created advantages, it has also created disadvantages. The history of interstate custody disputes and child snatching illustrates clearly one of these disadvantages.

The full faith and credit clause[1] of the Constitution requires that each state recognize and enforce the judgments of the courts of the other states. Thus a civil judgment in New Jersey can be, must be, enforced by the appropriate court in Alaska. Custody decrees were, however, unlike other civil judgments. Other civil judgments normally were (and are) fixed and not capable of challenge or variance once the period for appeal had passed. But custodial judgments were (and are) always capable of modification until the child reached the age of majority if it was subsequently decided that a sufficient change in circumstances had occurred to make a change of custody in the best interests of the child. Since the state that entered the original custody judgment could modify its order, any other state faced with the issue of custody of such child had the same right. Thus, a state unfamiliar with the child's history, not privy to the facts attendant upon the existing custody decree, and having jurisdiction solely because one parent had fled there with the child, could avoid the full faith and credit clause legally, hear the matter of custody anew, modify the existing order, give profit to child-snatching, and introduce massive insecurity and chaos into the field of child custody. That is what occurred.[2] A most revealing example of what evils this situation produced is provided by the issue of the *Wall Street Journal* for March 24, 1976,[3] wherein the exploits of one Eugene Austin of Foley, Missouri, were described. Reputedly Mr. Austin snatched more than two hundred children, usually from mothers for fathers, with only Florida on one occasion convicting him of law breaking (aggravated assault). Many, if not most, of the child-snatchings were committed by the noncustodial parents personally and often on the pragmatically sound advice of counsel.

In 1968 the Uniform Child Custody Jurisdiction Act (UCCJA) was issued by the National Conference of Commissions on Uniform State Laws and thereafter approved by the American Bar Association. To date the UCCJA has been enacted in 49 states. Massachusetts has a similar but different statute. The UCCJA specifically lists its purposes in detail because it is breaking "new ground not previously covered by legislation. . . ."[4] Capsulized, these purposes are:

1. To avoid interstate jurisdiction disputes
2. To have the Court that is best able to receive the relevant evidence hear the matter
3. To promote stability for the child by discouraging continuing custody disputes
4. To deter child abductions[5]

The basic scheme of the UCCJA is to present rules for the designation in any custody case of the proper court to have jurisdiction both for the initial custodial determination and for any subsequent modifications of custody. It also legislates means by which other states with germane information should make the state hearing the matter aware of that information. Under the UCCJA the only state that should hear custody cases will usually be the child's "home state," "that state in which the child immediately preceding the time involved lived with his parents, a parent, or person acting as parent, for at least six consecutive months. . . ."[6]

Whereas the "home state" will be the usual state upon which the UCCJA will confer custody jurisdiction, there are three other potential bases. First, it may be a state other than the "home state" if the determination is made that such other state has a "significant connection" with the child and at least one parent (or custodial contestant) and "substantial evidence" is available in that state relevant to a custodial determination.[7] Second, it may not be the "home state" if the child is present in another state and has been abandoned, mistreated, abused, or neglected, or has been threatened with such treatment.[8] Third, it may be the state in which the action is brought if no state qualifies as a "home state," a state with "significant connection" or because of mistreatment.[9]

The UCCJA also includes the deterrent of the pocketbook to discourage attempts to use the wrong state. The court may charge the petitioner to pay the counsel fees and the "necessary travel and other expenses . . . incurred by other parties or their witnesses."[10] This is the kind of exposure that should make petitioners and their lawyers very cautious. Additionally, consistent with the spirit of the

UCCJA, Section 8 thereof grants to the court the option to decline to exercise jurisdiction if the petitioner "has wrongfully taken the child from another state or has engaged in similar reprehensible conduct."[11]

Laws on books and laws in practice may, of course, be utterly different. As recent as 1977 two very respected legal commentators could state:

> The practical result is that under the criminal law of most states child-snatching is not prosecuted. Moreover, police and prosecutors usually are uncooperative, viewing a custody dispute as one example of a family fight that had best be avoided.[12]

Whereas it is our sense that the readiness of prosecutors to enforce child-snatching statues has increased measurably in the past ten years, we also believe that some reluctance to prosecute still exists. No matter how deplorable we may think it is that a parent or an agent may take a child without vigorous police action resulting, it is still easy to understand why from time to time police will be reluctant to become involved. It is, after all, an act different in crucial ways from kidnapping for money by a professional felon. It also is an act that creates in the minds of many onlookers sympathy for the kidnapper rather than concern for either the child or the custodial parent. Superimpose these views on the traditional police and prosecutorial view that this should really be civil business, and you have the reasons why child-snatching parents are not on the whole, have never been, and will probably never be as vigorously pursued by law enforcement personnel as other kidnappers are.

This same type of truth may impair the efficacy of the UCCJA. The type of local bias that in the days before the UCCJA gave custody to child-snatching parents Machiavellian enough and fortunate enough to have a sympathetic home base has not been eliminated just because the UCCJA has passed.

The history of interstate custody disputes is one full of chauvinistic refusal of one court to honor the decisions of a prior, out-of-state court when such decisions *could* have been honored by a refusal to modify them. There is still wide room for "hometown" judges to slide by the UCCJA if they find it an imposition so long as the petitioner makes the necessary jurisdictional claims. Even if they should be so sloppy as to rule in a manner clearly contrary to the UCCJA, not every loser will have the means or the fortitude to appeal, especially when the child in question will stay with the petitioner while the appeal pends. It is not surprising that one commentator has accused the UCCJA of the weakness of "intrinsic naivete" for presupposing "sweet reason and cooperation between trial courts in different states."[13]

In addition to the various criminal statutes for child-snatching the states have enacted and the UCCJA, another attempt has been made to stop the same evil. This is the Parental Kidnapping Prevention Act (PKPA) of 1980.[14]

Congressional findings that necessitated the passage of PKPA were, in part, that the number of interstate custody disputes were increasing, that state courts were inconsistent and conflicting in some of their decisions, that the limitations of our federal system contributed to child abduction and excessive relitigation of custody cases, and that there was a failure by the courts to give due recognition to the decisions of other jurisdictions.[15]

It is not our intent here to treat either UCCJA or PKPA in depth, either individually, or as they differ from each other. For our purposes we wish only to include their primary features and, most of all, be certain that the reader knows of their existence and where to obtain more details if desired. We think that it is worth noting that PKPA makes the Federal Parent Locator Service available in child custody cases and is also available in cases of parental kidnapping.[16] Moreover, PKPA makes the Federal Fugitive Felony Act apply to child abductions interstate and to interstate or international flight to avoid prosecution under applicable State Felony Statutes.[17] Important, too, is the fact that PKPA has been held to articulate "a federal policy of pre-emption in this area and under the Supremacy Clause of the United States Constitution must be accorded priority."[18] The effects of these aspects of PKPA are to make the fugitive abductor subject to be located by the Federal Parent Locator Service for child abduction, to make the FBI qualified to join in the hunt, and to make PKPA superior to UCCJA in the event they differ, as, in fact, they do. We have mentioned PKPA thus far essentially as a police measure. It should be noted and stressed that it also and primarily exists for the purpose of establishing "national standards under which the courts of the various states will determine jurisdiction to decide custody disputes and the effect to be given to custody determinations of other states." Thus, under PKPA, for a court to qualify to modify an order of another state, its own law must give it jurisdiction *and* the prior ordering state must either not have jurisdiction under its own law or decline to assert it.[19] Not surprisingly, this has already resulted in situations where a chosen state would have had jurisdiction under UCCJA Section 3(a)(2) but did not qualify under PKPA.[20]

International Custody Disputes

The full faith and credit clause of our Constitution applies only to the United States; it does not require obeisance to the decrees of other nations. Our states may, however, under the doctrine of comity recognize and enforce a foreign nation's decree. Comity, being a discretionary doctrine, will normally be extended by a state court only if it is satisfied under all of the facts that so doing will not be contrary to the public policy of that state. If the legislation of that state has met the issue raised, then the particular public policy in question will be set forth in such legislation. If the legislation has not specifically articulated public policy, then the court will glean it from the state constitution, from statutes not specifically in point, and from prior court decisions. Comity is extended depending not only on the issue raised but also on the procedures followed by the foreign court. Regardless of the nature of the decision sought to be enforced, if it was reached without what the state court views as reasonable notice to the parties and an appropriately fair chance for the parties to be fully heard, comity will not be extended.

With the passage of UCCJA there was for the first time a basis for the recognition and enforcement of foreign nation decrees that went beyond the doctrine of comity. Section 23 specifically extends the principles of UCCJA to international situations.

Pursuant to this section State courts have already enforced foreign decrees of Australia[21] and England.[22] Quite clearly there are on this planet a large number of judicial systems, not only not in the common law tradition, but also operational on principles unsatisfactory to our courts to whose decrees the UCCJA will show no deference.

The PKPA makes the Fugitive Felon Act applicable to parental child abduction, not only interstate but also internationally. But it applies only if the state in which the abduction occurred treats such abduction as a felony. Delaware,[23] Maryland,[24] Massachusetts,[25] Nebraska,[26] Nevada,[27] New Jersey,[28] New York,[29] South Dakota,[30] Virginia,[31] and West Virginia[32] all have statutes that for various reasons do not or may not make an abducting parent a felon for unlawfully removing a child from the state. In Arizona,[33] Illinois[34] Kentucky,[35] Minnesota,[36] Montana[37] Pennsylvania,[38] and Texas[39] the abduction charge can be avoided or mitigated if the child is returned by the abductor by a certain time. Thus in all these states the involvement of the FBI will either not be warranted or will be subject to delays, and thus the effect of PKPA is weakened.

We simply note here that European attempts have been made to counter the child-snatching problem there. Although these efforts do not as yet directly involve the United States, they are mentioned in the hope that they signal a concerted international march toward treaties eventually capable of reducing this particularly pernicious form of kidnapping.

Visitation

A noncustodial parent will normally be granted rights of visitation with the child in the divorce judgment. These rights of visitation may be fully defined, partially defined, or left to the parents to be explicitly defined. In this latter instance the judgment will generally grant to the noncustodial parent the right of "reasonable visitation." While this language is not specific and obviously leaves to the parents the task of defining it, nonetheless, it establishes a standard of reasonableness that allows a court to determine, if asked, whether or not the visitation the custodial parent has allowed, or the noncustodial parent has requested, is consistent with the order or is in contravention of it.

The fully defined visitation order will specify, often to the minute, precisely when the noncustodial parent may have the child. A common order, for example, would in part provide that:

The child shall be with father on alternate weekends commencing Friday at 5:00 P.M. through Sunday at 7:00 P.M.

Such an order, fully defined, would also grant precise visitation rights for the school vacation periods, other holidays, and such special days as Father's Day, father's birthday, child's birthday, etc.

In some cases the noncustodial parent may have one or two specific visitation requests but be willing to have the balance of the visitation rights left "reasonable" rather than specific. A common situation where this form of order is appropriate occurs when the noncustodial parent lives at too far a distance for frequent, regular visitation to be practical but wants to be certain that the major visitation period is specified. Example:

Mother shall have the child with her in Phoenix, Arizona, each summer from July 15 through August 31. She shall also have the right of reasonable visitation with the child whenever she shall be in Hartford, Connecticut (child's residence).

Visitation, like custody, is a right that can be taken away or modified for cause. The standard that underlies "cause" is the best interests of the child. But a right is different from an obligation, and neither custody nor visitation rights is an obligation. Thus a court cannot order a parent to be a child custodian if the parent does not wish to be, and it cannot order a noncustodial parent to either acquire visitation rights, or having acquired them, to exercise them. The court may, of course, impose obligations as limitations on these rights, but this does not transform the right into an obligation. For example, while a court cannot compel a parent to take custody, it can compel a custodial parent to allow rights of visitation, and while it cannot compel a noncustodial parent to visit, it can compel him/her to return the child by a specific time if visitation occurs.

A custodial judgment that grants custody to one parent and rights of visitation to the other parent carries with it other implications. First, tax consequences generally ensue. The custodial parent will almost always have the child in residence primarily and thus will be the probable recipient of the right to take that child as a dependent for income tax purposes. This is presumptive, however, not absolute, for the ultimate determination will depend on the amount of support being paid by the noncustodial parent, but it is still true that the custodial parent starts out ahead in this quest. Moreover, the custodial parent will be also probably the parent who qualifies as a "head of household" and thereby is entitled to a more favorable tax rate than is available to a single person who is not head of a household.[40]

Second, the noncustodial parent lacks certain abilities that flow only from an order giving full or joint custody. The noncustodial parent cannot authorize a medical procedure in an emergency and usually will not as of right be entitled to medical reports. The noncustodial parent may be entitled in law to such things as school reports but may find that they will be denied by the issuers who think they should be sent only to the custodial parent. What should be thoroughly understood is that not only *should* access to such information be available to noncustodial parents, but also it can easily be made available by a simple, supplemental order in the judgment. Such an order would provide:

> The noncustodial parent shall be entitled to prompt notice of any occurrence of importance in the life of the child, and therefore, the custodial parent shall immediately execute written authorizations and deliver them to the noncustodial parent allowing all school personnel and medical personnel to give to the noncustodial parent all reports and information they may now have or issue in the future concerning the health and educational progress of child. The custodial parent shall provide the noncustodial parent with additional authorizations in the future as said medical and/or school personnel shall change so that the noncustodial parent shall at all times during the minority of child be able to keep current respecting child's health and educational progress.[41]

Such an order need not, of course, be limited to health and medical information and should also be complemented by an additional order compelling the custodial parent to give the noncustodial parent prompt notice of the occurrence or the potential occurrence of *all* meaningful events in the child's life such as awards, sports activities, trips, etc. The major point here is that no noncustodial parent needs to be in the dark about a child's life simply because that parent lacks custody or joint custody. A request for such an order would very rarely be denied.

Third, depending upon the jurisdiction, a noncustodial parent with the right of reasonable visitation could be rendered powerless if the custodial parent should without notice vacate the state and take up residence far away. The Connecticut Supreme Court has ruled that an order of reasonable visitation, made without contemplation that the custodial parent would leave the state, and made when the custodial parent was in fact residing in Connecticut, was not violated by the custodial parent's removal to Florida.[42] The court in effect said that reasonable visitation is the same right wherever the child may be. To the father who anticipated visitation close by, however, the effect of this ruling was to give him a far reduced ability to see his child, a practical result that should have dictated the Supreme Court's decision. The Court chose, however, to render this strange decision, and therefore, the recipient of an order of reasonable visitation should have an accompanying provision in the judgment that bars the custodial parent from relocating out of the state (or beyond "x" miles from the present residence) if the recipient is to have any protection against such a move. A lesser protection would be an order not barring such a move per se but barring such a move without sufficient advance notice to the noncustodial parent to provide an opportunity to litigate whether or not the intended move is a proper reason to change the orders of custody and/or visitation.

One cannot fairly condemn custodial parents who remove children beyond the reasonable, frequent access of noncustodial parents even though the upset and loss imposed upon the noncustodial parent by so doing is great. The right to live where one wishes is a basic one and one not lightly to be denied or impaired. One also cannot aver flatly that it will be against the best interests of a child to move even though a result of the move is to intensify the separation of the child and the noncustodial parent. But surely where the noncustodial parent has not left the jurisdiction wherein that party resided when the custody decree was entered, or has moved closer to the child, the custodial parent should not be allowed the opportunity to move unilaterally so far away as to negate visitation without the prior approval of the court. We suggest this as a need because we are convinced that effectuation of the noncustodial parent's access to a child is entitled to be presumed to be in the best interests of that child and therefore entitled to judicial protection.

How do we protect it?

1. We begin by mandating that every custodial judgment contain an order prohibiting either parent from removing the residence of the child more than "x" miles away from its present residence and also from removing the child itself away from the then residence for more than "x" days without the written agreement of the parties or permission of the court.[43]

2. We provide that upon the occurrence of such inappropriate removal, and upon the filing with the court of an appropriate motion, with proper notice to the offending parent, the court shall have the authority, if such unauthorized removal has persisted to the date of hearing, to fine the offender and/or terminate, suspend, or reduce the noncustodial parent's support obligations and/ or to then determine whether such unauthorized removal has so violated the child's best interests as to warrant a change of custody or visitation.

This provision would operate to protect not only the noncustodial parent with rights of visitation, but every parent, custodial or visitational, who is victimized by an unauthorized removal. The fact that now, without such a proposed limiting order, such an unauthorized removal would usually violate a custody or visitation order is no argument against the proposal because the ability of a court to hold such a violator in contempt of its custody or visitation orders is not sufficient to solve the problem. After all, the offender will by definition be outside the state when the finding of contempt is made and thus not reachable by the court and surely not jailable. Thus the court must have alternatives. It should have the power to fine and fine heavily, but fines will be ineffective if the offender has wealth. It should have the power to terminate support, but again, if the offender is wealthy, withdrawal of support may have little or no effect. The power to terminate support must in some jurisdictions be supplied by new statute because there is authority for the view that the duty to support "is wholly independent of the right of visitation."[44] Most of all it needs the authority to alter custody if it finds that such removal was so inimical to the child as to make a change in the child's best interests. We do *not* recommend that custody be changed as a means of punishing the offending parent. We do, however, consider it quite possible that unilaterally taking a child away from the other parent and its presumably more secure environment may be bad for the child. Thus we see such an act as an appropriate trigger for custody reevaluation. We also see such a reevaluation as a deterrent, along with fines and terminating support payments, to unilateral removals. We consider it more important that the child be returned so that a full study can be made of the wisdom of removal than that the offender be punished and thus would negate any penalties if the child is back in the home jurisdiction at the time of the hearing. While we are sympathetic to any parent deprived of the chance to stay in constant or least frequent contact with a child, we are more concerned about the upset to a child that a thoughtless removal can create. The proposal we make is, therefore, primarily one for the protection of children.

Nonparental Rights

Although one generally thinks of divorce-based custody disputes as arising only between the divorcing parents, it is nevertheless true that persons other than parents are increasingly being heard as alternative custodians and as persons entitled to rights of visitation. Most often nonparental custody and/or visitation is sought by, and granted to, grandparents, but the nonparental class is not restricted to grandparents. Though the grandparental right to visitation has been statutorily made available only if the parent of the child (who is the child of the grandparent in question) has died, received no visitation rights, or failed to exercise visitation rights previously bestowed, nonetheless, such restrictions are rare.[45] In a few jurisdictions visitation rights have been specifically extended to great grandparents,[46] stepparents,[47] other family members,[47] other relatives,[48] and to other persons, not necessarily related, if the best interests of the child so require.[49]

With respect to custody there are many states in which the statutory language does not restrict the court to parents only as custodial designees.[50] In most of the states whose statutes seem to contemplate nonparental custody orders, the standard for choosing the custodian is simply the best interests of the child, but in some jurisdictions the court cannot award nonparental custody without first determining that an order of parental custody would be detrimental to the child.[51]

There is a great difference between a statute that permits a court to grant custody or visitation rights to a nonparent and one that permits a nonparent to seek actively to obtain such orders.[52] It is the difference between passive and active, between simply receiving rights because the evidence of others points that way and intervening as a party, with counsel, entitled to present evidence and wage judicial war.

To understand how unnecessarily complicated this question of nonparental custodial/visitational rights can become, let us examine the present state of the law in Connecticut.

Under the primary custodial statute[53] (hereinafter called 46b−56), the court may grant custody "to the parents jointly, to either party or to a third party," and it may also "make any order granting the right of visitation of any child to a third party including but not limited to grandparents."

Section 46b-57[54] allows the court to let "any interested third party or parties" intervene "in my controversy . . . as to the custody of minor children" and it "may award full or partial custody, care, education and visitation rights of such child to any such third party. . . ." The court may do this "in any controversy before the Superior Court as to the custody of minor children." Any order it enters should be made "guided by the best interests of the child."

Both 46b-56 and 46b-57 authorize court action only when there is a controversy before it. This is not the case with 46b-59,[55] which simply allows the Superior Court to "grant the right of visitation with respect to any minor child or children to any person, upon an application of such person." Thus under 46b-59 a nonparent may initiate litigation to obtain visitation rights to a child whose parents are not divorcing and could be quite healthfully married. Any such order of visitation could, under 46b-59, be later terminated if the custody of that child should later be litigated because of divorce or otherwise. Practically speaking, any divorce action subsequent to a

46b-59 visitation order would certainly address the feasibility of such an order and would modify it, terminate it, or order it anew.

In 1981 the Connecticut Supreme Court interpreted 46b-57[56] and in so doing severely limited the previously supposed breadth and utility of the ability to intervene. This case—Manter v. Manter—held that one could intervene in a divorce only if there was a prior controversy regarding custody or visitation existing independently of the motion to intervene. In other words, if grandparents wish rights of visitation, they *cannot* intervene to press for these rights unless the parties to the divorce have before that time engaged in a then pending controversy about custody and/or visitation relating to (presumably) the same child the grandparents want to see. In the same Manter case the trial court ruled against allowing the proposed intervenor to intervene, not only because there was not a preexisting controversy but also because he was not felt to have a close enough relationship to the children to qualify for custody and/or visitation—in spite of the fact that the statute speaks of "any interested third party" and appears, therefore, to impose no a priori restrictions on who may apply to intervene. Indeed the statute reads as though the only test (ignoring arguendo the controversy requirement) should be the best interests of the child. The Supreme Court did not address the question of who could intervene in the Manter decision, because the appellant was fatally wounded by the court's requirement for a preexistent controversy, but in its discussion the court does provide this dictum:

> We do, however, observe that under its mandate to give "paramount consideration in custody matters" to the child's welfare (citations omitted), the court may employ a flexible test of interest in harmony with the broad language of the statute.

> The traditional family model, never itself strictly limited to the nuclear unit, is today one among numerous variations on the extended family. (Citations omitted.) Courts in other jurisdictions have responded by granting visitation rights to such nontraditional parties as stepparents where the child's welfare dictated that result. (Citations omitted.) Our decision today is in no way intended to prejudge future interpretations of the phrase "interested third party" under 46b-57 where the controversy requirement is met and the trial court finds a prospective intervenor to have a significant concern for the welfare of the child.[57]

As a result of these three statutes and the Manter case, the present situation in Connecticut respecting nonparental rights of custody and visitation appears to be as follows[58]:

1. If the parents are not divorcing, have not divorced, and no other court controversy exists respecting custody, 46b-59 allows a nonparental aspirant for *visitation only* to seek such rights by initiating court action for that purpose.
2. Since 46b-59 allows "any interested third party" to seek rights of visitation, and since this is almost identical to the "any person" referred to in 46b-57, we presume that to qualify under 46b-59 an applicant will have to satisfy the "significant concern" test of the Manter case.
3. No one knows who qualifies under the "significant concern" test or for that matter what the test is.
4. Once a divorce action is commenced, 46b-59 becomes inapplicable and any order previously entered pursuant to this authority is subject to termination, modification, or continuation by the divorce judgment. Whether or not a beneficiary of a visitation order under 46b-59, outstanding at the onset of a divorce between the parents of the child in question, would have standing by virtue of such an order to enter the divorce as a party, is unclear.
5. When a divorce is pending, the court, under 46b-56, can grant custodial and/or visitation rights, inter alia, "to a third party." This is a passive right, however, allowing the court to grant but not allowing "a third party" to seek. Again it is probable that to qualify as a suitable "third party," the person in question would have to satisfy the undefined "significant concern" test of the Manter opinion.
6. For a nonparent seeking to assert a claim for custody and/or visitation once a divorce has begun, as the result of Manter, there *must* be a preexistent controversy. Almost always this will mean that there must be a dispute pending between the parents. Thus the court is powerless to hear the claim of a nonparent if two negligent parents make a negligent agreement about custody and thus raise no dispute on the subject. This is a result so bizarre and so unmindful of the best interests of children that one can get vertigo from the mere contemplation of it.

We believe and assert that the best interests of children should be the determinative tenet that pervades all provisions of the law of custody. Thus we recommend that:

1. Any person be allowed to seek rights of custody and/or visitation whether or not a divorce is pending, regardless of that person's relationship to the child, and with the full status of a party to any existing controversy.
2. The best interests of the child should be in any action the sole barometer utilized to apportion custodial and visitation rights. Accordingly, joint custody should be an available arrangement, not only between parents, but also between parents and nonparents. The fact that these arrangements are often not likely to commend themselves is no reason to bar them. Human affairs are unpredictable and thus the impossible tends to occur and the improbable tends to occur frequently.

We do not make these recommendations unmindful of the usual heavy emotional investment of parents in their children. We fully understand the sorrow that generally attends parental losses of custody. But children have a right to be reared in the most healthful alternative available and society has an interest in the healthful rearing of its minor citizens. These considerations must precede parental desires. Children must not be parceled out to parents because of sympathy for the parents' prospective loss. Obviously, therefore, we oppose statutes that impose a parental preference upon courts facing custodial decisions such as that in Nevada where "Before the court makes an order awarding custody to any person other than a parent, without the consent of the parents, it shall make a finding that an award of custody to a parent would be detrimental to the child. . . ."[59]

We are also mindful of the body of law, emanating from the United States Supreme Court, inter alia, that describes and enunciates a parental right respecting children of Constitutional basis.[60] This constitutional right of parents is not, however, absolute.[61] It is rather the creation of a presumption in favor of parents, a "parental preference," which should be superseded by the child's best interests if they conflict. The real issue is not the protection of parental rights per se but whether or not placing the "best interests of the child" ahead of parental rights as a determinant will result in nonparental custody when there really *ought* to be parental custody. The real fear is that nonparents of solid, middle-class accomplishment and character will take custody away from loving, bonded, but bohemian parents or that rich uncle will raise the child because the parents cannot afford preparatory school, college, and a big house. This is a genuine and proper concern, but not one of sufficient merit to be determinative. One could just as easily be concerned about a situation where two parents are living happily with each other, not even considering the possibility of divorce, but at the same time being abusive and/or neglectful of a child or children. Under these circumstances it would surely be preferable to afford a civil action for custody to a close relative or even an unrelated person with close ties to the child or children involved.

The way to deal with the issue of nonparental custody is not to prohibit or deter custody in nonparents but rather to do one's best to create criteria for custody that will lessen the chances of custody being granted to whatever persons are not likely to serve the true best interests of the child.[62] We believe that the criteria set forth in this work serve that aim and would effectively give such nonparents as the hypothetical rich uncle no chance of receiving custody if properly applied, certainly less chance that they now would have with our present vague, essentially subjective criteria. We cannot either promise or predict that this standard would always lead to the right choice, but nothing born of human beings or administered by human beings can attain perfection—it is surely sufficient to commend a recommendation that it reduces the chance for error. We believe we can claim this.

We also believe that for a nonparent to achieve custody under the criteria we propose there would have to have occurred such a failure of parenting that the demands of this doctrine of parental preference would be normally satisfied.

Custodial Relocation

Given the extraordinarily high degree of mobility that characterizes our society generally, it is not surprising that often spouses wish to leave their residential area after divorce. This can create vexing problems when the desire to move includes the desire to move a child. When should children be moved *away* from a nonresidential parent to a different locale preferred by the custodial parent? What criteria should be used to answer this question?

In thirty-four American states no special statutory criteria have been articulated to govern the removal of minor children from the jurisdiction after divorce.[63] The general standard of "the best interests of the children" is applied to this question, as well as to every other aspect of child custody. In sixteen states there are statutory provisions,[64] which differ markedly. The Georgia Code provides only that "the court entering such judgment shall retain jurisdiction of the care for the purpose of ordering the custodial parent to notify the court of any changes in the residence of the child."[65]

The Illinois statute[66] *requires* the Court's permission before minors can be permanently removed; the standard for removal is the best interests of the child. Improved employment opportunities,[67] improved educational facilities for the child,[68] and improved child health and welfare[69] are among some of the factors Illinois has found justifying removal. The simple desire to move has been found insufficient to justify removal.[70] The inconvenience alone of the noncustodial parent that the removal would create is not sufficient to bar removal.[71]

In Indiana a custodian who wishes to relocate a child's residence that is outside Indiana or one hundred miles or more from the prior county of residence must file a "notice of that intent" with the court clerk and to each noncustodial parent.[72]

Iowa simply lists "changes in the residence of a party" as a factor for the court to consider in a custody modification hearing.[73]

Kansas requires a relocation notice of twenty-one days before a change of residence or a removal exceeding ninety days. Additionally the failure to give notice subjects the custodian to potential contempt punishment and to claims by the aggrieved parent for counsel fees "and any other expenses incurred . . . by reason of the failure to give notice."[74]

Louisiana's statute[75] requires no notice, restriction, or penalty provision. It simply provides that where parents were domiciled in Louisiana and an order of joint custody ensued, the presumption in favor of joint custody ceases if either parent thereafter moves out of state.

New Jersey's statute bars the removal of minors from New Jersey where they are "natives" of New Jersey "or have resided five years within its limits" if the children do not consent, "if of suitable age to signify the same, nor while under that age without the consent of both parents" unless the court shall so order.[76] The statute of Massachusetts is similar.[77]

Minnesota flatly prohibits the custodial parent from removing a child out of state except by court order or the noncustodial parent's consent if such noncustodial parent has visitation rights. It further orders that such relocation be denied "if the purpose of the move is to interfere with visitation rights. . . ."[78]

Missouri likewise prohibits any residence relocation or child removal for more than ninety days except by court order or "the written consent of the parties with custody or visitation rights." This statute then provides: "Violation of a court order under this section may be deemed a change of circumstances under section 452.410, allowing the court to modify the prior custody decree."[79]

In Montana a change or intended change of residence by a custodian out of state qualified as a factor to be considered if custody is sought to be modified.[80]

New Mexico requires written, thirty-day notice if either parent "plans to change (a child's) home city or state of residence. . . ."[81]

North Carolina addresses only the potential problem of a child whom the custodian is obligated to return to the state but may not. Its statute provides for the possibility of bond or other security to insure the child's return.[82]

North Dakota requires that a custodial parent not change the child's residence to another state without court order or the noncustodial parent's consent if the noncustodial parent has rights of visitation *unless* the noncustodial parent "has not exercised such visitation rights for a period of one year."[83]

Pennsylvania's statute allows for review of the existing custody order if *either* party "intends to or does remove himself or the child" from Pennsylvania.[84]

Wisconsin requires statutorily that the custodian must get the written approval of the visitation parent or a court order to remove the child out of state either to live or to stay longer than ninety days. Failure to do so can allow the court to modify the custody order.[85]

Minnesota prohibits a custodial parent from removing a child's residence out of state "except upon order of the court *or with the consent of the noncustodial parent* (emphasis added) if such noncustodial parent has rights of visitation.[86] This statute specifically bars such a removal "if the purpose of the move is to interfere with visitation rights given to the noncustodial parent. . . .

Massachusetts and New Jersey have judicially created as a test for relocation the weighing of the advantages and disadvantages that would result. In New Jersey's leading case[87] the court opined that what would be advantageous to the new family unit (the one with the children to be relocated) would also be in the best interest of the children. If the parent desiring to relocate can demonstrate that relocation would be advantageous to this unit, and thus to the children, then the court must ascertain the true motivation for the proposed relocation, whether the relocating parent will comply with future orders respecting access of the children with the other parent, why the other parent objects to relocation, and whether adequate access will be available if the relocation occurs. In Massachusetts judges must consider all of the advantages or disadvantages of the proposed relocation, including the noncustodial parent's relationship to the children, the relationships between the children, the relationship of the custodial parent to the children, the well-being of the custodial parent, and the preferences of the children,[88] and, in addition the noncustodial parent's ability to see the children at their new address.[89]

The state that has enunciated the most stringent test for removal is New York. Here the case law requires a custodian desiring to relocate to show that "exceptional circumstances" exist to justify relocation.[90] The judicially avowed purposes of this rigorous criterion is to "provide an incentive for the custodial parent to avoid relocation if possible, thereby furthering the public policy goal of assuring that children of divorcing parents have meaningful access to both parents."[91]

We feel the answer to whether or not a primary custodial parent should be able to relocate a child's residence out of the jurisdiction wherein the other parent resides, and wherein the parties resided when the operative orders of custody and visitation were entered, is one that will necessarily have to vary from case to case. The answer must be gleaned from all the available facts that bear upon which living arrangement will be in a given child's best interests. It is, once again, a facet of custody that deserves inquiry unburdened by presumptions in order that the best results be obtained.

Specifically, we reject the "exceptional circumstances" test not only because it supplants the best interests of the child as the basic criterion but also because it is clearly capable of including results *not* in a child's best interest.[92] This is so because it elevates the visitation parent's ease of access to the unjustified level of a presumption that must be overcome. Custody decisions should be clearly and solely focused on the *child*. If it is better for a child to be removed despite a total or partial loss of visitation, then that child should be removed. This does not mean at all that we fail to recognize the importance normally of continued, qualitative access to the noncustodial parent; it means only that we object to elevating *any* single factor above others as a matter of law because such elevation serves to stifle investigation into the given child's particular needs.

The "advantages and disadvantages" test is also objectionable. In practice it appears to be a rephrasing of the best interest test and thus one might be tempted to see it as inappropriate but innocuously so. We object to it because we see the best interest test as satisfactory and would apply it throughout the field of custody decisions. After all, if it is the appropriate test for custody itself why should it not be appropriate for a custodial issue of lesser importance? Experience tells you that once you use different words, even if you mean to say the same thing, someone will conclude that you have said something different. "If you meant to say the same thing the second time," he will argue, "why didn't you say it the same way?" Thus, to avoid some judge or judges making decisions under an "advantages and disadvantages" test that would not be made under the best interest test, do not create an "advantages and disadvantages" test.

There is in our view no need for a special relocation statute at all. If a custodian wishes to remove a child, and if the other party has objection, the other party is free to raise the issue by seeking to modify the outstanding custody order in order either to obtain custody or bar the child's removal.

What *is* needed in order to provide an opportunity for such a motion to be filed timely is a statutory provision requiring that *any person*, who by order of a court of competent jurisdiction, has a right of custody *or* visitation, must give notice at least sixty days before such person makes a change of address.[93] This notice should specify the full new address, the date of removal, and whether or not the person intends to have the said child at such new address when the child is in the person's possession. Note that this statutory provision would apply to *visitation* address changes also.

With this type of statute each concerned person is entitled to notice and can seek modifications of existing orders before the move occurs. It is not sensible to make *only* the primary custodial parent give notice; it is quite possible that the custodian may object to the visitation parent's having the child in the intended abode. This notice would not be necessary only if a proposed move were out of state; it would be necessary *whenever* the mover intended to go. The in-state out-of-state distinction is useless. Obviously a move out of state that is two miles away from the prior residence will cause less disruption in the custody-visitation pattern than a move hundreds of miles away but within the same state. Such a notice statute further ensures that the parties will notify each other directly, not simply use the child as a conduit for oral or written messages. It would also save the end of protecting the child against potential feelings of anxiety and guilt caused by abrupt movements of those close to the child, for presumably, with such a statute at least *one* of the custodial figures would tell the child of the proposed move at least sixty days before it was scheduled.

There is a tendency in this phase of child custody, as there is also in the making of the basic custody award, to forget that the child is a person whose best interests should be the sole focus of inquiry. Instead one sees states focusing on what is fair to the noncustodial parent or on what type of behavior or attitude impels a parent to move. Factors like these should not be allowed to supplant the best interests of the child as the operative criterion for custodial decisions. Minnesota, for example, in its removal statute, provides that "If the purpose of the move is to interfere with visitation rights given to the noncustodial parent by the decree, the Court shall not permit the child's residence to be moved to another state."[94]

Since it is possible that a custodial parent can wish to move away from Minnesota wholly or primarily to create distance between the child and the noncustodial parent *and*, if successful in so doing, will remove the child to a new location that will better serve that child's interest, the Minnesota statute can create harmful results and should be repealed. We repeat: if an act is unfair to a parent but in the developmental future of a child it is beneficial, that act should be ordered. The strength of this assertion does not mean we easily or at all remove the noncustodial parent from the custodial equation; it means only that the whole is greater than any part and the noncustodial parent's custodial input is only a part.

We think it important to add that the right of a custodian to relocate should never require the specific consent of the child. We have spoken earlier in this work of the need to protect children against guilt, which so easily accrues when they think they are making decisions a parent will dislike. We have also spoken of the reasons why children's decisions under these circumstances can easily be the opposite of what they really desire. The same need to avoid damaging guilt and poor decisions exists in the area of relocation as exists in the larger area of custodial placement. The burden of decision should never be on the child. The child may speak, and should be heard, but others must determine what the child really means and really needs.

Perhaps the most objectionable aspect of the law that has been enacted in this area is that represented by the statutes of Missouri and Wisconsin. These states have provided statutorily that a custodian who unlawfully removes a child from the jurisdiction may well for that reason alone lose custody of that child. We cannot stress too strongly how inappropriate and dangerous it is to use the custody of a child as a punishment. While it is thoroughly understandable to wish to punish a custodian who flouts the law and acts with extreme rudeness to the other parent, it can never be in the best interest of the child to change that child's custody without a full consideration of all of the relevant factors. This is not to say that we object to punishment for one in contempt of court orders in general or in the field of custody. We can certainly subscribe to the approach of Kansas wherein removal of a child contemptuously may incur not only court-imposed sanctions but also the payment to the aggrieved person of counsel fees and monetary damages.

We must not forget how complex the issue of custody is. We must remember always how many factors must be expertly weighed in order to reach the right determination. We must also constantly remember that the sole purpose of this often agonizing process is to protect the children whose lives require custodial definition. Only when we forget these truths and become deflected in our purpose do we make custodial disposition possible solely because one custodian has done something wrong or another custodian has been victimized.

TWO

CLINICAL APPLICATIONS

6

A Developmental Model for Parent Evaluation

Parent Personality Organization

It is an incontestable fact that at the time of marital dissolution, parents acting in concert are the persons most qualified to make custody decisions. Parents, motivated by love and disciplined by objectivity, know far better than any court what is best for their children. Unfortunately, such objectivity sometimes does not exist. It becomes necessary, therefore, for third parties to influence or render those decisions.

A thorough custody evaluation begins with interviews with the parents and the child and usually the family as well. It includes data collected from teachers, pediatricians, therapists, and others. If necessary, adjunctive procedures such as psychological testing or an educational evaluation will be requested. It is the evaluator's task to synthesize this information in order to answer the question of interest to the court and parents alike: which parent can more successfully further the healthy growth and development of the child?

A holistic method of child custody evaluation—one that does not rely on gender presumptions or succumb to rigid dogmatism—must appraise two major components: parent and child personality organization and the psychological tie between child and parent. We understand that neither factor is to be considered apart from the other nor emphasized at the other's expense; parent and child personality and the parent-child affiliation are complementary. Maturity in the parent and positive development in the child strengthen the tie between them, which in turn promotes further growth and healthier parenting.

One might contend that it is presumptuous for anyone, regardless of expertise or skill, to identify which of two parents will be more fit to parent their child. At present the mental health field can do no more than identify some of the components of good parenting. Furthermore, these components seem to interact synergistically; there is seemingly no way to precisely predict the effect of any particular combination.

Notwithstanding the impossibility of creating a precise and formulaic method of evaluating parents, it is still desirable to improve the process of parent selection, and this is the measure of what we propose to do here. Nonetheless, we are fully aware that there will always be the final "intangible" qualities that sometimes make for good parenting in spite of seemingly insurmountable deficiencies in parent personality organization.

Further, since there are so many factors that bear on the developmental process—the child's constitutional endowment, the total family function, and extrafamilial influences comprise but a few— we cannot identify a strict causal relationship between parenting ability and the child's emotional development. Anyone familiar with development and family process will testify to the complexity of the forces that shape a child's personality. Therefore, the effects of parent personality organization on the child should be thought of as probable outcomes rather than conclusive predictions. The fact that a custodial recommendation is based on empirical evidence should not disguise the element of speculation inherent in choosing one parent over the other. We are dealing with a process that is both complex and in the end only one of the contributors to a healthy childhood.

In addition, the evaluator must be aware that the principal sources of information in child custody evaluations are potentially vulnerable to bias and subjectivity. This understanding applies not only to the persons being interviewed, as well as to the sources of collateral information, but also to the evaluator. These facts should impart a sense of humility to the professional vested with the responsibility for rendering custody recommendations.

This methodology is, therefore, at best a modest attempt to improve the means by which custody recommendations are made through an examination of the personality development of both parent and child, and the reciprocal connection between them. With its acknowledged limitations, we believe it offers that hope of maximizing the child's contact with the parent who can better promote growth.

Developmental Focus

To even a casual observer watching a healthy parent and child, the chemistry is obvious. To describe and define in words what is so clear to our eyes and ears is impossible. But if we search our observing selves, we can recall the telltale signs: a parent happy for a child's achievement regardless of how small it may be, a parent compassionately involved in a child's disappointment or experiencing the sheer pleasure of the youngster's presence. This child basks in the sunlight of the parent's approval or pleasure and responds appreciatively to the sensitivity.

The personality qualities that allow this kind of parental investment are generally subsumed under the term *maturity*. Thus, the ability to parent is considerably influenced by maturity. Every adult has achieved a certain level of maturity, each component of which developed within a specific epoch of childhood. Although development begins in childhood, one hopes it does not end there. Everybody has the opportunity to progressively mature throughout life. Naturally each person's level of maturity will fluctuate, within a certain range, on a daily or even hourly basis, depending on environmental stresses. Nevertheless, the level of developmental progress achieved by each adult, and therefore each parent, produces stable and relatively enduring character traits. Many of these traits govern major aspects of parent-child interaction.

Further, the components of parent development that result in specific character traits and thus influence relationships with children can be defined, examined separately, and, more than that, measured in a rough quantitative sense. By gauging a parent's progress in these areas, that person's level of maturity can be ascertained. We have identified five components of particular importance. A parent with healthy personality organization in these areas will be better able to encourage the child's psychological growth; therefore that parent will be a better custodial candidate. A parent's impairment in these areas of personality organization can potentially lead to stasis and perhaps even regression in the child's personality development.

What follows is a methodologic approach for parent evaluation using the aforementioned personality components. In the ensuing chapters we refer to the custodial aspirants as parents. We do this for simplicity, and because in the vast majority of cases, the aspirants will be parents. This does not mean, however, that we do not believe that, in unusual cases, the appropriate guardian may not be a grandparent, sibling,[1] stepparent, other relatives, or even an unrelated person.[2] Parent personality organizational features to be used will include the following:

1. nurturance and empathy
2. degree of personality separation and individuation
3. impulse control
4. reality testing
5. identity organization

These components can be designated parent personality functions.[3] Later in this chapter they will be explained in detail.

However condensed, they represent the capacity to emotionally invest in a child and put the child's needs before one's own, what is ordinarily considered love; the ability to foster independence and the child's unique personality; sufficient control over one's anger, aggression, and sexual impulses to help one's child develop normal self-control; sufficient objectivity and clarity to help the child correctly assess the environment; and enough strength in one's personality to project a secure sexual identity and healthy values and beliefs.

Thus, they are attributes that will contribute to how well or how poorly parents will interact with the world around them and, more specifically, with their child. Since the areas chosen for assessment are such crucial components of personality organization, adults who have achieved relative health in those areas will have a positive influence on developing children in their care. The converse is not necessarily true. If a parent should experience conflict along the designated parameters of evaluation, it may or may not adversely influence the developing child. Only an evaluation will verify the presence or absence of a correlation between psychological disturbance in a parent and the child's deviation from normal development.

All but the last of these parent ego functions, or developmental lines, operate along a continuum from low level to high level. Identity organization, in contrast, does not exist as a graduated continuum of maturity. Some identity qualities are healthy and others are not, and it is the presence or absence of these traits, rather than relative progress in identity organization, that is of interest to the evaluator. Progress or the lack thereof along these continua and the extent to which identity has evolved in a healthy or unhealthy fashion will result in certain behavioral and emotional qualities. To a custody evaluator these qualities should be readily identifiable.

Let us offer an example of how problematic fixation along a parent developmental line may adversely influence a child's development. It would appear that a child's personality is often most vulnerable in those areas that coincide with the parent's own unneutralized conflicts.[4] For example, development may proceed reasonably well until a child begins to test authority as a result of growing independence. This testing may awaken the parent's own unresolved conflict with authority. As a consequence of parental overreaction, independence seeking may be transformed into rebellion.

One might question the wisdom of using adult personality functions as a means of conducting custody evaluations. But in fact, parent developmental lines are used on a daily basis by mental health professionals in an attempt to understand parent-child relationships, being routinely invoked to explain the impact of a parent's overprotectiveness on a child's school phobia or the causal effect of a father's or mother's excessive investment in a child's achievement generally— and that youngster's school performance in particular—to name but two applications.

To the best of our knowledge, however, no attempt has been made to formally use a series of parent personality functions as a means of determining that person's capacity as a custodial guardian.

Since the parent developmental lines operate on a continuum, those who have progressed substantially can be quantitatively distinguished from those who have advanced very little. We believe there is a significant correlation between the degree of progression and the capacity to parent. The measure of movement can be roughly assessed by the personality qualities and behavior reflected in those persons' daily lives and in the interview setting. By locating the extent of an adult's growth on the various continua and evaluating that person's identity organization, not only can the parent be identified who is less likely to promote the child's growth and development, but also the one who is more likely to do the same can be elicited, through the recognition of their strengths. Thus, both parenting strengths and weaknesses can be ascertained. As a result, affirmative reasons for recommending custody can be offered in addition to negative ones.

Another advantage lies in being able to discriminate along any one developmental line between those factors that should be considered of major importance and those of minor influence. In addition, assets along one particular avenue of development can be compared with liabilities along that same or other lines.

Other parent personality functions or developmental lines might have been chosen but were not. In our experience, a parent's development along the selected lines bears most strongly on the emotional development of children placed in that adult's care. Certainly we hasten to add that the proposed system is intended only as a point of reference, as one tool in the evaluator's repertoire of approaches.

It is important to recognize that it is not the primary aim of the evaluator to describe, identify, or diagnose adult emotional disturbance. Certainly these should not be excluded from consideration; emotional disturbance may indeed affect how a parent functions and therefore may influence the children in that family. But it is relevant only insofar as it affects actual parenting ability.

We are instead attempting to draw a clinical correlation between parents' maturity in several areas and their children's development, presuming one exists. We want to know, therefore, how a parent functions, as a parent, not specifically how disturbed or not disturbed he or she is. Thus the application of the approach allows custody evaluators to avoid the practice followed by many, that of identifying the parent with the greater level of psychopathology and recommending custody for the other parent. For this reason, the classifi-

cation method we have chosen is different from the standard classification scheme according to the *Diagnostic and Statistical Manual
of Mental Disorders,* the DSM-III-R.

We are fully aware of the danger inherent in this system. First and
foremost there is the risk of generalization. One must take care not
to treat a parent's development along a maturational line as prescriptive of a particular constellation of behavioral qualities. An adult who
falls roughly at a particular level of development may have none,
some, or all of the suggested qualities. Other qualities may be present
that were not suggested in this discussion. In the experience of the
authors, though, the identified traits are valid, frequently occurring
examples of personality features and behaviors of parents who approximate a certain level of growth along that developmental line.
They are presented, however, only as examples of characteristics that
commonly correlate with a particular degree of progression. They are
employed to illustrate how a measure of advancement along a developmental line can affect parenting and to demonstrate the relatively graduated nature of the developmental lines. But in no way
should they be viewed as categories that will universally exist. Parents' functional capacity defies categorization. Any attempt at relating movement along a particular developmental line with a specific
constellation of characteristics would represent a clear overgeneral-
ization. The experienced evaluator knows that one identifies a constellation of qualities in a person being interviewed as a means of
assessing that individual's development, but the converse is not true.
One cannot presume to isolate a particular set of characteristics that
will universally serve as the markers of maturational progress.

Another point must be emphasized. Parent developmental lines and
identity interlock and interact with each other. To use a particular
ingredient in a parent's personality drawn from one specific developmental line, whether positive or negative, as a sole criterion for
recommending for or against that person's obtaining custody is as
harmful as making no recommendation at all—perhaps more so. The
same can be said for drawing simplistic conclusions from superficial
correlations. An adequate family evaluation consists of assessing parent personality functions, including progress along each developmental line, coupled with a comparison with the child's evaluation
data. When this is compared with collateral information, a reason-

able basis for making a recommendation will have been established. The experienced evaluator is aware that clinical judgment entails weighing all the factors in the parents' development and balancing those against all the information obtained from a child's evaluation. Understanding adult developmental lines and identity organization, and their connection to children's development requires an appreciation of the intricacy and complexity of these interwoven relationships. Even then, the mysterious chemistry that lies at the heart of a child's development will be beyond the depths of our ability to plumb.

When using these developmental lines to evaluate personality functioning, we make the assumption that progress along one avenue of development will be paralleled by progress along another, an assumption borne out by our experience and by theoretical reasoning. It is extremely uncommon to find a parent whose relative development along different axes of personality organization is remarkably discrepant. In fact, it would be practically unheard of to discover someone who functions optimally in two areas of personality development and at the bottom of the other two.

Another salient fact is that development along these axes is relatively enduring. The resultant behavioral qualities, because of their roots in the organization of personality, do not fluctuate beyond a certain limited range. This endurance is useful in assuring the evaluator that recommendations based on the proper application of this proposed methodology should not vary between evaluations done by different people at different times.

The enduring nature of these qualities will also assure contesting parents that no one will be able to deceive the evaluator by painting a rosy self-picture during the evaluation interviews. Recommendations should be based, not on either custody candidate's opinion of self or of the other candidate, but instead on the relatively permanent personality organization of each. The term "relatively permanent" is used because whereas these qualities are enduring and will not change in and of themselves, they are mutable. A parent may fluctuate on a regular basis in the development level of behavioral expressions, within a certain range. We all know that we are more mature on some occasions and less so on others. The level of maturity we exhibit in any facet of our personality at any particular time depends on the internal and external stresses to which we are subject and our motivations in that particular situation. This means that a parent who wishes to change can, with effort, do so. Although this can happen through psychotherapy or simply through consistent effort at self-awareness coupled with a determination to brave the uncomfortable emotions triggered by attempts to change, the latter is more difficult.

This is important for two reasons. A skillful custody evaluator should consider if a parent has the potential and motivation to improve parenting skills. Consequently, once a particular quality has been elicited, whether positive or negative, its chronicity, the extent to which it falls within the parent's self-awareness, and the degree of its tenacity can be ascertained. The evaluator may believe the positive or negative quality in combination with other findings does not warrant a custody recommendation in that parent's favor. If, however, the quality is very affirmatively influential in the former instance or quite modifiable in the latter, a recommendation for some type of greater visitation might be made. The opportunity for greater parental involvement might well enhance the influence of a positive quality or it might give a parent with a modifiable negative quality an opportunity to improve parenting involvement. In addition, a custody decision rendered previously may be reevaluated at the request of one or both parents on the basis of a change in one candidate's personality organization.

As an advocate for the involved children it behooves each custody evaluator to explain to parents how their offspring may benefit from improved parenting and also, within reasonable limits, to provide opportunities for it to happen. Using developmental line findings, a parent can be helped to see in behavioral or personality terms when progress might be made to improve parenting skills.

In this light it should be apparent that the custody evaluator's task is not to search out the factual truth of all allegations. Custodial aspirants, judges, lawyers, and especially evaluators themselves must all clearly understand that the best result an evaluator can normally achieve is to recommend the custodial arrangement with the best probability of success, based on an understanding of the reciprocal interaction between the parents and children and its impact on the latter's emotional growth.

Children's Development

Whereas the developmental level of parents is a major subject of focus in this methodology, the developmental level of the child must also be considered in rendering custody recommendations. D. W. Winnecott, in coining the term "good enough mothering," clearly demonstrated that good parenting is not independent of a child's age.[5] Rather, parenting skills must be adapted to the scale and scope of children's needs at various phases in their emotional and intellectual development. This adaptation, without requiring wholly different parental qualities at different ages, does require a flexible parent willing to understand and address the variety of maturational issues that arise over the course of childhood, both during the current developmental phase and through future phases. To restate the point, it is not a matter of searching for different parenting skills in each phase of development. Healthy parenting will be represented by the application of the same parenting skills with different emphasis and foci based on the child's changing needs.[6]

Formal Parent Evaluation

What follows is a discussion of the aforementioned parent developmental lines and identity organization. As one examines the developmental lines it will be apparent that there is considerable overlap between lines. It is the nature of personality formation that the components are interwoven. One element triggers or is reliant upon another, and any one quality or behavior may be prompted by factors along two or more lines. Consequently one must be discerning so as not to take intricacy for redundancy.

Nurturance and Empathy

In the course of many custody evaluations, one heartfelt conviction is common to both opposing parties: that the parent being interviewed deeply and unconditionally loves the child and that the other parent does not display equivalent love. Of course, this poses an impossible task: to determine which of two parents more loves the child. In fact, it cannot be accomplished inasmuch as love is defined so differently by each person using the term. It may, however, be possible to determine to what extent each parent has a positive and growth-promoting emotional investment in the child. Not only is this likely to occur only in the presence of love, but also it is a rough index of the degree of healthy love. For very young children in particular, developing reciprocal investment is manifested by a mutual, preferential attachment. The form of this attachment will depend to a certain extent on the age of the child.

Two of the most crucial, even essential, ingredients in such an investment are nurturance and empathy. Empathy is the capacity to instinctively and intuitively put oneself in another's place, to share another's feelings. To do so is to temporarily suppress one's own self-interest for the sake of the other person.[7] This quality of empathy is a core component in the attachment process.[8] In its presence attachment flourishes, in its absence attachment never germinates.

For our purposes, nurturance will mean responding to the developing child's need for security, love, affection, instinctual gratification, and verbal support. By these means love is expressed, and development is promoted.

Prerequisite to the development of nurturance and empathy are self-esteem and the ability to value others apart from the purpose they serve.[9] Nurturing others and emotionally putting oneself "in the shoes of the other" require a sufficiently large measure of self-worth to rest confident in the knowledge that one's own needs will be met in good time, making sacrifice for the sake of a child both possible and worthwhile. Further, one's own development must have progressed to the point where others are no longer esteemed for the purpose they serve but rather for their intrinsic value as people. In this context, babies are not "prized possessions" intended to pump up a parent's self-worth or a failing marriage, nor should they be expected to serve as the sole or even primary determinant of their parents' mood. They are persons who have their own needs apart from the satisfaction they provide adults. Enduring feelings of self-worth and the capacity to truly value others, the requisite constituents of a parent's ability to project nurturance and empathy, are governed by a dual developmental path: the ability to love and value oneself and the ability to love and value others.[10]

Evaluating Parental Capacity for Nurturance and Empathy Although nurturance and empathy are especially crucial during the first three years of the child's life, they remain important throughout childhood. Secure in the knowledge of available parental love and understanding, the school-age child can transfer trust in the parent to peer relationships that compete with those earlier ties. Such trust prepares these children to handle the enormous number of potential and actual insults to their egos inflicted during this developmental phase: academic disappointments, rejection by peers, and competitive failures. Similarly, in adolescence, peer relationships, particularly evolving love relationships, and academic endeavors are forums for feelings of rejection and failure.

To the parent who has achieved substantial progress along this developmental line, the nurturant response is preferential—based on the young child's needs and time frames and, within reasonable limits, without regard to the adult's need state at the moment. Parental needs are balanced against the intensity and urgency of the baby's distress.[11]

As children advance in age, what were formerly absolute needs for gratification, protection, and parental assumption of responsibility become relative. The parent of the school-age child and adolescent expresses nurturance and empathy by looking behind moody and even rebellious behavior to understand the tortured feelings concealed by the child's reactions.

The picture we have of the empathic parent is that of a secure person, motivated by the high value placed on the intrinsic worth of others, and on the child in particular. Therefore, this person responds to the reality of the child's state, not merely that portion refracted through adult needs and anxieties. When this parent errs, normal guilt is triggered. The empathic parent is not consumed or punished by guilt but is rather guided by it toward a better dispatch of future responsibilities. The empathic parent is the good enough parent.

A parent who falls at the lower end of this developmental continuum may present in several different ways. Basic child caring responsibilities are often ignored, reflecting weak attachment. It would seem that this father or mother disregards some of the basic ingredients of child care.[12] Not only is there a deficiency in motivation to solve problems, there is often a mood state evidenced in bland responses that challenges one to distinguish between depression and apathy. Just as empathy is lacking, so is there a deficiency in self-regard,[13] often manifested by severe detachment. Further, self-esteem impairment triggers the conviction that one is a total victim of the world.[14] Apart from the "bad days" common to all parents, these persons regularly substitute verbal attacks for emotional support and discipline when faced with the occasional displays of immaturity and misbehavior demonstrated by every child.

Other parents who suffer self-esteem deficiency are need-gratifying. Commonly vain, pompous, and arrogant, this person may be pleasure-seeking—habituated to drinking or carousing. However, the basic problem lies in a proclivity for self-indulgence, and more specifically, self-absorption or self-interest.

Although more emotionally invested in others[15] than the parent with extreme self-esteem deficiency, the parent who inordinately seeks security still does not display investments that operate at a consistently high enough level.[16] An expressed wish or demand on the part of another adult, who is a security providing figure, will compel this parent's time and attention to the exclusion of commitments to the child. All intense love relationships provide security, but when the relationship is measured by the degree to which it quells anxiety, it is predominantly security-providing as opposed to loving.

Whereas the young child cared for by the extremely self-esteem deficient parent may experience a "failure to thrive,"[17] older children may suffer in other ways. Often failing to form attachments early in childhood they sometimes display uninhibited indiscriminate friendliness, are attention seeking, and lack the capacity for guilt and the ability to form lasting relationships.[18] Others become parentified. Still other children, representing narcissistic extensions of their parents, grow up with the entitled conviction that the pampered preferred treatment accorded by the parent is their just due.

The Impact of Nurturance and Empathy on Custody Considerations In the field of custody determination there is probably no area of investigation that has greater importance than the ability of a parent to emotionally invest in children. This is especially so for the young child who is in the midst of an intense attachment to one or both parents. The intensity of the tie between child and parent, either father or mother, will be roughly proportional to each parent's healthy, consistent and repetitive attendance to the child.[19] Such attendance means emotional responsiveness in contrast to simply physical care. Naturally this will be commensurate with the emotional investment of that adult. And that in turn will be indexed by the capacity for nurturance and empathy.

Therefore every person conducting a custody evaluation involving infants, toddlers, and even preschool children should bear this in mind. Observing a baby with its parents will provide evidence of who are the principal and subsidiary attachment figures. It has generally been assumed that since mothers have traditionally been primary caretakers, they will predominantly be the principal attachment figures. Neither of these assumptions is necessarily true.[20] Recent work strongly suggests that the ability to nurture is not gender specific.[21] It is entirely possible, therefore, for children to have, in addition to two equal caretakers, two principal attachment figures, father and mother, to whom there is an equal but different tie. Further, the intensity of attachment is not necessarily related to the measure of physical care provided. It behooves custody evaluators to look beyond the point of simply who the primary caretaker is. Of equal and sometimes greater importance is with whom is the child most emotionally involved.

Apart from the significance of particular attachment figures, careful consideration must be given to the level of sensitivity of the baby's current developmental stage. Beyond the first few weeks of life, but prior to five or six months, removal of an infant from a parent to whom a baby is predominantly attached should be effected very cautiously.[22] During the stage of greatest attachment, roughly from the sixth to the fourteenth month, extreme care must be exercised in considering such a change, and then only for the most cogent reasons, e.g., serious parental neglect or abuse.[23] This consideration will be less compelling as the child approaches the third, fourth, and fifth years.[24]

It is not simply age, however, that determines the child's ability to be separated from an attachment figure. As a child approaches the time when longer separations can be tolerated, there is far less need to be in the proximity of an attachment figure, separations of one to several days are tolerated without distress, mutual interest in and ties to both parents and to other subsidiary attachment figures are demonstrated, and there are displays of increasing interest in playing with peers. In addition, shifting parental moods are handled without undue anxiety. For some children this may occur at an earlier than expected age; for others it may occur at a later age.

Given that the evaluator must exercise great caution in removing a child from the domicile of an unrivaled principal attachment figure during sensitive periods of attachment, it is still very important to identify that parent who is better able to promote the emotional tie, bring the phase to a successful conclusion, and foster growth past the point of intense attachment. It is possible for a variety of reasons that the parent who more possesses these qualities did not become a principal attachment figure. While the relative importance assumed by a principal attachment figure during the highly sensitive period is profound, it is also temporary. Further, if an apparent principal attachment figure is very deficient in the other areas of personality organization, the evaluator must question the validity of the attachment. Despite a child's urgent need to be around this parent, the actual mutual emotional investment of parent and child may be weak and the apparent attachment may in fact represent dependence, insecurity, and clinging due to the parent's inability to separate. The child's dependence may also be intensified by the other parent's relative unavailability as an attachment figure. In any case, after the child has emerged from the most sensitive period of attachment, both parents, provided each is either a principal or subsidiary attachment figure, may compete for custody on the basis of their total constellation of parenting skills.

In most custody evaluations at least one parent will generally make the point that he or she carried the major role in raising the children. One must, however, distinguish between obligatory and loving child rearing. It is not enough to inquire about who fed, diapered, and put children to bed. In conversation with the parent who acts out of obligation, it may be apparent that responsibilities were handled with a sense of duty but emotional support was not available. When a child was injured, the proper physical care was provided, but the emotional wound was not bathed with nurturance. In contrast, the parent who is more empathic will show the desired feeling response when coping with children's difficulties. For instance, in the office setting, the parent's compassion and understanding, coupled with firm direction, will show through as the youngster's academic deterioration precipitated by the marital separation is discussed.

The pleasure arising from a shared empathic experience is also to be distinguished from the artificial pleasure displayed by the parent who is manipulating to obtain cutody. At times a spurious request for custody arises out of a desire to obtain a better financial settlement or to retaliate against a rejecting spouse. For this reason an evaluator must give significant consideration to continuity of care and consistency. Adults who have been continuous in their involvement with children have demonstrated commitment.[25] A parent who is manipulating will attempt to persuade the evaluator that he or she has been the more involved of the two parents, albeit for a relatively short time. If a parent is committed, that person's intent is clear. It is unnecessary to "sell" the evaluator. Not only does the longitudinal record of involvement speak to the point of intent, but also when the committed parent talks of assuming responsibility for child care, for example, it is clear that he or she is ready to cope with expected adversities. Despite this, on balance, a pleasurable experience is anticipated. Similarly, one can use the nature of parental pleasure and pride to distinguish between truly nurturant parents and seemingly nurturant parents whose child actually represents an extension of their own ego. There is a significant difference between the shared pleasure of a mutual emotional investment resulting in affection and the pleasure arising from the child's accomplishments fanning the flames of the parent's ego.

A phenomenon common to many marital dissolutions is undervaluation of one's spouse as a parent. This may simply represent the lack of regard arising from normal anger, which is a common element in the breakdown of every marital relationship. It may also, however, represent a characterologic defect emanating from a parent's tendency to undervalue others. This is especially true in the case of parents with need-gratifying qualities, who are often so committed to their own need gratification that they lack the capacity to truly value a marital partner as a person.[26] By probing this person's initial attraction to the spouse, the evaluator can gauge the undervaluing parent's ability for self-scrutinization and objectivity. The more objective person can be helped to recognize how the anger arising from marital conflict has clouded the recognition of the other parent's value.

Frequently the matter never reaches the point of a custody evaluation because the undervalued partner, complementing the devaluing partner's point of view, does not pursue custody. In point of fact, this person may be the better custodial parent but needs encouragement from legal counsel to seek that goal. The denigration of a marital partner can spawn a variety of problems. Among these is the practice of arbitrarily restricting visitation because the other parent is not considered sufficiently worthwhile to warrant the requisite investment of time and energy or may, in the opinion of the residential parent, be such an inadequate person as to be a bad influence on children.[27] Whereas a child should not be put in jeopardy by being placed in the care of someone who is reckless, impulsive, or dangerous—e.g., drinks while driving—by the same token, the mere fact that the residential parent considers the former spouse characterologically flawed should not be adequate reason for restricting visits. There is a distinction between deficient character resulting in truly hazardous actions and the marginal risk of questionable but not really dangerous practices. Visitation restrictions should be based on documented evidence of danger, not on suspicions and fears, which flourish in the adversarial environment of divorce and evaluation.

In contrast, the empathic parent seeks to understand the good, as well as the bad, qualities of the former mate and attempts to recognize and accept personal mistakes, including those that contributed to the marital failure. Because this level of self-regard is matched by equal regard for others, this adult possesses the ability to ascribe worth to the other parent.

Pivotal importance has been accorded to the ability to share and involve the other parent.[28] Only if one appreciates the growing child's ongoing need for the other parent, especially as a role model, can one grasp the importance of recognizing that person's good qualities. Even if the other parent seems to have few redeeming qualities, it is important that the child have visitation contact. If it serves no other purpose, it will, at least, decrease the youth's propensity for developing an idealized image of that parent. This would not apply, naturally, to those parents who represent serious physical, or even psychological, threats to their children. Also, the more confident a child is that the residential parent can accept the good aspects of the other parent, the more comfortable that youngster will feel about criticizing the other adult without experiencing guilt. Finally, children identify more realistically when they are able to recognize both the positive and negative blend in their parents' personalities.

Because persons with security-seeking elements in their personalities are subject to anticipatory rejection in any intense emotional relationship, they have a tendency to triangulate: feeling jealous or stirring jealousy in others. In the context of a divorcing family, the security-seeking parent may become jealous of a former spouse's relationship with their children. This may entail involving the children in loyalty struggles as a means of increasing security. It may entail one parent's severely criticizing the other parent, either to the children or in their presence, in order to win their favor. It can lead such a parent to indulge the children in order to curry their favor. It can even lead a parent to seek custody, not necessarily because of deep convictions about the relative suitability of each adult, but because it may alleviate insecurity or serve as a means of retaliation. Although rejected by a former spouse, retaining the children will at least cushion the loss. Or it may "even the score" and thus provide vindication and bring about "justice."

In any custody dispute, the available evidence can present conflicting portrayals of a parent's personality.

> For example, a forty-one-year-old man asking for custody of his eight-year-old daughter seemed to consciously manipulate the arousal of her anger with her mother. For her part, the thirty-seven-year-old mother was self-centered and preoccupied with her own interests to the relative exclusion of her daughter. Against this was a background of the father's having been deeply invested in this youngster since early childhood. Further, the evaluator was convinced that whichever way the custody decision went, the father wanted the best arrangement for his child. In the evaluator's opinion these two factors were cogent reasons for rendering a recommendation in favor of the father, notwithstanding his manipulative efforts.

Self-esteem injury and insecurity can affect the involved children as well. Because of feelings of rejection and abandonment, a child, especially an adolescent, may refuse visitation. Or because of an identification with the parent they view as a victim, overprotection of or an alignment with that parent may result. Also, children may get caught up in an attempt on the part of one of their parents to overindulge them in order to ensure their allegiance. In situations like these, a parent's tolerance and ability to empathetically appreciate the meaning behind the child's behavior will be taxed to the limit. A parent must tread a fine line between empathy and surrender. Suffering must be appreciated without encouraging or identifying with it, and the parent must seek to understand the "real" hidden emotions rather than simply react to the surface behavior. To do these things, even with great difficulty, speaks more eloquently for a person's capacity as a custodial parent than any noble sentiments voiced.

Separation/Individuation

The term *separation* refers to independence: the ability to function separately from other people, both physically and emotionally.[29] Individuation refers to uniqueness: the development of personality characteristics that identify one as a distinct individual.[30] Separation and individuation, as characteristics of a parent's personality organization, play important roles in the parent's discharge of child-caring responsibilities.

The individual who has achieved personality separation can be alone without anxiety, make independent decisions and be comfortable with, validate, and sustain the separateness of personal thoughts and feelings. Characteristically the person who is individuated may emulate others and unconsciously adopt another's personality characteristics through identification. Once adopted, however, those qualities become part of an integrated personality. The individuated person does not attempt to mimic others or to rebel against an identification with others.

Successful parenting requires both an unequivocal desire on the part of the caretaker to foster independence in the child and the capacity to take pleasure in the child's pride in his or her evolving uniqueness as a human being. Parents who are gratified by their own personal separateness and autonomy wish their child to share the experience. Unencumbered by doubts, this person is emotionally available to foster the child's progress. Encouragement is given the youngster to seek whatever level of autonomy is within that boy's or girl's capability, regardless of age. This parent desires the offspring to become a unique person. Therefore, no attempts are made to mold and shape the youth into an image of the parent's making.

Assessing the Capacity for Separation/Individuation in Parents
Although separation and individuation are dual developmental paths paralleling each other, in this section we will primarily address the extent to which progression toward separation and independence affects parenting. A discussion about personality uniqueness is best left for the section on identity.

A word that graphically characterizes the parent who has not advanced substantially along this continuum is "fearful."[31] Convinced that their sometimes horrifying fears will translate into reality, this person may be unable to distinguish between the end point of fears and the beginning of reality.

Since the child is often the object of the fears, any physical distancing is forcefully suppressed. Not only this person, but frequently the entire family become prisoners of the basic fear of abandonment.[32] Because the child is viewed as an integral part of the parent, thoughts, fears, beliefs, and fantasies are projected onto the boy or girl. Thus fears, wishes, and beliefs belonging to the adult are attributed to the child.

Naturally there are parents who have advanced more substantially along this developmental line and therefore possess qualities that promote dependence to a lesser degree. Usually, however, to whatever degree the traits are present there are certain common features; indulgence, infantilization, and overprotectiveness. Indulging infantile wishes fosters dependence because it facilitates regression. Encouraging immature behavior or infantilization has the same impact. Owing to considerable ambivalence regarding independence, this parent is overly protective and unwilling to grant freedom.

One consequence of a parent's lack of discrimination between personal emotions and those of the child is the assumption of personal responsibility for the child's feelings. As a consequence, the adult feels compelled to relieve the youngster of any worry, anxiety, or fear.[33] An extension of this problem is the proclivity for projecting anger and even rage onto the other parent,[34] which, when compounded by an identification with the child viewed as victim, results in the other parent's being seen as inimical to the child.

For the adult who has become developmentally more autonomous, there is great pleasure in a child's increasing age-appropriate separation, growing independence, and evolving personality uniqueness. Utilizing the precepts of graduated development and "good-enough parenting," at the proper time and in a phased fashion, the child is urged to explore the house, the yard, and ultimately the community. If it should be the parents' judgment that any such step is premature, it is restrained until readiness is demonstrated. A high priority is placed on the acquisition of such independence-fostering skills as self-care, assuming a higher level of self-expectations, and coping with personal problems.

Not immune to the troubling emotions that accompany independence seeking, the parent who possesses considerable autonomy tolerates them, taking them as a signal for action, when action seems appropriate. Likewise, the children of these persons are encouraged to accept and handle their unpleasant emotions rather than regress when faced with them. For instance, aware that separation anxiety will attend major separations, going off to school for the first time, being left for the evening with a babysitter, etc., the child is encouraged to cope with the situation, confronting and therefore learning to live with unpleasant emotions.

Beyond teaching acceptance of personal emotions, an independence-promoting parent encourages individual expression. Great pride is taken in the child's ability and willingness to think independently and to develop independent ideas even when they are diametrically opposite to those of the parents.[35] Finally, for this parent, the right to be alone at times is not only respected but also encouraged. It might be said of parents who value autonomy that they neither sanction nor condemn overly dependent behavior. Instead, they attempt to kindly and firmly alter it.

The impact of dependency-promoting parenting on a child will vary according to the extent to which the other parent is assertively independent and will also depend upon the age of the child. The very young child, for example, will come to view any physical separation as dangerous, missing opportunities for independent exploration, and thereby becoming incurious and cautious in relation to the environment. Growing older, the youngster may develop a reluctance to express opinions or feelings that would deviate from those of an adult, lest disapproval and perhaps abandonment ensue. The child is more likely to display this fear through behavior than to verbalize it. For the school-age child age-inappropriate habits such as thumb-sucking may seem necessary to create security. This child may also seek inappropriate protection by adults from real and imagined tormentors, frequently peers. In addition to the innate psychological damage that these behaviors represent, they will also increase the child's social isolation. The adolescent may continue this withdrawn pattern or may instead rebel as a substitute for independence and individuation.

Separation/Individuation as It Relates to Specific Custody Considerations   Parents who have difficulty separating their emotions from those of their children will be very anxious to remove those children from any worry, whether it has to do with friends, school, or family. It is this person who is most likely to suggest that divorce will not be considered because of the children.[36] Likewise, it is generally not this person who chose to separate. Fearful of triggering criticism and disapproval, this parent may hinder an objective custody reevaluation by refusing to discuss the parenting deficiencies of the spouse.

To this parent there are probably few threats that evoke more fear and anxiety than the possibility of losing custody. It strikes at the most intense source of the anxiety, the anticipation of possible separation and loss. For this person every fear is at risk of becoming a reality; therefore, possibilities are transformed into certainties.

Anticipating the loss of their child, this person may predict dire consequences if not granted custody. Clearly, this message is transmitted both to the involved child and to officials of the court. Many a custody evaluator has been intimidated by such threats. If such warnings can frighten a professional adult, one can imagine their effect on a vulnerable child. In point of fact, through intense dependence and a willingness to make subjective predictions about the horrifying consequences of a separation from the child, this parent is very often able to manipulate an evaluator into recommending custody be granted to him or her. This parent is very sincere, and therefore, very convincing.

Through the projection of parental fear onto the child, which reinforces the youngster's already existent fears, separation anxiety is easily triggered at the visitation interface. Even though the crying, clinging, and begging to remain with the residential parent rapidly cease once the child leaves, this person is convinced that the other parent is the source of the distress. When the crying and agitation are reignited upon returning home, this parent quickly concludes that something untoward happened on the visit.

In contrast the parent who functions more autonomously is emotionally available,[37] provides verbal and physical support, remains understanding, tries to verbally put the disquieting experience into perspective, and encourages the youngster to go on visitation.

It should not be surprising that the parent who has not been able to achieve differentiation from the child believes that anyone who endorses separation and independence is bad. This includes the custody evaluator. Consequently, one of the premises upon which the evaluation rests, placing the child in a circumstance where he or she can achieve the greatest level of independence, renders the process adversarial and the clinician an adversary.

It may be beneficial to offer the parents a few clarifications. It is not the purpose of the evaluation to take a child away from either parent but rather to place the child in an environment that will most promote growth. Because one person might be better able to accomplish that at present does not automatically make that person a better parent. Second, while everyone agrees, in theory, that independence is healthy, no one likes the anxiety and insecurity that accompany its progression. But since anxiety is a concomitant of all growth, one must learn to accept it. Whether or not these comments are reassuring and stimulate motivation to handle anxiety, they may serve as a diagnostic tool to plumb the depths and rigidity of the parent's dependence.

For example, a forty-one-year-old woman who was marginally alcoholic and who had been the primary caretaker of her ten-year-old son all of his life complained bitterly that her more rigid and self-righteous husband was attempting to woo their son away from her. She feared her husband might obtain custody. Discussing the child's emerging identification with his father as an indication of growth and encouraging her to handle the feelings of anxiety and rejection stirred within her led to a commitment to encourage greater closeness between the father and son. As a result the evaluator was able to recognize her ability to cope with growing independence in a more positive fashion than she had previously demonstrated.

Finally, the important distinction between dependence and attachment must be clarif d. Dependence is easily confused with attachment. Dependence represents a reliance on others, age appropriate or inappropriate, which diminishes anxiety. Attachment is a relatively time-limited tie constituting a mutual emotional investment arising from survival need, containing but not wholly consisting of age-appropriate dependence and culminating in a reciprocal respect for the intrinsic value of the other person and the ability to separate, externally and internally. It is common for any parent who has promoted substantial dependence in the children to contend that the children's extreme dependence on the parent is evidence of overwhelming attachment. Clinging and an unwillingness to stray out of sight are interpreted as love and affection. Such a dependent youngster is a far cry from the independent, adventurous, and affectionate preschooler at the end of the period of attachment. Notwithstanding this distinction, many agree that dependence and attachment are synonymous and coincident. Perhaps this is because it is so tempting to yield to dependence and so difficult to be separate and independent.

Impulse Control

The reasonable and satisfactory control of one's impulses should be a fundamental component of every parent's repertoire of personality skills. Impulse control is important, not only as a determinant of the relative enrichment of the family's intellectual, social, and emotional environment, but also as a catalyst for the child's own development of autonomy and self-esteem. Throughout childhood, a youngster's development will be directly affected by a parent's expression of instinctual drives.

In homes where there is satisfactory impulse control, children have a better chance to feel loved and cherished. They have little reason to fear either unprovoked verbal eruptions or physical assaults. In other words, they enjoy a state of security and trust that the environment will reflect continuity and stability. This continuity and stability, as well as the model of successful impulse control provided by their parents, enables them to develop better self-control and mastery of their bodies. With these successes come a sense of inner assurance and tranquility; self-control engenders self-confidence.

Evaluating Impulse Control Capacity in Parents The range of impulse control problems in parents at the time of a divorce is as broad as that of dependency-related problems. The spectrum runs from severe abuse to the parent who, under the stress of the divorce, has mild temper outbursts due to a fluctuating mood state. Impulse control, like separation, operates on a continuum and, at any one time, emotional stress will play an important role in determining a parent's ability to display impulse control.

Impulses, however sophisticated, are based on instinctual desires for oral, anal, sexual, or aggressive gratification. The person on the lower end of the impulse control continuum, one with relatively less control over these instinctual desires, may be given to extreme excess in one or more areas, including substance abuse, physical abuse, and sexual abuse of children. Additionally, problems with impulse control are cross-instinctual in that a higher incidence of one difficulty is frequently found in populations who suffer from another.[38] Thus, those who have impulse control problems commonly share characteristic personality patterns. Cardinal manifestations of the parent with impulse control problems include projection of responsibility,[39] denial,[40] rationalization,[41] serious self-esteem deficiencies,[42] role reversals and distorted identifications—especially in the case of physical abusers.[43] A core characteristic of the abusive parent lies in a deficiency in empathy that results in impaired attachment to the children.[44]

There is no question but that impulse-disordered parenting in its most extreme form is profoundly destructive to children.[45] But the manner in which their emotional suffering manifests itself depends to a great extent upon the child's gender. Boys who have been the victims of physical abuse become bullying and aggressive themselves, indiscriminately taking the possessions of others or initiating unprovoked assaults. Girls who have been physically abused are more likely to display a great desire to be held and a reliance on autoerotic activities such as hair-twirling, thumb-sucking, and clinging behavior.[46] As these children grow up, violence becomes a prominent part of their lives and frequently results in their becoming abusers themselves.[47]

Abused children of both genders will display social withdrawal, fearfulness, anxiety, eating and sleeping disturbances, depression and low self-esteem, somatic complaints, poor peer relations, eroticization, repetitive sex play, sexually destructive behavior, substance abuse, running away, and a decline in school performance.[48] Boys in particular may react to sexual abuse by internalizing their aggression through self-destructive activities leading to such characteristics as obesity, anorexia, self-mutilation, suicide, or self-medication and by becoming depressed; or they may externalize their aggression as they grow older through child or spousal abuse or even murder. Other male victims suffer hyperactivity, excitability, recurring fears, nightmares, and crying spells. Girls who have been sexually abused frequently act self-destructively or may become sexually promiscuous. Both boys and girls may become involved in homosexuality.[49]

Poor impulse control need not imply stereotypically uncontrolled behavior. Indeed, one example of poor impulse control is that of the person who is overly restrictive. Such excessive self-control is commonly associated with self-denial, a preoccupation with cleanliness and neatness, and a compulsive desire for perfection that may translate into controlling behavior. Inordinately circumspect, this individual is frequently ambivalent regarding discipline, fluctuating between restriction and permissiveness.[50]

In contrast, the parent who is under better emotional control will manifest self-control in a healthy, growth-promoting fashion. Such a parent will administer discipline using some methodologic approach and will apply steady, consistent limits with love and compassion rather than through the imposition of "seat-of-the-pants" punishment. This parent may employ a variety of disciplinary measures including corporal punishment, deprivation, isolation, and induction. Further, discipline is tailored to the particular act of misconduct and to the child's developmental level. This parent will seek to contain the breaches of impulse control that do occur. Whether such fractures involve alcohol consumption, sexual expression, or excessive discharge of anger, they are kept within reasonable boundaries and they will trigger appropriate guilt, which will serve to facilitate self-control.

Impulse Control As It Relates to Custody Considerations Allegations of loss of impulse control are common in custody disputes. Many charges center around physical aggression, ranging from excessive and/or harsh discipline to physical abuse. Other accusations focus on improper sexual behavior, again operating within a range from seductive actions to outright sexual abuse. These allegations are generally denied, the branded parent accusing the other of lying in order to gain a stronger position in the custody battle.

For someone embarking on an assessment, understanding the evaluator's role in such conflicts is crucial to carrying out the task. It is the job of the custody evaluator to draw a probable conclusion about what took place. This will be based heavily on the evaluator's convictions regarding the accuracy of what was reported by various family members. These convictions will arise, not only from the evaluator's observations about the likely truthfulness of each involved person, but also from an understanding of the individual, interpersonal, and family dynamics. Generally those dynamics will point toward one inference over another but will not necessarily be conclusive.

An important piece of evidence in evaluating such claims is the presence or absence of personality qualities typical of abusive persons in the accused parent. It is known that certain qualities are more frequently manifest in the personalities of serious abusers: self-image impairment, role-reversals, rationalization, empathic deficiency, denial, and, especially in physical abusers, projection and distorted identifications. These last two qualities would appear to be essential psychopathologic elements in parents who physically abuse their children. These parents project their distorted perceptions onto their young children and respond impulsively in accordance with their own misperceptions.[51]

While the presence of these mechanisms obviously does not serve as specific, confirmed evidence of abuse, their presence or absence, especially when it centers around the child, may be used to a substantial degree to corroborate what has already been partially or largely concluded. It should be a part of every custody evaluation where such allegations exist to diagnostically challenge these qualities so as to test their depth and rigidity. If the magnitude and frequency of their operation is great, at the very least, this person is heavily reliant on self-deception. This may be especially so with regard to adult behavior directed at children.

In some instances children may share a parent's inability to discriminate between fact and fiction. Young children are heavily influenced by the opinion of adults to whom they are strongly tied, often to the point of reporting either what they believe this adult believes, or what they think this adult wants to hear, possibly for both positive and negative reasons. While it is not a factual truth, neither is it a lie; it is a distortion! Adults who have some selective impairment in their capacity to assess reality and who have experienced a rejection or even an abandonment may project their worst fears onto that abandoning and/or rejecting person. These fears may relate to sexual or physical abuse. This is not a lie but, rather, a misperception. Those perceptions may be complemented by a child's need to accept a parent's misperceptions, transmitted when the parent reinforces unconscious suggestions made to the child.

It is important that the evaluator remain dispassionate in investigating these charges. Few practices will arouse more emotion in an evaluator than physical or sexual abuse. If these practices, or substance abuse, is suspected, it is crucial that the evaluator address questions regarding discipline, sexual practices, and substance use straightforwardly and without apology. An inhibition to do so may arise either from the interviewer's presumption that the parent is guilty or a concern that the parent will suspect that such is the case. Or, without being aware of it, the evaluator may be intimidated by the anticipation of a hostile response. Although many child abusers, physical and sexual, are passive, dependent, seemingly compliant, and perhaps even self-effacing and taciturn, an equally characteristic pattern is for the parent to be suspicious, and often pervasively hostile. Anger permeates the personality of this individual and may be triggered by seemingly minor stimuli.[52] Nevertheless, the evaluator must press these questions without prejudice or pause.

Short of outright sexual abusers are those parents who are insensitive to the impact of sexually stimulating situations on their children. For instance a parent may introduce the child to a person with whom the parent is having an affair. Even more potentially startling and stimulating is the practice of entertaining casual sexual partners during a child's overnight visitation. While the parent might justify the practice on the grounds of being open and forthright, it usually arises from an unconscious attempt to alleviate guilt over that parent's role in the family dissolution. This person may believe sexual involvement more justified if sanctioned by a youngster's acceptance. Whatever the reason, at the very least, it places the child in a possible loyalty struggle and exposes the child to inappropriate sexual stimulation.

These more minor infractions of good impulse boundaries should not serve as reason in and of themselves for not recommending custody for the involved parent. But they should be weighed along with other developmental line characteristics. Naturally the extent to which they operate alone or in concert with other developmental line problems, are acute or chronic, have or have not impacted the child's emotional state, and are or are not likely to be time-limited will be crucial. Further, one must take into account the extent to which available insight, motivation to change, and parental mutability can influence their modification.

During custody contests, it is a frequent criticism that one of the parents intermittently loses control, threatening both spouse and child with punishment and abandonment. An important distinction should be made between those "explosions" that represent chronic, periodic assaults, often on one particular child, and those that reprsent a stress-related, episodic loss of control. Their motivations and impact on the child may be quite different.[53]

In the former instance the loss of control could be due to a characterologic defect, and thus the hostility and anger expressed toward the youngster are usually of long standing. It can result from a parent's inability to methodically set consistent behavioral limits, which, ironically, may arise from an ambivalence toward discipline stemming from the parent's own childhood experience with arbitrary and excessive punishment. The loss of control may also be the consequence of an identification of the child with some hated or feared figure from the past: a parent, sibling, or even more frequently, a spouse, or it may occur for other reasons. On the other hand, stress-related outbursts of anger emanate from a general loss of self-control chronologically keyed to the initiation of the divorce. It is usually characterized, therefore, by quicker parental recovery, is generally not directed at one particular child, and is likely to be more time-limited.

The extent to which either one of these types of parents is able to gain insight from the evaluator's comments regarding the probable impact of physical or emotional abuse on the child and from becoming aware of rationalizations or a disturbing identification will provide the evaluator with information about the extent to which the qualities can be modified. Naturally one would expect more flexibility in the capacity of the adult with a stress-related problem.

A case example might illustrate a number of factors that play a role in allegations of abuse.

At the time of marital dissolution, a forty-three-year-old father was accused of exposing himself to, and fondling his five-year-old daughter. Purportedly these acts were initiated by the father in concert with the girl's fifteen-year-old brother. Although the girl was persuasive in an initial interview, subsequent meetings failed to replicate the disclosure. Although the father had engaged in seductive behavior such as walking around the house almost completely naked and occasionally allowing his daughter to sleep with him, he did not have the personality characteristics that would have strongly suggested the profile of a sexual abuser. He was, however, given to silly regressed behavior, pomposity, and showing off. On the other hand, the thirty-nine-year-old mother was profoundly dependent, was deeply wounded by her husband's rejection, and regularly misperceived other people's intent, these misperceptions being reinforced by distorted perceptions on the part of her parents. This resulted in a projected conviction, at the end of her marriage, that all of her husband's friends had turned against her and were gossiping about her. The five-year-old child experienced a school phobia to the point of refusing to attend school for roughly one week at the time of her parents' separation. The fifteen-year-old brother was an outgoing, extremely confident young man who had many friends, including healthy relationships with girls who were friends. In addition, he was an honor student who was engaged in considerable community service.

Abuse could not be demonstrated, and after embarking on a postdivorce arrangement of residence with the mother and liberal visitation for the father, the allegations disappeared. It was the conclusion of the evaluator that within reasonable probability, the father had not abused the child, but neither had the mother "lied" in the commonly accepted sense of the word. It appeared that the mother's traumatic ego wound triggered profound regression with intense dependence and a marginal rupture of her reality-testing capacity. She truly believed the father was malevolent and dangerous. This was complemented by the child's strong identification with her mother as the victim, coupled with heavy dependence on her. This led the girl to pick up her mother's messages and validate them.

It is a common occurrence that dysfunction along one parental line, in this instance, nurturance and empathy, triggers dysfunction along other developmental lines, i.e., separation/individuation and reality testing. In a parent who was reasonably mature under normal circumstances and able to be satisfactorily nurturing and empathic to her child, the self-esteem blow resulting from her husband's rejection led her to become severely depressed. This in turn triggered a deterioration in her capacity to promote independence and in her reality testing. Her fears ran out of control when they were triggered by the immature, marginally seductive behavior and inappropriate boundary intrusions displayed by her husband.

This is a graphic example, not only of how family dynamics interact to create misunderstanding and misperception, but also how each developmental line is intimately tied to another. Thus, a regression along one line will trigger a similar regression along another. Also, this is an illustration of how the stress of marital dissolution can prompt an acute deterioration in parental functioning in an otherwise competent parent. Further it points out how each parents' developmental lines are influenced by the other parent's behavior. Finally, it is a demonstration of how one must take account of a child's developmental level and that youngster's dependence on a parent figure in evaluating the accuracy of statements regarding abuse.[54] Repeated interviews over an extended period of time may be helpful in this regard.[55]

Reality Testing

Reality testing is a term that describes the ability to distinguish between stimuli arising from the external world and stimuli originating in the wishes and impulses of the internal world. We will use the term *reality* to denote the external world and all stimuli arising in it.[56] When a person's perceptions coincide with reality, that person has achieved objectivity. Discrepancy between the two constitutes subjectivity. Although there are gross distortions of reality, including hallucinations, delusions, and illusions, more common is the unconscious manipulation of sensory information so as to conform to internal, emotionally driven realities.

Everybody is subjective to some extent. When we "read between the lines" of someone's behavior, we may be reading a script of our own creation. This is to be distinguished from the empathic posture, in which one seeks to intuit the true meaning of another's behavior. The distinction arises from the motivation: the empathic person desires honest and truthful communication. Thus, when necessary, this person will go beyond the literal meaning of another's words and actions in order to define what the person is really "saying." In contrast, persons with impaired reality testing impose their own interpretation upon the thoughts and actions of others regardless of whether such an interpretation is true or if it even makes sense. These persons have an emotional need to perceive a particular message and will not be thwarted by reality. We often, for instance, ascribe nonexistent characteristics to people on the basis of their economic status, gender, appearance, and racial, ethnic, or religious heritage. Most particularly, we tend to invest authority figures with exaggerated emotional and physical characteristics, perceiving them as extraordinarily benevolent or malevolent.

Many subjective thought patterns tend to be self-reinforcing. We intuitively recognize persons with a "chip on their shoulder" as people whose behavior, being only loosely related to reality, is likely to be unpredictable and unpleasant. Therefore the wariness accorded their presence will, in many instances, simply reinforce the already embedded conviction that one must be ever watchful of others.

The Importance of Reality Testing in Parent Evaluation   A person who experiences gross psychotic distortions, arising from a serious mental disturbance such as schizophrenia[57] or a major depression[58] is very noticeable. Neglect, when it occurs, results, not from deficient emotional investment, but rather from an inability to focus on environmental surroundings. Owing to the extreme level of reality distortion, custody contests rarely involve such persons.

More commonly custody evaluations involve people whose ability to judge reality is better; nonetheless, their thinking might be quite impaired. Inordinate mistrust of others, suspicion, and fear are experienced regularly, especially of those in authority, including mental health professionals and, in particular, custody evaluators. Such persons do not tolerate anger well; they unconsciously externalize it onto someone in the environment. Likewise, they seem not to experience fear in the absence of an external source. Many of those persons seem cold, humorless, and unemotional. Given to extreme polarization, these adults think in terms of absolute rights and wrongs—someone must be blamed for problems. Often hypersensitive and overly reactive to the mildest criticisms, they almost appear to search for criticism directed at them.[59]

In contrast, the more objective adult is generally able to see things as they are even in the face of compelling emotional pressure to distort reality. Certainly the more objective parent tolerates anger and criticism well. The subjectivity of others is handled with grace and ease; tolerant of self, the same tolerance is extended to others. This capacity is rooted in the ability to comprehend people as complex mixtures of good and bad.

One can see that the more objective parent remains flexible and committed to understanding the truth about situations, no matter how unpleasant that may be. This represents a quiet commitment to reality and the pleasure that accompanies the accomplishment of confronting the whole of life: the joy, the pain, and the revelation of one's own character.

Parents with impaired reality testing frequently ascribe information to their children that is actually known only to themselves. Thus a child, allowed to help with the wash, might be punished for including some dry-clean-only clothes. This represents a disturbance in referential thinking and is commonly found in families with disturbed children.[60] In addition, nonreality-based thinking in parents may inhibit a child's development of the ability to "de-center,"[61] which essentially represents the capacity to discriminate between one's own point of view and that of others.

Parental subjectivity may have its greatest impact on the preschooler,[62] who has not yet established a firm border between the self and the surrounding world.[63] However, distortion in a child's perception of reality, derived from an identification with an adult who has a tendency to do the same, may continue for several years.[64] Both parent and child often believe that external causes account for one's good fortune or misfortune.[65] Teachers are blamed for scholastic failure, teasing is held responsible for a child's ostracism from a peer group, and accidents, injuries, and other misfortunes are not accepted as a part of growing up. Children in this group do not learn how to objectively assign responsibility to themselves or how much guilt one should appropriately feel for some act of misconduct.

The Impact of Reality Testing on Custody Considerations   There are few phenomena more common in a marital dissolution than the vilification of one's spouse. Most marital dissolutions result in anger and a temporary inability to take "ownership" for some of the problems. However, since this response is the natural consequence of the loss reaction, it should be temporary and mutable. During the interview the evaluator should therefore be able to facilitate more objective thinking by pointing out the reality of bilateral participation in and "joint ownership" of marital problems. Further, this type of reality distortion is confined to the marital relationship.

In contrast, adults with impaired reality testing display generally polarized perceptions of people and events, which are characterized as either totally "good" or "bad." In particular this polarization will lead such a person to hold the spouse wholly responsible for the breakdown of the marriage and to hold oneself entirely blameless. To these parents the aim of the assessment is to prove themselves the "good parent" by proving the other parent "bad." Characteristically the custody interview is transformed into an opportunity to blame the other party for the existing problems and to present oneself as guiltless. In the interest of validating this claim, the evaluation is approached with a "laundry list" of complaints. In this instance the blaming is often total and unalterable and covers most aspects of the couple's relationship. Attempts to shift the discussion away from the spouse and back to the parent being interviewed are usually futile.

The evaluator should confront this parent's tendency to externalize blame, in order to gauge this person's capacity for self-scrutiny and objectivity. If the proclivity is deeply embedded and rigidly held, pointing out the illogic of totally allocating blame to the spouse will trigger a defensive, evasive, and sometimes overtly angry reaction. This happens because the interviewee experiences the evaluator's challenge as an attempt to shift the entire blame back upon him or her. If the personality organization should operate at a higher level, there may be more self-questioning and an acceptance of greater responsibility for the marital problem. This will be accompanied by a diminution of the attack on the other party.

A less extreme form of impaired reality testing is that of hypersensitivity. Rather than display overt hostility, this person is instead extremely defensive. Blaming the other party is not the primary aim: self-defense is. In the interest of proving their fine parenting qualities, these parents may offer to ask friends and relatives to write letters of reference. Any emotional support offered by the evaluator is quickly taken as an endorsement of parental competence, resulting in a diminution of the defensive posture.

In this instance too, the depth and fixity of this quality should be plumbed. As is the case with all the parent development lines, some discussion will determine to what extent hypersensitivity is a product of the guilt and vulnerability of the divorcing process and to what degree it is a result of a character quality. Further, even if it is part of this person's personality, if it should substantially diminish as a consequence of some insight, this person lies at the upper end of the continuum.

A case example may illustrate some of the points that have been made.

A forty-six-year-old dentist and his forty-two-year-old wife were divorcing after seventeen years of marriage. A somewhat compulsive, perfectionistic, and rigid person, the father was accused, by his wife, of gross insensitivity throughout the years of their marriage. Defensive and highly charged in her discussions, the wife described incident after incident of her husband not coming home during mid-day when she was ill, of not taking charge of the children on weekends when she wished to rest, and of criticising her for what he considered to be her irresponsibility in caring for the house. She insisted that the evaluator's objectivity could best be demonstrated by agreeing with her charges. During the evaluation the clinician learned that she was erratic in her daily responsiveness to the children's caretaking needs.

While the fifteen-year-old son was strongly identified with his father, the nine-year-old daughter made claims similar to those of her mother. She accused her father of not appearing on time at her school performances and of refusing to readily provide transportation when she wished to go to her friends' homes.

In a family interview attended by both children and their mother, the girl demonstrated her security seeking by curling up next to her mother and sucking her thumb. This was in contrast to her more independent behavior in her father's presence.

The evaluator concluded that the father's rigid personality structure led him to be less than optimally sensitive to the needs of his wife and children. However, a further conclusion was that, on balance, the wife's charges were largely based on her hypersensitivity. This resulted from a projection of the hostility arising from an underlying self-esteem deficiency onto her husband. Further it was believed that the father provided a greater level of stability and consistency and was more independence promoting. Therefore, joint custody was recommended for both parents with the children to be in primary residence with their father.

A child's alignment with the parent who distorts reality commonly results in that youngster's "taking sides" against the nonaligned parent. Perceiving the latter as an invidious persecutor of the aligned parent, the child may inform the custody investigator that this parent is totally responsible for the marital problem. As one might expect, this child will express a clear and decided preference for the aligned parent, exhibiting no insight or self-scrutiny regarding the wisdom of this posture. The rigidity of self-deception may be an index of the extent to which the child has endorsed and accepted the imposition of the parent's distorted thinking.[66]

While caution must always be exercised in giving custody choices to latency-age children,[67] we urge prudence in offering too much option to adolescents as well. Although the custodial preferences of adolescents should always be elicited, and their choices given much credence because of their presumed ability to offer considered opinions, they should be made unequivocally aware that their parents or the court will be making the ultimate decisions about their custody and residence. To leave this point vague or ambiguous arouses in them unnecessary guilt, loyalty conflicts, and a polarization of attitudes toward their parents.

Seeing oneself as one truly is, under the best of circumstances, is a painful process, but it can be nearly impossible when adolescents are encouraged to avoid unpleasant knowledge and to blame some external source for their problems. Thus the examiner must be mindful of the inherent difficulties in seeking the custodial preferences of children who are not their own masters and who may not even know themselves very well. Conclusions must be drawn based upon all available data, with the children's preferences but one piece of those data. Armed with this evidence, the evaluator must search for parents who struggle to understand things as they are rather than as they wish them to be, or fear they might be, and who endorse the same in their children.

Identity Organization

It is widely held that heredity or constitutional factors and parental and societal influence are the primary contributors to formation of personality in children. As the nature/nurture controversy has yet to be resolved, we cannot be fully certain which factor or combination of factors plays the most significant role in determining a child's personality formation. Although we have often ascribed causation of certain characteristics to one category, we have later discovered that causation must be attributed to the other category. For example, in cases where children were born with some degree of anatomic sexual ambiguity, having physical characteristics of both sexes to some extent, they adopted gender roles "consistent with their sex assignment and rearing, even when the latter contradicted chromosomal sex, gonadal sex, hormonal sex, the predominant internal accessory reproductive structures, and the external genital morphology."[68] On the other hand, Autistic Disorder, once presumed to be some species of emotional illness presumably induced by environmental factors, was later identified as, at least, predisposed by certain constitutional factors.[69] Although we cannot always ascertain whether a child's development is predominantly constitutional or environmental in origin, we can be sure that parental influence will always be powerful and significant. Crucial to a child's development is the parent's ability to reflect a positive and healthy image.[70] Projecting to one's child those personality attributes that will best foster development of a sound sexual identity, a strong conscience, and a high level of achievement orientation will greatly increase that youngster's chances of developmental success. This bears significantly on the selection of a custodial parent. Naturally those persons whose personality inspires admiration and imitation by their children will be better able to transmit to those children qualities that will make them happier and more mature.

As with all parent personality functions, the qualities that make someone a sound identification model are not completely clear. Also, the process of identification is an unconscious one: neither the child nor the parent is aware that identification is occurring. The adult cannot force it to happen. Regardless of how much a parent wishes a child to admire and to become like him or her, it cannot be imposed by force of will or wish. Despite the fact that its overall impact cannot be easily assessed, identification continues to be a powerful force in a child's life well into adulthood, long after the other parameters of parental influence have diminished or been extinguished.

In general, the parent's personality image to which we are referring is the parent's identity. The degree to which it has crystallized in a healthy fashion will determine, to a large extent, how strongly growth-promoting messages from the parent will be reflected in and acted upon by the child. Self-assertion, strong convictions about high-level principles, confidence in one's own sexual identity, and powerful achievement aspirations are some of the modeling projections that represent positive identity organization.

Healthy and Unhealthy Identity Projections   Comprising many aspects of a collective "sense of self," a person's self-identity might include, among others, sexual, social, and moral components and an achievement or occupational component. It is hoped that these will be refined and revised throughout adulthood, progressing toward a state of better integration, greater strength, and more coherence.[71] Healthy parenting in this area will entail projecting an image after which children might model themselves in crucial aspects of personality organization.

During early childhood, the child is very susceptible to parental attitudes and opinions. As the child ages, identification with parents is more selective.[72] Healthy image projections encompass a number of factors: dominance, salience, quantity and quality of involvement, self-awareness, and the possession of positive sexual, occupational, and ethical aspects of self.

The relative dominance or passivity of a child's gender-same parent can exert a powerful influence on the child's personality identification and adoption of sexual role. Children of both genders identify well in families where the parents alternate leadership.

Up to a certain level of dominance of one parent, for whatever the reason, boys and girls will identify both in sex-role preference and in personality with the dominant parent, provided that parent is gender-same to them. In a home where the dominant parent is gender-opposite, boys are affected far more than girls, whose sex-role preference and personality identification will be little affected, if at all.[73]

Although some parents who are domineering, as opposed to dominant, use tyranny and intimidation to keep power in the family, others rely on controlling by engendering guilt. Frequently a domineering parent is complemented by a passive parent who neither attempts to participate in decision-making nor assumes responsibility for decisions already made. In such cases the domineering parent may also be dominant and the aforementioned sexual and personality identifications probably obtain. It is clear that parental dominance or, more precisely, parental salience, is a major component in determining sex role preference in children, at least for boys. It appears that girls tend to identify with their mothers in sex role preference to a greater or lesser extent regardless of which parent is dominant. It has been posited that the weak identification of boys with nondominant fathers is due, at least in part, to the relative "father absence" of our society.[74] As a consequence unless the father projected a forceful image in the family, he was not sufficiently ubiquitous to inspire identification, in the absence of a salient family role. As our society evolves in the direction of a decline in the relative quantitative involvement of mothers and a (hopefully) concomitant increase in the role of fathers in family life, these identification principles may change.

Parents facilitate their children's achievement orientation by encouraging independence, by providing a model of such an orientation, and by encouraging and supporting their youngster's efforts.[75] Relative to academic achievement, a primary driving force behind intellectual functioning and scholastic endeavor for many children lies in the premium placed on education by one or both parents a well as the presence of positive parental self-image, warmth, nurturance and accessibility.[76] If the youth's confidence fails, whether in the area of academic performance or some other area of achievement, the parent who models well urges perseverance and completion.

It is perfectly healthy for children to wish to please or pattern themselves after their parents, but parents must carefully avoid using their power to stir children's motivation so as to satisfy the parent's need for their success.[77] It is hoped that every parent will be interested in a child's peer group activities, scholastic performance, and age-related stylistic and friendship choices. That interest, however, should be focused on the child's welfare, not motivated by an unconscious desire to vicariously relive a past experience in order to make it come out right, or to do so because it was so rewarding.

In matters of discipline, good modeling entails the use of different disciplinary methods according to the appropriate application of the "good enough" parent principles. Excessive physical punishment, or uncontrolled anger especially accompanied by threats of rejection as a form of punishment may project the notion that adult disapproval transcends ethical principles. Healthy guilt is elicited if it results from a child's misconduct rather than from adult anger.[78]

A parent who models well is not satisfied with merely correcting behavior. Utilizing the principles of respect for justice and human dignity, he or she will attempt, through the use of induction, to elevate the child's level of empathic understanding about misconduct and its effect on other persons.[79] As a result, a dedication to moral principles that are independent of adult mood is modeled.[80] Furthermore, this ethical stand is encouraged even when it comes into conflict with the parent's opinion.

Crucial to healthy parenting that projects sound sexual, occupational and moral aspects of self are nurturance and intense involvement. Through warmth and a readiness to supply emotional support, these parents reinforce positive identification. Committed to steady and consistent parenting, priority is given to the quality of involvement, presuming quantitative involvement is sufficient.

The Impact of Identity on Custody Considerations   An important part of a custody examination is an evaluation of the parent's sense of identity in those areas relevant to a discharge of parental responsibilities and to that parent's ability to serve as a model of identification. To project clear and decisive messages, a parent's identity must be circumscribed and integrated. If it is not well bounded, or is composed of too many conflicting or contradictory fragments, the parent will be prone to project inconsistent or paradoxical messages to the child.[81]

A parent may endorse certain values simply on the basis of idiosyncratic wishes. This can govern a whole range of behaviors from

slavish conformity to societal standards, to irresponsible noncon-
formity such as some instances of partial or total nudity in front of
latency age or adolescent children, to adults' adopting teenage standards in their dress, curfews, and companionship. Such parents might
even relinquish all choice over curfews to their children and may actually become their companions.

Because of a gut-level belief in his or her own superiority, many
a domineering parent believes the marriage failed because the spouse
could not meet certain expectations. If that parent does not obtain
custody, or chooses not to pursue it, he or she may undermine the
residential parent's efforts. Consciously convinced that he or she is
not only the better parent, but is also the sole protector of the children's best interests, this individual is not open to advice, persuasion,
or criticism.

In contrast, a parent who is quite passive may believe that the
marriage failed because he or she was the one who failed to meet the
spouse's expectations. One of the children may dominate such a passive father or mother. Owing to an insufficiently cohesive sense of
self, such a person, in chameleonic fashion, may be willing to shift
opinions or values depending upon what he or she believes the evaluator would like to hear. Although the desire to pursue custody vigorously may be weak, this person may be the better candidate, notwithstanding the presence of considerable passivity.

Parents who live vicariously through their children generally believe those children require their vicarious involvement. They frequently take personal credit for the apparent success realized by their
overly achieving children. If, on the other hand, the youngster rebels
against the heavy pressure, which happens most often with adolescents, the conviction is held that a hard line is required to counteract
the other parent's supposed permissiveness. In neither instance does
this parent make the child's actual needs a priority. Of course, the
criticism of the other person may be accurate. But when the emotion
behind the condemnation of the former spouse for not placing enough
emphasis on athletic, academic, or social achievement is too intense,
it signals an inappropriate need to live through the child.

It behooves the evaluator to assess the measure of self-awareness
possessed by these parents. Certain insights will reflect more favor-
ably on custodial competence. These include the ability to recognize

that the motivation for obtaining custody, at least in part, arises from a desire to maintain a position of power, or from a wish to vicariously live through one's child. For more passive persons, it is important that they be aware that further passivity might reinforce an already existing role-reversal between parent and child.

The boy or girl who has rebelled against an excessively demanding parent may be strongly opposed to being in that person's custody, and often rightfully so. However, caution must be exercised about simply accepting the youngster's perceptions. The hated person may simply be someone who stands for limits and firmness, albeit perhaps in too exacting a fashion. Further, because of a conviction that the lofty but critical parental model could never be matched, an underlying existent identification does not manifestly emerge.

In contrast, the child who overachieves because of a wish to please, impress, or satisfy a parent may strongly desire to be in that parent's custody. An idealized view of the parent should not be confused with love. Nor should sympathy for a needy adult be confused with empathy and true identification. In either case, the evaluator's recommendations must take into account the reality behind the child's perception, how much damage has been inflicted by parental pressure, and to what extent the other parent possesses reasonable expectations.

A parent with a flexible sense of self is able to gracefully and easily change roles. Such a person can be a parent in an intact family sharing leadership, a single parent vested with the responsibility for making decisions, or a visitation parent for whom supporting the other adult's role is a major task. Another role requiring considerable patience and flexibility is that of a visitation parent whose child is living with a stepparent. Controlling any feelings of threat are important for a few reasons. Children need the vote of confidence projected by the nonresidential parent that a tie to a stepparent will not diminish that biological parent's love for them.[82] It also helps the child avoid being caught in a loyalty struggle between two same gender parents.

As to the matter of homosexual parenting, it is a clouded issue. Emotions so color thinking in this matter that decisions are often based upon bias rather than reason. Before discussing homosexual parenting, however, one must first address some of the theories regarding the development of homosexuality. In addition to the evidence of some possible genetic and prenatal hormonal influences on the evolution of a homosexual orientation, theories of psychological causation or at least influence have been offered.[83]

At this point, however, the development of sexual identity in children is not well understood. It has been postulated that boys subject very early in life to an overly involved mother, to whom they are fused, especially in the presence of an emotionally distant or absent relationship with their fathers, are at risk of a gender opposite sexual identity.[84] Although one cannot be certain about the meaning of this hypothesis, homosexual males, more so than heterosexual males, cited father-son relationships which were characterized by uninvolvement, absenteeism, and passivity.[85] We know that the seeds are probably sown early because boys who later became homosexual reported a strong predilection for cross-gender-role behavior early in life. They preferred to dress like females, chose female playmates and adopted stereotypic feminine interests.[86] For girls the matter is less clear. According to one author, often girls who become transsexual move into a vacuum created by the sadness of a tired, long-suffering, mother who is left alone too much by her husband. Feeling protective toward the mother, the girl has conscious thoughts of taking care of her as would a husband, and then receives positive reinforcement for her masculine behavior.[87]

Regarding homosexual parenting, several studies point to a lack of correlation between mothers' homosexual orientation and a developing child's sexual identity.[88] Studies have focused almost exclusively on lesbian women with one exception, a paper discussing the unique situation of the homosexual father.[89] There are, however, no data to support the notion that sexual orientation development in children is primarily the result of modeling a significant adult.[90] Drawing upon these findings one might conclude that it is advisable to treat a custody case involving a parent with a homosexual orientation like other custody cases. It would appear that custody decisions are best determined by which parent can better facilitate growth and development.[91] This will be especially true in situations involving mothers with a homosexual orientation since the data, in that circumstance, is far more plentiful. One should also keep in mind that male homosexuals frequently report cross gender behavior at an early age; consequently, if one is concerned about the impact of homosexual parents on boys, the concern should be less after roughly seven years of age. Of course children raised in the home of a parent who chooses a lifestyle that is at variance with the cultural mainstream are subject to teasing from peers and potential loyalty conflicts.

Although the actual choice of a homosexual preference does not seem to occur as a result of uncomplicated linear identification one should not assume that the usual principles of identification will not operate between a dominant parent and child. Thus, for example a parent who engages in regular cross-dressing in full view of a child may, at the very least, confuse the youngster. In addition exposing children to the knowledge that a homosexual parent has a series of lovers who might spend periods of time in residence with the parent and child is just as indiscreet as the heterosexual parent who does the same thing. The same can be said for the homosexual parent who exposes a child to a homosexual companion who is attracted to the child.[92]

A clinical example might illustrate a few of the salient features. After a three year absence, during which time he had relatively little contact with him, Harry, a thirty-eight-year-old father, filed a motion to obtain custody of his eight-year-old son, Matt. The child was living with Sylvia, his thirty-five-year-old mother, and Sylvia's homosexual partner, Lillian thirty-four. Although the mother had demonstrated bisexual preferences prior to her separation, it was not until her divorce that she became openly committed to homosexuality. Since that time she has had a committed relationship with Lillian. It was Harry's contention that Matt was in jeopardy of becoming homosexual by his association with Sylvia, Lillian, and their homosexual friends.

Harry maintained that it was only with great reluctance that he had relocated away from Matt and his ex-wife as he had suspected at the time that his wife was homosexual. Unfortunately, the demands of his career took him out of state. Now that he was engaged to remarry, he felt in a position to "rescue" Matt from what he called "an unnatural way of life." His fiancée, he said, agreed with him that Matt should come and live with them as soon as possible. In addition, Harry noted, his fiancée was very warm and would be able to provide Matt with all the love he would need. He added that he personally neither approved nor disapproved of his former wife's way of life. He simply thought it was harmful to Matt's sense of masculinity and to his self-esteem, for he would have to bear the taunts of friends when they learned his mother was homosexual.

Neither Sylvia nor Lillian displayed cross-gender role behavior; their friends were similar; they lived quiet, unassuming lives and were both emotionally involved in and committed to the care of Matt. In school and in his relationships with other children, Matt was prospering. In addition he was involved in age-appropriate peer activities such as Little League Baseball and Cub Scouts. As a result of the evaluation it was determined that Matt was a normal child displaying no cross-gender role behavior.

In contrast, his father had not demonstrated a deep and continuous interest in Matt's upbringing, and in fact had pursued little contact in his absence. His preoccupation with his own ego needs precluded his interest in more substantive issues: close family relations and a sense of community. Indeed he was prepared to uproot Matt from institutions and peer relationships in which he was well-ensconsed, displaying little sensitivity to his secure role in the community. Sustaining the continuity of a child's tie to his community, including school and peers, should always be given some albeit not overriding consideration.

The evaluator concluded that Matt was progressing satisfactorily in all developmental areas, and there was no reason to be concerned about the care or modeling influence provided by his mother, Lillian, or their friends. In addition his mother demonstrated a significant continuity of care. Therefore, reason could not be found to consider a change in residence.

Parents who model healthy identity are aware that the shadow of parental identity will be cast upon an offspring regardless of whether their status is that of a custodial or visitation parent. This should diminish this person's urgency about obtaining custody. In its place should appear a desire for a decision that truly reflects the child's best interest, whether or not that decision coincides with parental wishes.

Where the child, and a teenager in particular, is free to identify with both parents' arrays of personality features without encumbrance, shared custody is often indicated. Given the opportunity to alternate time with each, the adolescent will be able to selectively and unconsciously choose those qualities, attitudes, and values that best match his or her sense of self. This is a distinct advantage of shared custody. Ultimately, elements of both parents will be refined into any child's own unique style to a greater or lesser degree. The crucial aspect of the identity organization process is that the youth become who he or she is. This will, of necessity, be different from either parent, and from anyone else for that matter. We would do well to recall Polonius' advice to his departing son Laertes, from *Hamlet:* "To thine ownself be true . . . for then thou canst not be false to any man."

7

Child Evaluation

As a means of evaluating children a clinical examination is conducted. In addition to a standard mental status examination, with more emphasis on attachment and identification factors than might ordinarily be utilized, this evaluation will also include an exploration of custody and visitation preferences. An example of a mental status examination adapted to preschool and school-age children will be discussed. It will be applicable to some adolescents although many teenagers will adapt better to the mental status examination used for adults.[1] Very young children may require a still different approach more suitable to their age.[2] Another component of the clinical evaluation, a psychodynamic formulation, will be included in the summary of the evaluation report relating the child's psychodynamics to those of the parents and family. Certainly the clinical examination may reveal any emotional disturbance present in the child, but perhaps equally important, it will elicit the child's personality strengths as well. Not only will this bear on the selection of the custodial parent who can promote these strengths, but also it will allow the evaluator to better predict the character of the child's postdissolution recovery from the aftermath of divorce.

For the young child, attachment factors are very important. The evaluator should identify principal attachment figures and subsidiary attachment figures. As the child progresses, preferential attachment will be less necessary to psychological well-being; therefore, though significant throughout childhood, attachment decreases in importance as the child ages. Once the child reaches preschool and school-age, identification with one or both parents assumes greater prominence as an index of unconscious parental connections. Clearly the parent with whom the child is positively identified is in a better position to promote psychologically healthy developmental progress. The youngster's custodial and visitation preferences should also be obtained whenever possible. Whereas the teenager's preference is always given great weight, it is equally important to determine the preference of younger children, although their opinions may not exert as great an influence.

Additional Evaluations

While the clinical interview is the cornerstone of the minor child's evaluation,[3] other assessments might be conducted if necessary. These might include a psychological evaluation, educational assessments, or a neurologic evaluation. Such additional evaluations might be performed for a number of reasons including: concerns about the child's ability to adequately understand reality, an educational problem that might warrant special education assistance, or to rule out an organic problem such as a neurologic disorder. By no means are these evaluations generally and universally recommended. It may be that even if one of these concerns is initially present, the clinical appraisal will suffice to answer the questions and determine the proper course of action. If an additional assessment should appear necessary, the evaluator might call upon the services of a clinical psychologist, educational specialist, pediatric neurologist, or some other specialist to provide a consultation. In certain instances selective psychological evaluation of a parent may be carried out as well.

It should be remembered that though the primary purpose of this evaluation is to offer a recommendation regarding custody, the child's other mental health needs must be kept in mind. If the evaluator should identify an emotional disturbance in the child, it should be assessed to the best of the evaluator's ability within the constraints of the evaluation procedure. If necessary the evaluator can refer the youth to another clinician for a more nearly comprehensive diagnostic assessment and possibly for therapy.

Secondary Contacts

In any evaluation the primary basis for conclusions are the evaluator's own observations. A secondary source would be the various professionals who have been involved with one or more parties. The child's pediatrician should be contacted to supply developmental and historical medical information regarding the child's attainment of certain milestones and the presence of past illnesses or surgery that might have significantly influenced the youngster's development or family relationships. Further, the pediatrician might be able to offer some objective observations on the family's interrelationships.

Generally the child's current and possibly previous teachers, as well as the school principal, will be contacted to supply information about the youngster's intellectual abilities, academic performance, and classroom behavior, as well as any insight into the family's relationships that might bear on the custody recommendation. Of importance will be any change in the youngster's scholastic productivity or behavior since the onset of the parents' separation.

If any member of the family should be in therapy, it will almost invariably be of value to contact the therapist. In contrast to the two aforementioned sources of information, this professional's perspective will be primarily focused on individual or family problems. One should not conclude, however, that a parent's emotional problems will necessarily affect the child's development. Nor should one assume that emotional disturbances observed by a child's therapist were necessarily the result of impaired parenting.[4] In each instance one must draw one's own conclusions from the data. Information obtained from therapists may simply point the evaluator in a particular direction or confirm impressions derived from interview material.

Frequently parents will ask the evaluator to obtain information from various family members or friends, often in the hope that the friend or relative will give a testimonial to their parenting ability. Nonprofessional observers recommended by the parties are rarely useful. There are, nonetheless, occasions when such persons might supply helpful information, such as when they have served as a live-in babysitter.

As a means of determining the potential value of such a contact, the person recommending it might be asked what information the evaluator can expect to acquire from this source. Only if the expected information is sharply at variance with conclusions drawn from primary and secondary sources is the inquiry likely to be beneficial. In those instances the evaluator must carefully weigh the objectivity of the informant and therefore the reliability of the information.

Whenever information is obtained from a third party the principle of informed consent should operate. Not only should the person supplying the facts and impressions be aware of the use to which it will be put, but also the person should be asked if there is any part of the material that should not be entered into a report. Because these persons may wish to sustain a personal or professional relationship with the person or family about whom they are serving as informant, not only do they have a reason and right to know what information they provide is being transmitted to the family and how the information is being used, but they have a right to exclude portions from the report. However, none of the information provided is privileged. The evaluator, therefore, should advise informants that any information received, even if omitted from the report, may be elicited at trial.

Finally certain documents and reports may have value: Hospital records may shed light on the physical or mental health of one of the parties; school report cards are always of assistance; police reports can clarify some of the facts about a family altercation; previous custody evaluations may offer another point of view about certain key factors; and judgments from the court give information about previous decisions sometimes centering around the same custody and visitation issues currently being contested.

Mental Status Examination

A number of standardized approaches to the mental status examination have been described.[5] One such version, useful in custodial evaluations, especially for preschool and school-age children, includes the following categories:

Mental Status Examination

1. Size and appearance
2. Motility
3. Coordination
4. Speech
5. Intellectual function
6. Modes of thinking and perception
7. Emotional reactions
8. Manner of relating
9. Fantasies, dreams, and play techniques

Other outlines include ethical structure. Any discussion of this examination will necessarily be limited to those features germane to custodial evaluation.

Size and General Appearance   A child's physical characteristics, gestures, and mannerisms may bear a striking resemblance to those of one of the parents. The physical resemblance is of course, due to a genetic transmission of characteristics, whereas similarities of manner and demeanor probably represent a psychological identification. A parent may favor that child who most resembles the parent. The other parent may, as a consequence, harbor animosity toward this child. As a marital relationship deteriorates, the parents frequently displace their anger toward the other partner onto the children in the family. A ready target for such displacement will be the child who resembles the other parent. If the real object of this adult's anger, the spouse, and the displaced object, the child, are of the same gender or possess similar personalities, the physical similarity will promote psychological congruence, prompting even greater misdirection of anger onto the child. If the parental enemy favors this youngster, the hostility may be even more intensified. Gender-role behavior will also be important if there is a question of the child's sexual identity.

Motility   Either hyperactivity or decreased activity are significant clues to a child's emotional state. Slowed motor movements may indicate depression. This commonly occurs in children whose parents are getting divorced. However, one must search further to determine if a depression exists for some other reason: rejection by a parent, school failure, medical illness, etc.

Hyperactivity, along with an inability to concentrate and impulsive behavior, are common concomitants of a childhood disorder referred to as an Attention-deficit Hyperactivity Disorder.[6] Although hyperactivity may be psychologically caused, it may also have a neurological source. Psychologically induced hyperactivity may reflect a parent/child conflict whereas neurological hyperactivity arises from a dysfunction of the central nervous system. One must be careful not to universally ascribe behavioral characteristics to flaws in parenting: a child with neurologically based hyperactivity might resist self-control to a greater than average degree and, in fact, require better than adequate parenting in order to improve impulse control, and to ensure the child exercises full capacity for control over his or her activity level and develops a healthy self-image.

Coordination   Gross and fine motor coordination may have great significance to parents. The child with outstanding coordination may provide a parent, through athletic accomplishments, with an opportunity for vicarious gratification. Conversely, the child with poor coordination may be a grave disappointment to a parent hungry for the pride and accolades that accompany athletic accomplishment. It is important to be aware of the possibility of such ulterior motives in a parent's investment in the child.

Speech   When present, poor articulation may call for speech therapy.[7] It will call for a parent sensitive to the child and committed to obtaining the required intervention.

Intellectual Function   The ability to grasp the significance of the family breakdown will to an extent depend on the child's intelligence. Brighter children with a greater capacity for abstract thinking will think through the possible consequences of a divorce on their future. Their ability to recognize parental manipulation could render them less ambivalent in dealing with such a parent.

Creative talent or some other manifestation of substantial intellectual ability may render a child the object of parental pride and favoritism. On the other hand, the child's intellectual competence may threaten a parent. Mental retardation can trigger overprotection or rejection, either subtle or overt. The existence of discriminatory behavior, either for or against the child, on the basis of the youngster's intellectual capacity, may have a significant impact on the evaluator's deliberations.

Modes of Thinking and Perception   Impaired reality testing in the child may suggest the influence of a family member who is similarly handicapped. The capacity to make reality based differentiations should be appropriate to the child's age. By three or four, the child should display some ability to discriminate between fact and fantasy. By six or seven most children should fully possess that skill.[8]

One must carefully analyze children's perceptions to determine their accuracy. Caught up in a flood of emotions and witness to scenes laden with charges and countercharges, youngsters from families in the process of divorce are taxed by mixed loyalties, fears of rejection and abandonment, rage, and feelings of protectiveness. One common result is a tendency on the part of especially young children to distort events and issues. Their interpretation of an incident may change, consciously or unconsciously, to match the perception of their favored parent.[9] They may interpret every criticism of them as a sign of parental rejection, strengthening their already biased point of view. Sometimes they may believe that a victimized parent needs their protection from the more aggressive or critical parent. Obviously it is unhealthy for a child to be caught in parental conflict this way. Careful scrutiny may determine the extent to which and the means by which parents reinforce an impaired view of reality.

Emotional Reactions   In contrast to their parents, children enter an evaluation interview with extremely mixed feelings about the involved adults. Almost universally, each adult holds the other responsible for at least months and often years of emotional pain and suffering. Therefore, their feelings of anger and rejection are intense and relatively undiluted. Children, however, usually love both of their parents. While they might experience disappointment and anger with either or both, these emotions coexist with fear, affection, and love. As a consequence, they are fearful of injuring one or both of their parents by their actions, their thoughts, and their feelings.

Very young children do not discriminate between their feelings and facts.[10] Thus, they ascribe great power to their emotions; to feel anger is to do damage. One consequence of this is that any anger they feel readily triggers guilt. Since they are angry with their parents for divorcing, the attendant guilt arouses in them a sense of responsibility for the divorce. This complicates any discussion of their parents because it impedes their ability to express anger and disappointment. Guilt is especially inhibiting when the topic of discussion is their custodial preference. As a consequence of these facts, children are fearful and tentative. They are concerned that the evaluator will encourage them to say something they do not wish to disclose or to speak critically of their parents. The wise evaluator will respect those feelings because pressure to discuss forbidden topics will probably precipitate their withdrawal and failure of the interview. Children respond best to someone who respects them. Like adults, children can develop trust only in someone who behaves in a trustworthy fashion.[11] Making jokes, clowning, and talking in an artificially enthusiastic, childish fashion triggers in children the belief that they are being manipulated.

In interviewing children, one must be creative in order to get them to surmount their anxiety sufficiently to generate sincere responses and provide useful information.[12] The interviewer should clearly transmit the message that the interview is being conducted for the purpose of getting to know them as persons and not simply to extract information. This entails learning how they think and feel and what their opinions are. This is crucial, not only for the aforementioned reasons, but because one should treat the youngsters for who they are—individuals.

Beginning the interview with this understanding will set the stage for a dialogue as free of unnecessary pressures as possible. This can be accomplished by explaining to children at the outset that, while the need for the interview was created by the parents' divorce, the evaluator wants to get to know them. In addition to learning about their family, the evaluator wants to know about interests and friends. Although it will be necessary during the interview to ask very specific and direct questions, the more open-ended the interviewer can make questions, the more individuality will be encouraged in the children. For example, it is better to ask them what they like to do for fun than to specifically ask if they like baseball.

In contrast to many adults, children generally do not spontaneously and openly discuss their emotions. Often their emotions are expressed only through their behavior. One must "read between the lines" to understand what they are feeling. Throwing a ball against the office wall with great force immediately after discussing the topic of a father leaving the house upon separating from a mother may indicate the power of emotions regarding that event. One can only speculate about the nature of that emotion. It may represent anger with the father or mother or it may depict fears of abandonment. In order to understand the significance of behavior, one must look for some verbal interchange or other interactional event in the interview that served to trigger it, what function the behavior serves, its underlying significance, and what emotions it might conceal.

Feelings are an important part of a child's life. As such they should be elicited and given strong and careful consideration. Very young children may fear abandonment or deprivation of nurturance. School-age children may feel jealous of a younger sibling or shame that they cannot live up to a parent's academic expectations. Adolescents may feel suffocated. The presence of such emotions does not document that a parent threatens abandonment or is nonnurturing in the first instance, fosters jealousy or imposes too high academic standards in the second, or is controlling and overly protective in the third. Nonetheless, one should search for parental qualities that complement the youth's fears and therefore might have a causative or perpetuating effect on the worrisome feelings. Children need parents who will scrutinize their participation in a child's emotional state and accept the extent to which the youngster's views are accurate. Regardless of the validity of the perceptions themselves, the growth-promoting parent will accept and validate the emotions emanating from the child's perceptions. The growth-promoting parent of the teenager who felt

suffocated would, for example, discuss that adult's control and protectiveness with the teenager, watchful for evidence that the criticisms
are partially or completely valid. If indeed, there is evidence that the
criticisms are wholly or partly valid, the adult will acknowledge the
problem, apologize, and make a commitment to change. In the absence of any such evidence, the parent will indicate that while there
is a different point of view, the parent does appreciate the youngster's
feelings and will request that transgressions be pointed out when they
occur. It is this kind of parent-child relationship that frees children
to examine the authenticity of their own point of view.

Manner of Relating   It is at the interface between the waiting and
interview room that some of the most prominent displays of separation anxiety occur. Having been told the purpose of a custody evaluation interview, most children will display some tension. In addition, some degree of stranger anxiety is to be expected, especially
since that stranger is a person who will be making important recommendations about the child's life. There is, however, a palpably
distinct difference between tension arising from an understandably
stressful circumstance and an age-inappropriate degree of separation
anxiety.

Preschool-age children commonly display some fear and withdrawal, accompanied by security-seeking behavior, when approached
by a total stranger. This will be especially true if the child senses the
accompanying parent's own emotional strain. However, when the
internal stress leads to severe clinging, outbursts of temper, and
pleading for removal, even in a preschooler, the interviewer should
suspect age-inappropriate dependence and incomplete separation. This
suspicion will be even stronger if a four- or five-year-old child is able
to enter the interview room only in the company of a parent. Certainly if this same behavior is seen in a school-age child, incomplete
separation is even more probable.[13]

Aggressiveness is a commonly observed pattern among children in
diagnostic custody evaluations. Again, one must keep in mind that
these are high-stress interviews. Therefore, a youngster's behavioral
expressions may be exaggerated inasmuch as maladaptive behaviors
are frequently final common pathways, or expressions of last resort,
for anxiety in children. As was the case with separation anxiety, every

effort should be made through history taking and careful clinical observation to distinguish between aggressiveness arising from situational tension and aggressiveness embodied in a child's developing characterologic changes. Aggressiveness related to the stress of the interview will be more situation specific, occurring when the child's awareness of the uncomfortable emotions attendant to the parents' upcoming divorce is triggered. In contrast, developing characterologic aggressiveness is more pervasive: it is manifest to some extent in most environments, under most circumstances, and with most people. Because aggressiveness often masks underlying emotions, the evaluator must vigilantly watch for the presence of such feelings. A child's attempts to verbally demean the evaluator may reflect a wish to retaliate against adult authority figures out of a perception of being injured by them or it might have some other dynamic significance. The specific importance of this or any other behavior can be ascertained only by analyzing it in the context of other pieces of information acquired during the interview.

Since children from dissolving families have frequently been subjected to threat-laden conversations or have themselves been the direct target of threats of rejection or abandonment, they are commonly approval seeking. Understanding the source of such behavior is important since it is imperative that one ascertain whether it arises from acute interfamilial stress or is the consequence of long-standing family problems. In the latter instance, the conclusions may bear directly on the custodial decision.

Whereas the primary subject of the interview is the child, valuable information about a parent-child relationship can be derived from the interaction between the two in the waiting room. Similar information about relationships between various family members can be obtained in a family interview. For this reason, many custody evaluators regularly conduct family interviews. In this setting, not only is the presence of separation anxiety, aggressiveness or approval seeking behavior in the child important but so is the manner in which the parent responds. By virtue of the parental interchange with the youngster, the maladaptive behavior might be fostered or discouraged. Thus some parents will encourage separation anxiety by welcoming the clinging instead of reassuring the fearful boy or girl, or it may be discouraged by the parent setting a limit on clinging confident that the youngster can handle it. A parent may respond to a child's expression of uncomfortable emotions such as anger, fears of disapproval or feelings of rejection by accepting the emotions and thereby promoting tranquility; or that person may respond in such a way as to make the unpleasant feelings flourish, becoming defensive at the child's anger, rationalizing decisions and actions, or becoming angry with oneself.

Fantasies, Dreams, and Play Techniques   There are a variety of fantasies and play techniques that are valuable in eliciting less consciously available information. These include the Despart Fables, magic wishes, stories, and early, best and worst memories and ambitions. Dreams can serve the same purpose. To some extent, the choice of fantasy material will be contingent on the child's age. Despart Fables and magic wishes are more appropriate for younger children whereas best and worst memories and ambitions might fit teenagers better. But there is considerable crossover. Young children reveal a good deal about their developing identity through discussing their ambitions. One must also bear in mind that the choice of fantasy material is more dependent on maturational age than chronological age. Some school-age children find fable responses infantile whereas some adolescents are more attuned to telling stories than discussing their ambitions.

A variety of play or projective techniques can be used for the same purpose, tapping into the child's preconscious or unconscious feelings, fears, wishes, convictions or identifications.[14] In addition, one can learn about the extent, nature, and depth of the child's personality or ego skills including that youngster's ability to tell the real from the unreal. For example, an eight-year-old child who, while playing in a doll house, becomes so stimulated and aggressive that the interview must be ended is displaying an inability to emotionally extract himself or herself from the fantasy.

Very young children may use fantasies and play as their major if not the only route of communication. School-age children also communicate extensively through fantasies and play. They are in a period where many of their emotions and thoughts have been buried in the unconscious. Consequently, they find discussing their feelings or wishes very threatening. Fantasies, play, and dreams discharge those affects and express their desires without their conscious awareness or complicity. Thus a fable, completed by an eight-year-old child, about a lamb who feels rejected by a mother and who is subsequently eaten by a wolf may take on a vivid meaning. A story by a ten-year-old child about a girl who falls from a tree while listening to her parents argue not only expresses some of her feelings about her parents very graphically but also may demonstrate her guilt. But notwithstanding the richness of these fantasy expressions, they lack the validity and accuracy of interpretation of direct, conversational discussion. By the time a child reaches adolescence, communication in a direct conversational fashion occurs more easily although this is not universally so.

Evaluating Emotional Disturbance

The mental status examination represents a vital contribution to the diagnosis of emotional disturbance in children. One must, however, take care not to oversimplify or draw quick conclusions. Upon observing severely withdrawn and regressed behavior in an eight-year-old boy: sitting in the corner with his face turned to the wall, making no verbal or eye contact, putting his thumb in his mouth, one might draw a tentative conclusion that he is emotionally disturbed. Tentative is the key word. Diagnostic conclusions evolve from the compilation of a substantial history and converging impressions of the origin of various feelings and behaviors. As is the case in any interview, one must take care not to overly generalize from a single impression or piece of data. Recommendations should not be based on conclusions derived from prematurely singling out one particular explanation as the likely cause for a symptom constellation. Conclusions can be accepted as valid only if they are the product of several converging or at least compatible pieces of information.[15]

Emotional disturbance may emanate from a variety of sources including constitutional and ecologic factors, as well as parental and other family disturbance; one cannot simply assume that it results from an unhealthy parent-child relationship. Nor should one presume, to the extent that a disturbed parent-child relationship is responsible, that the disorder lies with the most visibly problematic adult. It is generally accepted that emotional disturbances do not arise from linear relationship problems. Any one family relationship may be seriously impaired. But childhood disturbance of psychological origin is the consequence of a network of conflictual interactions acting upon the child's internal equilibrium.

A mother may, for example, suffer from episodes of depression and crying ending in frequent withdrawal to her bed. The child in the family, ostensibly because of his strong identification with his mother, also withdraws from stress by retreating to his room. What may not be so apparent is that his quietly hypercritical father subtly rejects both his wife and child; they do not measure up to his standards of coping with problems. His comments, indicating that he appreciates and understands his wife's and son's emotional distress, conceal the rejecting message. To the casual observer it may appear that this youngster's difficulty simply arises from the strong pull of his mother's influence. But the more astute clinician will realize that the real difficulty is a network problem. The father's rejecting messages foster his son's identification with the mother, who, like the boy, is a victim of him. In turn their rejection of the father furthers his resentment. He has rationalized that the only reason for his anger lies in his disappointment with his wife and son when, in fact, his feelings of being rejected have rendered him bitter.

A conclusion that the boy's mother had a singularly damaging influence on him resulting in a recommendation that the custody be awarded to the father would be hasty. Naturally, comprehending emotional disturbance in children as resulting from a network of problems makes custody determination more complicated. But development is complicated. One should not assume that any clinician can predict with certainty the ingredients of successful development. The conviction that one can or should be able to do so only leads to premature conclusions based on a paucity of information or incomplete judgments regarding the cause and effect influence of linear relationships. This does not serve children's best interests: it merely reduces the evaluator's anxiety.

One must accept that there are no perfect solutions. A belief in this fiction will lead only to a tendency towards premature conclusions. One must also give up the belief that clear and definitive recommendations will be apparent. As a guide to decision making when the factors are complicated, the least detrimental alternative has been proposed. The least detrimental alternative is the placement that satisfies three components; in accordance with the child's sense of time, on the basis of short-term predictions, and given the limitations of knowledge, it maximizes the child's opportunity for being wanted and for maintaining on a continuous basis a relationship with at least one adult who is or will become a psychological parent.[16]

Finally, if one identifies a probable interlocking pathological relationship between a parent and child, it is insufficient to demonstrate the presence of the complimentary pathology in both parent and child. One must also determine the specific ways in which the parent's pathologic influence affects the child's development. For example, an evaluation might reveal the presence of antisocial behavior in a young adolescent. It is not enough to point out that the parent promotes poor impulse control. One must determine how that parent telegraphs unconscious encouragement to "act out" and, if possible, the manner in which the child uses the signal as a sanction to misbehave. One must keep in mind, however, that it is not the essential function of a custody evaluation to ascertain which parent is the more disturbed, nor is it of sole importance to determine what negative influence that parent might have inflicted on the involved child or children. The optimal custodial parent is the one who can best promote the child's growth and development. Indeed, it is important to identify how parents might negatively influence their children. This must be balanced, however, against that parent's positive influence. Let us offer an example to illustrate this important point.

A parent who has fostered excessive dependence in a child, contributing to that youngster's clinging to adults, a reluctance to attend school and withdrawal from peer associations is contesting custody. This parent is, at times, very empathic and understanding, stimulating in the child feelings of being loved. When an evaluator or other clinician points out the dependency-promoting effect of his or her behavior, that adult displays some degree of insight and ability to curtail inappropriate behavior. In contrast, the other parent is detached and relatively disinterested in the child's plight, demonstrating little capacity for self-awareness when attention is called to the detachment and its deleterious effects. Notwithstanding the detrimental impact of the dependency-promoting parent's behavior, the periodic empathic involvement and ability to change renders that person a positive influence at times, and actually more positive an influence than the uninvolved spouse.

Attachment and Identification Factors

Issues of attachment would be addressed in any examination of an infant or a toddler just as identifications will be explored in the routine mental status examination of a school-age child. Since attachment and identification are such crucial aspects of a custody evaluation, they will be discussed in a separate section. An informal approach to assessing attachment will be presented here. For more formal approaches to investigating attachment in young children other sources are available.[17]

Identifying a preferred attachment figure for the very young child is often best done in the presence of the parents. Young children display their preferential attachment to an attachment figure, often but not necessarily the mother, through attachment behaviors such as smiling, crying, crawling forward, following, and, perhaps most importantly, clinging and sucking. The baby terminates these behaviors when they elicit some response from the principal attachment figure, such as approaching the baby or picking it up.[18] By observing these behaviors, the evaluator can get some indication of to whom the baby is more tied. For instance, a small child may specifically crawl to one parent, whereas an older child may choose to sit on the preferred parent's lap.[19] If that parent should choose to distance himself or herself during the interview, the child's response will be rapid. Anxiety will be readily apparent and the youngster will quickly seek that parent's attention and reassurance. Likewise, if that child should become injured or, for some other reason, anxious during the interview, the same response will occur. Naturally, this parent's reaction, as well as that of the other parent, will be of importance. If the nonpreferred parent supports the child's choice verbally, by facial gesture or body posture, a parental alliance is displayed and speaks well for that parent's ability to respond to the child's need. A warm reception from the preferred parent that quells anxiety, followed by encouragement to again be independent is evidence of good parent-to-child attachment. This represents optimal gratification of the child's impulse. On either side of this are growth-stifling responses. The overly protective person will encourage the child's clinging, while the detached parent may reject the child's overtures. In either case the child's independence seeking may diminish.

Preferential attachments to one parent will diminish with the child's advancing age. In fact, for some children in their second year, beyond the ages of the most intense attachment, their tie to each parent may become increasingly equal. Of course, this will be more true in those instances where both parents have shared caretaking responsibilities equally. A parent's description of preferential attachment may or may not coincide with the evaluator's observations. Obviously many parents who wish to view themselves as a preferred principal attachment figure will report their wish as fact, offering evidence to support their assertion, an assertion that may be inconsistent with reality. Since the evaluator's observations are generally less biased, any discrepancy between a parent's claim and the professional's perception should, at least, call for further inquiry and probably for a repeat observation. In the final analysis it must be the evaluator's opinion that is accorded greater credence. The evaluator's perspective, even if it was originally different from the parent's, may eventually coincide with that of the parent. But in the absence of convincing evidence that the evaluator's observations are in error, greater credibility should be attached to conclusions drawn from them since that person is professionally trained to make such observations and because less bias is likely to accompany them. In general, custody evaluators should not simply accept the veracity of parental statements without supporting evidence. Even if they are not consciously attempting to manipulate the evaluator's perception of their relationship with their child, most parents want to perceive themselves as the favored adult and will unconsciously interpret incidents in that light.

During very early childhood, children pick up parental qualities through mimicry and by incorporating images of the parent. As they progress, they eventually reach a point where they are able to clearly differentiate between themselves and others and are capable of tolerating physical separation from their parent and changing mood states; that is, they have sufficient personality organization to incorporate parent qualities through assimilation. This process, called identification, is selective in that boys and girls at this stage identify with particular feelings, attitudes, beliefs, or traits in their parents rather than necessarily adopting parental qualities indiscriminately. During school-age and adolescence children take on parental qualities in a discriminating, though unconscious, fashion. This is equally true for both positive and negative parental attributes. Children between roughly four and a half and six are in the midst of a developmental sequence in which they often become emotionally invested in the parent of the opposite sex and are in competition with the parent of the same sex.[20] Consequently, the information presented in fantasies and other affective assessments may reflect that alliance and competition rather than true preference.

Subsequent to the completion of this period, a new relationship develops between the child and the same sex parent. The identification with the parent of the same sex that evolves from this period may signify a sexual identification but it may not entail the comprehensive adoption of that parent's attitudes, aspirations and values. The other, opposite-sex parent could conceivably be just as, if not more influential in that regard.

A parent with whom the child is positively identified can greatly influence and support that youngster's attempts to cope with anxiety, meet expectations, risk failure and rejection in the pursuit of success and to negotiate friendships and heterosexual peer attachments. This can be accomplished through active intervention or by silent approval of such growth promoting activities. It can be said that this parent truly has "the child's ear." In and of itself this does not mean that this parent should be the logical choice for custodial parent, but positive identification does fulfill, at least partially, the criteria for psychological parent.[21]

On the other hand, a child may identify with the parent's negative qualities: feelings, attitudes, convictions or traits. A child may identify with a parent's anger and aggression, rendering that child aggressive as well. This particular identification is referred to as an identification with an aggressor.[22] The child may also mirror the parents' racial prejudices or negative opinions about the other parent. Besides mimicking a parent's attitudes, a youngster may come to possess some of a parent's less desirable traits, such as a propensity for impulsive spending or blaming others for problems. This identification is often reinforced by someone, commonly the other parent, vilifying the parent who serves as the object of identification. A typical circumstance might be one in which a mother is constantly reminding a son that he is just as irresponsible as his father. Or a father may repetitively tell his daughter that she is lazy "just like your mother." Certainly, identification with negative qualities will be even more readily reinforced when the identified child is of the same gender as the vilified parent.

Evidence of a child's identification with a parent may be obtained either in the dialogue portion of the interview or in the fantasy material or both. Thus a child may extol the virtues of a parent with whom positive identification has occurred. Because the process is unconscious, it is clear that the child is sincere and is not attempting to manipulate the evaluator. Frequent references may be made to the object of identification such as "My dad says," or "My mom thinks."

It is apparent that this youngster wants the approval of the parent with whom the identification occurs. While talking about a little league team, a desire might be expressed for the parent, with whom the child is identified, to attend practice sessions or games in order to observe the child's improvement. Although identification-related wishes and aspirations often correspond to culturally defined gender roles, this does not mean that identification is not cross genderal. A girl may wish her father to see her perform in a ballet recital so as to gain his approval, whereas a boy may wish his mother to watch him while he practices tying his newly learned boy scout knots. Culturally defined gender-linked roles exert a strong pull, leading children to crave the approval and encouragement of the same-gender parent. But a strong identification with a gender-opposite parent can be just as compelling, if not more so, at times.

Another common pattern is for a child to empathize with or relate to a parent's feelings of anger, disappointment, fear, or other emotion: "I can see how angry my mom must be," or, "Boy, is my dad worried, I don't blame him." This requires, of course, that the child have some capacity for empathic involvement.

The assimilation may extend to the point where the child assumes parental traits: gait, postural and speech characteristics, or gestures. Identification can also include personality patterns such as assertiveness or patience. And it can spread to such identity areas as occupation, religion, or morality, and, of course, sexuality. During the evaluation, the youngster may, through behavior or conversation, display any one of these identification components.

Even in the event of parental death identification can continue.[23] Therefore a nonresidential parent need not fear that because the child is seen less often, that parent's influence will diminish. This will happen only if that parent does something to mar the identification process.

A common means of detecting to what extent a parent is the object of a child's identification is through the use of fantasy. Children may display in their stories a perception of one parent in particular as strong, powerful, or resourceful. A more definitive confirmation of positive identification is obtained if the child aspires to acquire the same qualities.[24] Almost any positive quality can be so represented, ranging from the ability to give affection and nurturance to self-assertion. Identification can become manifest in stories, fables, doll or puppet play, magic wishes, or dreams. School-age and adolescent children may express their identification through ambitions to achieve an academic goal set by their parent, an occupational choice that falls within their parents' range of interests and choices, or by aspiring to a parent's set of values and moral code. Such aspirations may be expressed in the course of conversation occurring during the session, as well as pursuant to a discussion of the youngster's future ambitions.

Identifications with negative qualities are expressed in the same way. Through observation, direct discussion, and fantasies, the evaluator can learn, for example, that a boy sees himself as inadequate because his father failed, a girl feels bound to be rejected because her mother was, or that a child feels doomed to an impulse-ridden existence because of the precedent set by an alcoholic father or mother. Comments such as "How can you expect me to finish school, my mother quit when she was a sophomore?" or, "Sure I sleep around so does my father," clearly point to identifications with negative qualities. The parents' behavior is being used by the child to rationalize the youngster's action. This can be pointed out. But if this parent does nothing to acknowledge mistakes, attempt to correct them, or alter exploitive behavior, in short, does nothing to modify the image projected, this bodes poorly for that person's potential as a custodial parent.

One must further discriminate between healthy and unhealthy identification. All of the connections of a positive nature made by children with their parents that would promote their growth are healthy. Those that have been termed negative, because they foster maladaptive behavior or an adverse sense of self, are unhealthy. One form of identification, with negative characteristics, that has already been mentioned is the adoption of a parent's prejudices. A particular variation of this type of identification is the acceptance of one parent's prejudicial attitudes toward the other parent. Because marital deterioration frequently induces marital partners to perceive their spouses as the source of whatever malevolent victimization they may have experienced in their lives, these spouses are often vilified far beyond the scope of whatever malicious things they may have done. As relationships deteriorate, the door is open to the projection onto one's partner of the responsibility for all the terrible things that have been visited upon oneself by the significant adults of one's developmental and subsequent years. Parents sometimes share these feelings with their children as a means of reinforcing the validity of their perceptions. In this instance, children may identify with the prejudiced parent either because they have a strong tie to the distorting parent or because their security is threatened if they do not. Sometimes identification occurs for both reasons. Obviously, unless a parent is able to recognize subjectivity and strive to be more objective, it weakens that person's potential capacity as a custodial parent. In addition, the attempts of the prejudicial parent can backfire, causing a stronger identification with the scapegoated parent.

Finally, a distinction should be made between positive identification and age inappropriate dependence. From a developmental perspective, positive identification implies that sufficient internal independence has been achieved to allow for selective assimilation of parental qualities. Age inappropriate dependence means that insufficient internal independence has occurred to allow the child to feel comfortable handling age appropriate responsibility, tolerate physical separation from a parent, or cope with parental disapproval without a fluctuation in self-esteem. In individual interviews, children often display such dependence upon a parent, either in the course of discussion or in fantasy expression. They will be apparently unable to deal with some reasonable stress without the intervention of the parent upon whom they are dependent. This suggests that they need to be in that parent's presence or be assured of that parent's approval in order to feel secure. This is often mistaken by custody evaluators as evidence of a favorable tie between that child and that parent. It is not. Nor does it represent a propitious identification that will auger well for the child's psychological growth. Therefore, it should be looked upon as potentially handicapping and an issue to be resolved.

Custodial and Visitation Preference

Whenever possible, the evaluator should determine the child's preference for a custodial parent. One must be aware, however, that such determinations are sometimes secured only with difficulty, if at all. While this is especially true for preschool and school-age children, even adolescents may display considerable hesitancey.

Most preschool children and many school-age and adolescent children have not yet mastered internal separation. As a consequence, they do not believe they fully possess their own feelings and ideas. Neither do they possess strong convictions that they have a right to their own wishes. Children hopefully come to recognize, as their identity crystallizes, that their feelings and thoughts are their own property while the feelings, thoughts and ideas of other people belong to those people. When they have achieved that degree of internal independence, they will feel very compassionate and concerned about others, but will not be responsible for other's emotions. Thus they may be able to voice painful truths and feel empathy for the feelings of others, while avoiding guilt over someone else's expression of emotions.

Children who have not reached that point experience a deep sense of disloyalty and sometimes a fear of rejection if they choose one parent over the other as their custodian. The fact that internal separation is not fully accomplished means that their perspective on their emotions is not necessarily based in reality. They believe the influence of their emotions extends fully into the external world and that their feelings can exert powerful and baneful effects on others, especially their parents. It is, however, important to note that a certain measure of worry that a child experiences about parents' feelings arises simply out of compassion for the loved one.

Custodial preferences are expressed by different children at different ages in different ways. Young children express their preferences through their attachment behavior. Older preschool and school-age children who are already verbal can discuss their feelings and wishes to some extent. However, it is especially difficult for these children, because of their dependence, their possible reliance on magical thinking and other developmental factors, to articulate their desires, affects, and thoughts. Nevertheless, the matter must be explored. Fantasies may prove to be a fruitful route for exploration, for this is a frequent mode of communication for this age group. A five-year-old girl may offer valuable insight into her preference when, in her doll play, she places herself in the house with her mother and baby brother while placing her father in another house at a distance. A five-year-old boy might draw a family portrait containing his father, older brother, and himself engaged in play, excluding his mother from the picture. The evaluator should be careful, however, not to overly interpret these data nor accord it excessive import. Nonetheless, it has its importance. Also, one should not assume that a parent for whom a child has voiced a conscious preference will have the more influence on the child. One must take identification factors, as well as preference, into account when there is a discrepancy between unconscious identification and consciously voiced preference.

The question of custodial preference can be broached with young and school-age children in many ways.[25] Probably the simplest and least threatening is to ask in which residence they prefer to live. Small children invest considerable trust in their environment. While such a choice may represent a parent preference, especially for children whose parents are separated, one cannot draw more than tentative conclusions from the response because it could represent a security choice for an insecure youngster. One advantage to this approach is that it obviates the need for a direct question about the child's custodial choice.

A second avenue of inquiry lies in querying the child about what the pluses and minuses would be of living with each parent. Like the previous presentation, this approach avoids placing the child in a position of directly choosing one or the other parent. It has the further advantage of providing some sense of what factors might contribute to the preference. In this instance an eight-year-old girl might say "Dad is fun and gives me lots of nice things, but mom cooks good meals and puts me to bed." This girl is clearly saying that her father provides her with good times and possessions, neither of which are maturity providing. Her mother, on the other hand, gives her security. In another situation a 10-year-old boy may say "Mother gives me lots of kisses but she goes out every night. Dad is too strict because he makes me go to bed early and do my homework. He is not nearly as nice." He is telling the evaluator that although his mother is an affectionate person, her priority for the evenings, an important time for most children, is in going out. His dad, while he is not fun, pays attention to the essentials that will provide for his health and probably his self-esteem. This method of inquiry provides an opportunity to weigh the factors the child presents, allowing the evaluator to reach a considered decision regarding custodial preference based on the child's best interests.

In the final analysis, each child should be directly asked which parent he or she would like to live with. This question should be reserved for the latter part or end of the interview because its strong emotional impact may stifle further discussion. At this juncture it is usually helpful to tell the child, if it has not already been stated, and to reiterate it if it has, that a preference, like identification, does not determine the choice. It is only one ingredient in the final decision and that determination will be left to the judge.

As children approach and enter adolescence they are far more able to reliably state their custodial preferences.[26] Because they are growing increasingly independent from adults, and because their identities are crystallizing and becoming more secure, teenagers consider themselves as mostly separated and individuated persons.

Preschool and school-age children generally do not indicate a choice as far as visitation rights are concerned, unless they are not permitted sufficient time to spend with the nonresidential parent. If this is the case, younger children will become depressed or moody and older children may comment on their dissatisfaction with the arrangement. Depression will afflict the older child as well, and it may manifest itself in academic deterioration or social withdrawal. By the time adolescence is attained, the child is generally competent to negotiate a visitation schedule with the nonresidential parent. Most teenagers, because of their desires for independence, want considerable say in the matter. Unquestionably, as children get older they need more control over their visitation schedule inasmuch as their peer relationships become more important and their social calendars more crowded.

Some mention should be made of the child who is being "wooed" by the parent. In order to encourage youngsters to select them as their preferred parent, many fathers and mothers engage in a propaganda campaign. Obviously this places children in a difficult position. It clearly puts them in a position of control that in and of itself is problematic because it invests them with an inappropriate sense of power. Moreover, it gives them a vehicle for retaliation against adults and undermines parental discipline. Finally, it can trigger feelings of guilt if the child accepts the proffered indulgences, whether it be a new toy or the privilege of staying up past a bedtime. The "wooing" process will increase the child's feelings of disloyalty. Certainly it should be pointed out to the "wooing" parent if it is observed.

It is incontestable that children's preferences should be given great weight in rendering the custodial decision since, if it reflects a choice based on feeling loved, valued, and wanted, preference demonstrates a psychological parent selection.[27] One must remember, however, that it is only one factor in the custody consideration, albeit a very important one.

Confidentiality

Mental health interviews are, for obvious reasons, confidential by design. While this is equally true for both adults and children, it is especially important for children. Because of a certain degree of normal dependence on adults, children must necessarily trust the evaluator to handle with care and good judgment the information and expression of feeling imparted during the evaluation. Great caution must be exercised in protecting that trust. In the usual clinical interview, the confidentiality contract serves that purpose. That contract does not exist in a custody evaluation. It is important, therefore, that the child know that the material obtained from the interview will be reported to a judge; therefore, the parents will have access to the information. Despite the fact that this may limit the child's candid expression of thoughts and feelings, a lack of clarity on this issue could make the youngster feel betrayed.

By discussing the dilemma with the parents before the interview, the potential problems surrounding confidentiality can be mitigated. If they are aware of the psychological importance of their youngster's feeling unintimidated by their fears of disapproval and rejection, they can discuss the matter with the youngster in advance of the interview. If reassured by the father and mother that they wish an honest expression of feelings and opinions, regardless of outcome, because to them honesty is more important than any unpleasant emotions they may experience as a result, the child may be far less inhibited. Parenthetically, this is a good index of the parents' capacity for empathy.

Conclusion

Although custody interviews are frightening to some children, and anxiety provoking to all, they can be helpful and growth promoting. It should be kept in mind that it is anxiety relieving to children, just as it is to adults, to express their feelings. It is respectful to ask their opinions and preferences. Beyond this, the custody interview provides an opportunity to identify emotional disturbance that has been triggered or intensified by the divorce process, uncovering the need, if it exists, to obtain some assistance for the child. In the final analysis, divorce is an event that everyone in the family will have to live with and learn to handle in some fashion for many years after the final echo of the gavel in court. Children will cope better, although not necessarily comfortably, if they have been participants in the process.

8

Case Example

To illustrate the principles described in the previous two chapters, we have provided a simulated case evaluation, with fictitious names. This case example is a composite of features that have appeared repeatedly in the custody cases that have been a part of the authors' practice. It is comprised of (1) a case history that includes a marital separation history, evaluation procedures outlined in the first interview, and a family history including a history of the marriage; (2) the evaluator's assessment of each parent derived from personal interviews and information from a collateral source; (3) a summary of information obtained from family interviews; (4) a discussion of the childrens' developmental, medical and educational histories; (5) the evaluation of each child; (6) a summary statement including the evaluator's conclusions and finally; (7) a detailed list of recommendations.

Case History

Events Leading to the Evaluation Married sixteen-and-a-half years, Mary Longworth one day in October 1987 came across a receipt from a local motel, dated the previous evening, among her husband's belongings. She had long suspected her husband of engaging in extramarital affairs, and his practice of keeping late hours, which he attributed to the demands of his business, heightened her suspicions. She determined to bring the matter out in the open. That evening, when confronted with the motel receipt, he confessed his infidelity, which prompted an argument. During the angry interchanges, John Longworth insisted that not only did he not love his wife and had not for a long time, but also that he saw little hope for a reconciliation.

Within a week Mary visited an attorney and told him that she wished to file for divorce—an action to which she was resigned on the grounds that her husband no longer loved her. Besides, she felt that she and the children might do just as well without him, given that he was not around very much, so long as she was able to receive satisfactory financial support. This was necessary because she was unemployed outside of her home.

Upon learning that his wife had sought legal counsel, John too decided to visit an attorney, although it is unclear that he would have done so independently if Mary had not taken the initiative. Two weeks later, John was served with papers indicating Mary's intent to obtain a divorce and sole custody of the children. One month after that, John's attorney filed a motion to obtain sole custody of all three children.

The two attorneys met and agreed to the selection of an evaluator to conduct an evaluation respecting the custody of the three children. A stipulation was entered into the court record designating the evaluator. The stipulation became a court order by agreement and included a provision that John would pay the cost of the evaluation.

The First Interview At the initial evaluation session in December 1987, attended by both parents, some statistical data were obtained. This included the names of the family members, parents' ages and addresses, and the date of birth, school of attendance, and grade placement of each child. Both parents were asked about their attorney and whether the children had legal counsel. No counsel had been appointed for the children.

The evaluator then outlined the procedure for conducting the evaluation, informing the Longworths of the approximate number and nature of the interviews, the type of information the evaluator would request, the collateral contacts he required, the collateral contacts and information acceptable to the evaluator, and the nature of the report. In addition, the evaluator informed them of who would have access to the report and under what circumstances.

Both parties were advised that they enjoyed no privilege regarding confidentiality. Therefore, anything they said could be used in the evaluation or potentially in testimony. This same rule applied to the children. The limits upon traditional psychiatric confidentiality derive from the fact that confidentiality applies only in treatment situations. Normally the evaluator's conclusions and recommendations will be embodied in a written report that will become, in the event of a trial, an evidential exhibit. The evaluator's notes, recollections, and opinions, not contained in the report, may or may not become evidential; this generally depends upon the extent to which the dissatisfied party seeks to discredit the evaluator's conclusions.

The Longworths were told that the evaluator would require approximately four individual interviews for each parent, depending, of course, upon each parent's supply of pertinent and relevant information. In addition, each child would be seen for one, and possibly two, individual interviews, a second interview being necessary only if the child's anxiety level should be so high as to impair the quality of information the child was able to supply, or if the child should possess sufficient information and insights as to render one interview insufficient to fully obtain the relevant material.

Finally two family interviews would be held, one with Mr. Longworth and the children, the other with Ms. Longworth and the children. The purpose of the interview would be to obtain information about parent/child interaction. Under certain circumstances, although not in this instance, both parents might be asked to join in a single family interview if they can tolerate the other's presence without experiencing overwhelming negative emotions that preclude their participation.

Mr. and Mrs. Longworth were told that during the individual interviews considerable information would be obtained. In addition to assessing individual parenting capacities, the evaluator would collect from each of them a family and marital history, including specific dates of emotional importance, and an understanding from their own perspective of how the marital breakdown evolved; an appraisal of their relationship with each child emphasizing their own and their spouse's strengths and weaknesses as parents; a developmental history for each child, including milestones, a discussion of any developmental or medical problems, and information about each child's current school and peer relationship performance; a brief history of their family of origin; and finally, a discussion of their custody and visitation preferences.

The evaluator informed them that he would require the following collateral information: pertinent court documents, hospital and health records, police reports, information from any mental health professionals with whom any member of the family has had contact, school report cards, and any previous evaluation reports that might prove useful, such as pediatric, psychiatric, psychological, or educational reports for any of the children. The evaluator also requested to speak personally, by telephone, to the children's pediatrician, teachers, and to any therapists whom any member of the family may have seen. In addition, a personal interview would be conducted with any person who may be able to offer first-hand observations of the family in their home, such as a live-in babysitter or maid. The evaluator informed them that any information from friends or relatives would be considered but usually would not be accorded great importance.

Once the report is completed, they were told, a copy would be sent to the court and to each attorney, through whom each parent would have access to it. It was clarified for them that the evaluator is an advocate solely for the children and is not an ally of either parent, regardless of who pays the fee. While each parents' feelings would be given consideration and understanding, the children's best interest will be the only relevant guideline for the recommendations. Further, it was stipulated that no hints, information, or tentative conclusions would be offered to either parent or to their counsel before a submission of the report.

During this joint interview it was necessary to interrupt the conversation several times because the couples' discussion became tangential. In an angry tone of voice, Mary made it clear that she considered this process a sham. She had diligently cared for and raised the children while her husband was making a mockery of their marriage by having one affair after another. In a defensive fashion, John countered that he was sick and tired of her constant complaints and incessant fatigue and inertia.

Family History During her first interview it was apparent that Mary was indeed depressed. She gave a sad account of her relationship with John and its devastating effect on her life. Through five individual interviews with Mary and four with John, a detailed marital and family history was obtained.

John and Mary met during their junior year in high school. Each was the other's first serious romance. Both were shy and found their time together a chance for companionship, sexual experimentation, and an escape from the loneliness of their otherwise isolated peer experiences.

Upon graduation, each went off to college, she to an all-women's school one hundred miles from her hometown and he to the state university on the other side of the state. Weekends were lonely times for Mary because she did not make friends easily. Therefore, she generally went home on weekends. In addition, though she did not admit it to herself, she missed John and her family desperately. John too, because he was socially inhibited with girls, missed Mary. After her second year Mary left college for two reasons. First, she never felt entirely comfortable living away from home. Second, she and John were speaking of marriage; she therefore believed a college degree would be unnecessary since she did not plan on a career outside her home.

John finished college and received his bachelor's degree. Although he planned to enter the family business, his parents urged him to get a degree so as to better prepare himself for the administrative duties he would eventually assume. In January 1971, John and Mary were married at the Sacred Heart Church, their home parish. Their first year of marriage was like a renewal of their high school romance: warm, friendly, and pleasantly sexual.

During their second year of marriage Mary became pregnant. It was a difficult nine months. She had morning sickness and for a short time she was confined to bed because she was spotting. To make matters worse, John was away much of the time; his duties as vice president of the family business required him to travel frequently.

In November 1972 Gail Jean was born. Colicky and a poor sleeper, Gail soon wore out her mother, who was the child's primary caretaker. John shared in caretaking responsibilities such as feeding and diapering when he was home, but the task was still not easy because Gail kept them awake at night. As a toddler, Gail Jean was an adventurous youngster in everything. And while not rebellious, she certainly was independent and quickly displayed a "mind of her own." Increasingly she proved more than Mary could handle. Mary found herself in a position of needing to find, stop, and discipline Gail much of the time. For John, Gail Jean was an easier child, and he almost enjoyed her saucy attitude, often laughing at the way she walked away when she did not wish to follow her parents' requests.

By late 1974 the couple was having serious difficulties. John's heavy work schedule aggravated Mary's loneliness and sense of isolation, brought about by the extent to which she was confined by Gail's care. John, for his part, found Mary's complaints and continual state of depression burdensome, especially as he felt pressured by business concerns of his own. He avoided being with her, and as a result, she felt rejected and even more depressed. Her anger level with Gail rose steadily. Toilet training Gail became a battle of wills and Mary thought Gail a little rebellious. John did not perceive Gail in the same light. He enjoyed playing with the aggressive little girl. Mary cautioned him not to turn her into a "tomboy" with his rough ways. Partly in order to compensate for John's influence, Mary dressed Gail in pretty, dainty outfits. Invariably though, they were dirty within half an hour.

Because their state of compansionship had so badly deteriorated, and with it their sexual relationship, Mary suggested that they seek therapy. At the suggestion of a friend they consulted Dr. Nagle, whom Mary found very understanding. While John was concerned about their marriage and about Mary in particular, he hesitated to take the time from his already demanding schedule, so he proposed that Mary go alone. To Mary this was not a satisfactory solution. From her perspective, her problems were the result of John's absence and his spoiling Gail, although to herself, she acknowledged that he was always available to help when asked, and more than that, he frequently offered to help.

The marital therapy was short-lived, inasmuch as John believed that Dr. Nagle too quickly agreed with Mary that he was the cause of their problems and her depression. Each session followed a similar pattern. It began with a discussion of Mary's emotional state and ended with a discussion of how he was progressing in readjusting his schedule. John admitted to himself, as well as to Dr. Nagle and Mary, that his hours posed a serious problem for his wife. On the other hand, his father was talking of retirement and was placing increased responsibility in John's hands. When John found at least partially rational reasons why he could not make appointments regularly, Mary continued anyway. Soon the marital therapy became individual therapy for Mary.

In 1975 Mary again became pregnant. Both had wanted a large family when they married. In addition, John and Mary's relationship seemed to improve. Having become president of the company upon his father's retirement, John was able to delegate more responsibility. But of equal, if not greater importance, Mary's emotional state improved. This was a consequence both of John's increased attention and of the support she received in her therapy; privately, she could not really discriminate between the impact of each.

John Jr. was born in December 1975. An easy pregnancy and John Jr.'s calm temperament made him an easy baby for whom to provide care. As he grew, Johnny was as easy a baby for his mother to love as Gail had been difficult to manage. He did everything "on-time" and with spontaneity and ease. A dreary or lonely day was always warmed by his pleasant smile and happy disposition. He was indeed the sunshine of his mother's life.

As John entered his preschool years he came to enjoy his father's playful attitude. Because John was not so tired upon arriving home in the evening as he had been previously, he participated more spontaneously in his son's care than he had with Gail. Nonetheless, Mary continued to be the primary caretaker, though with Johnny it was not work for her, it was sheer delight. Each night Johnny would eagerly await his father's arrival and run to him when he entered the door. To Gail her position as daddy's girl was a little threatened by this engaging younger competitor. She did not fear too greatly, however, because whenever he was tired or upset, Johnny preferred his mother's waiting arms to his father's playfulness.

During the summer of 1979 calamity struck. Mary's father developed a highly malignant and rapidly progressive cancer. By late fall he was dead. This was a crushing loss for Mary, the more so because, of his two children—an older son and a younger daughter—she had been his favorite. He had appreciated the fact that Mary, during her childhood, made her family the center of her social circle and he especially liked that she doted on his every word. During automobile rides in the country, they had many long and pleasant conversations. Just thinking of those conversations made Mary feel warm all over. During some of her most difficult days, it was the memories of those times that buoyed her up. Her grief was intense and lasted for years; perhaps she never entirely got over it. Then too, her mother was becoming an increasing burden. Initially John was quite understanding, but after several months he felt drained by Mary's nearly nightly crying and continued state of depression. To himself he was thinking, "how long, oh Lord, how long?" During the summer of 1980, roughly one year after her father's death, Mary returned to see Dr. Nagle, who gave her the support for which she so deeply longed.

While Mary's mood state again improved as a consequence of her therapy, the couple's marital relationship waned. This occurred for a number of reasons. During her many hours in Dr. Nagle's office she recognized how angry she was with John and for how many years this had been so. Try as she might, she could not warm up to him. The frequency of their sexual relations diminished from infrequent to very infrequent. In addition she became able to voice her irritation with a nagging, demanding mother. She also discovered just how great a place Johnny had come to occupy as an object of her affection. His loving nature filled a void.

Meanwhile, John's business was an increasing success. After his father's retirement his work, innovative planning, and willingness to take calculated risks had paid off. He was proud of his success, a success that offered financial rewards for his family, of which he was equally proud. Mary did not, however, seem to share in his pride. She was too submerged in her unresolved grief, disappointment, and anger.

John had also lost considerable interest in his spouse, both emotionally and sexually. However, this was not so great a concern for him as it was for Mary, for he enjoyed subtle flirtations with a variety of women he encountered in his daily business life. While he thought they were simply flirtations, he was aware that at some level they satisfied a deep ego need. Within a short time what he had initially persuaded himself were merely business luncheons turned into social engagements and at some point they became sexual encounters. There were a number. To the end of his marriage John is not sure how many there were, although he agrees that they were not love matches except for the last. The word "escape" best characterized them. Most of all, for the first time in a long time, he felt appreciated and esteemed, if for nothing else, for his free-wheeling spending. Although Mary was very concerned about her husband's many evenings away and his growing social isolation—largely because it increased the amount of time she spent without adult companionship—at least it precluded having to deal with her ambivalence about him.

By 1982, the children were doing well scholastically. Gail, a 6th grader, was proving an exceptional student. Possessing a quick mind and an unquenchable curiosity, she soared. A leader among children, she was sought out as a friend and she seemed likely to blossom into a very attractive, vivacious, and poised young lady. She was finding less time for family because her social calendar was becoming crowded with parties and other peer excursions. To top it off, Gail was a gifted soccer player.

John Jr. likewise was a good student. His good mind was complemented by diligent effort and strong commitment. His mother worked with him long hours on his reading and spelling; this in no small way contributed to his success. Even, however, when he declined the help, Mary persuaded him that some extra tutorial assistance would not hurt. She recalled thinking to herself that it seemed so unfair: with little effort Gail was at the top of her class. Johnny reached that point only through endurance and hard work. His teacher commented that John Jr.'s work was even more commendable in light of the fact that a mild fine-motor coordination problem slowed him down.

In his peer relationships, however, John Jr. suffered. He was a little overweight and basically shy—much as his mother and father had been at his age. Johnny found it difficult to make friends. In addition, he avoided peer competition. His coordination and weight interfered with his efforts to some extent, but basically he did not like the competition. Rather, much of his time was spent at home watching television and enjoying his mother's company. This pleasure was reciprocated by Mary.

John Sr.'s pride in Gail could not be greater. It was matched by Mary's muted compliments. Regarding Johnny, he had difficulty distinguishing between his disappointment, and sometimes visible annoyance with his son because he made little effort to make friends and participate in any peer activities, and his clear resentment of Mary's treatment of Johnny. He felt that she babied him. Getting his clothes out for him, she dressed him if he dallied, and when the dinner was not to his liking she prepared him a different dish. Johnny was affectionate with his father and loved nothing better than to play games with him, especially when he won. John loved him dearly, but his embarrassment in his son was evident. If his father showed any anger, Johnny was clearly intimidated. The couple's conflict over Johnny mounted. One such characteristic argument ensued when Johnny got off the school bus crying because the boys were teasing him. Incensed, Mary demanded that John call the school principal to insist that the bullies be reprimanded, or else she would do so herself. In an angry tone, John told his wife that Johnny would never grow up if she intended to fight all his battles.

In an effort to save their ailing marriage, the couple went to Europe for a vacation in the Fall of 1983. Away from the children and their daily stresses they recommitted themselves to one another. No small part in their decision to stay together was played by their religious convictions and their belief that an intact family was better for the children. Several weeks after they returned, Mary discovered that she was pregnant.

In July 1984, she gave birth to their third child, Sarah. The pregnancy and delivery were uneventful. Sarah was, like Johnny, an easy baby for whom to care. Perhaps this was due to Sarah's mild temperament, possibly it was simply that they were by now experienced caretakers. John and Mary, when together, shared equally in caretaking responsibilities. Mary nursed her and enjoyed doing so. The attachment between mother and child was clear and firm. John was just as playful and fun-loving with Sarah as he had been with the other children.

Then, over the course of roughly the next three years, there was increasing distance between the couple. Each vowed to try harder, but it was to no avail. John continued his heavy schedule and affairs. Mary was dissatisfied with her life and remained depressed. Even though Sarah was a pleasure and she enjoyed the two older children, especially John Jr., she felt unfulfilled and unhappy. When she discovered the evidence of John's infidelity, she recalls thinking to herself, "it was a long time in coming."

John Longworth

Appearance and Behavior A handsome, friendly thirty-nine-year-old man, John tries with considerable difficulty to hide his pride in himself, a pride that borders on self-centeredness and pomposity. John's perceptions are extremely polarized. He is predisposed to adjudge people and situations as totally good or bad, right or wrong, beneficent or malevolent, ignoring the reality that few circumstances or individuals can be so sharply defined. Complementing this trait is the analytical and scrutinizing character of John's intellect. He is generous with his criticism, which he supplies without regard for the feeling and sensitivities of others. In short, John likes or dislikes people vehemently and immediately; how they experience his opinions and criticism is of less importance to him than is his right to supply it.

John rationalizes his critical and detached behavior with a philosophy that holds that it is his duty to those he loves to make them aware of their shortcomings, as painful as this is, in order that they may grow. Furthermore, he is engaged in a struggle to support his family and this struggle must take precedence over emotional involvement with his wife and children despite the fact that his income was sufficient to provide the Longworths a fair measure of affluence. In place of true emotional communication, John affects an affable demeanor, even when irritated. This superficial jocularity conceals his basically hostile nature, a nature that emerges in demeaning and sarcastic comments, especially about Mary.

Direct Discussion Inasmuch as John's self-righteous attitude precluded his feeling guilty about his extramarital affairs, much less apologizing for them, it was relatively easy for him to hold Mary responsible for all of their marital problems. In his opinion, the breakdown in their marriage stemmed exclusively from Mary's lack of affection, constant state of depression, remote mood state, and what he considered to be her alcoholism.

As far as John was concerned, while Mary was loving, affectionate, and a good, or at least a reasonable, sexual partner early in their marriage, their sexual relationship had steadily diminished to the point of vanishing. What could anyone expect but that he would seek sexual satisfaction elsewhere; he had no choice. As a matter of fact, if it were not for his regular affairs, he would not have met the woman who, at some point in the distant future, may become his second wife, Helen Crandell. To John, Helen was everything Mary was not. She was a business person herself. Appreciating his need for an independent life, she too wanted and treasured her space.

John described at great length what he termed Mary's "retreat to her bed." The children, John claimed, were left to fend for themselves. Gail, in particular, bore the brunt of responsibility inasmuch as she was often expected to prepare meals, do whatever cleaning that was done and look after John Jr. and Sarah on a regular basis.

As far as he was concerned, Mary's depression arose primarily from her weak character and inability to handle her own emotions. When confronted with the possibility that their marital problems served as a source of her melancholic state, John quickly diminished their importance by pointing out that he and everyone else had daily problems with which they must cope.

John considered Mary a confirmed alcoholic. The fact that she drank less during periods of marital tranquility, particularly when they were away together, did not, in his opinion, ameliorate this judgment in the least. Her drinking was, so far as he was concerned, just another manifestation of her weak character. One of his favorite sources of misplaced humor was a comment, delivered with sardonic pleasure, that he did not know which route was least cost-effective, her visits to the liquor store or to her therapist's office. When pressed on how much his wife actually drank, John was unclear, except that he believed that two or three quart bottles of vodka were disappearing weekly and she always had a drink in her hand. She began her day, he said, with an early morning eye-opener and ended it with a nightcap.

When the discussion turned to his business and friends, John became considerably less emotional and far more objective. His friendly attitude returned and at times he was even genuinely humorous. Although he had considered himself shy during his young adulthood, this quality became gradually less prominent as he gained confidence and achieved business success.

John's father had been satisfied to operate a small business, but John was more ambitious and visionary. Taking a calculated risk, John borrowed money for expansion purposes, and over a ten-year period his investment in the future of this type of manufacturing paid off. His pride in this accomplishment was considerable. As he described it he became, in fact, somewhat boastful. His ability to self-correct was considerable, however; as quickly as he began to brag, he just as quickly gained self-control by talking in more reasonable and rational terms about his business acumen and expertise.

His conversation about the children was especially revealing. As the topic was broached, he again lost his objectivity and became quite energized in his conversation. John's features became animated as he began to describe his eldest daughter's accomplishments. Whether discussing Gail's scholastic ability, athletic prowess, or her skill at initiating and sustaining friendships, his great pride was evident. There could be no doubt that she was his favorite.

While he was lavish in his praise of Gail's accomplishments, he was equally lavish in his criticism of John Jr.'s character. John considered his son to be someone who tried hard in school with modest success, despite the fact that he was not especially gifted. He said this in an almost apologetic tone of voice, as if he were fearful that he too would be judged by John's mediocrity. As he spoke of how readily John gave up at team sports and with friends, his concern about the interviewer's judgment of him seemed even greater. When the evaluator pointed out this apparently unconscious transmission, John seemed surprised and a little embarrassed.

As far as Sarah was concerned, John had relatively little to say. She was a delightful baby with whom John greatly enjoyed playing. But she was, after all, a baby and little could be said about her yet.

Family of Origin   Raised in an intact family, John was the oldest in a line of two, having a sister Susan three years his junior. His family was clearly patriarchal. His father had presided over the family business founded by his grandfather. The business dominated his father's life, as indeed it dominated John's as well. Consequently, John became very attached to his mother. As he grew older, this attachment was fortified and intensified by his unsuccessful attempts to win his father's approval. It seemed that, try as he may, John could never do enough, well enough, to gain commendation from his dad.

John's relationship with his sister was somewhat strained. Far more competitive than Susan, and possibly more gifted, John was successful in all of his youthful pursuits except for his considerable shyness. Academically and athletically John was the family star, especially in the eyes of his mother. While John loved Susan, clearly he did not respect her laid-back attitude, which he considered a form of laziness.

Although John's father was not openly critical, by the same token, he provided little emotional support. It was not as if he did not feel emotionally pulled toward his son and proud of him. Rather, his inability to express his affection and pride arose from the combination of exceptionally high standards and a deep conviction that expressing emotions was a weakness not to be exposed, especially in a man.

When John met Mary during their high school years, he was considered a "catch" indeed. Handsome, a star athlete, and a good student, John, despite his shyness or perhaps partly because of it, was well liked. He was immediately attracted to Mary. It was not simply that she was pretty and possessed a warm personality; her nurturing acceptance struck a resonant chord deeply with him. It was like coming home.

Custodial Preference   So far as John was concerned, there could be no doubt about Gail's custody. She belonged with him. He shuddered to think how she would turn out if she had to live with his "Milquetoast" wife. When asked if his sometimes overdetermined pride in Gail, actually out of proportion to her accomplishments, could have the negative effect of creating inappropriate expectations for her, John grudgingly acknowledged that as a child he had felt that he could never please his father. In retrospect, however, he believed that this had given him the push he needed to achieve success.

John believed that John Jr. also belonged with him. He needed structure, discipline, and mandated responsibility to pull him out of

his "babyish" ways. Queried about John Jr.'s need for encouragement, John replied that this was implicit in what he called his "tough
love" approach.

As far as Sarah was concerned, he was ambivalent. While he believed himself the better of the two parents for the aforementioned
reasons, John could clearly see that Sarah was strongly attached to
Mary; therefore Sarah probably should remain with his wife.

Mary Longworth

Appearance and Behavior   A very pretty thirty-nine-year-old woman,
Mary's moderately overweight condition does not conceal her basically attractive appearance. Soft-spoken, Mary is articulate as she expresses the relief she feels since learning of John's affairs and since
their separation. It is surprising to the evaluator that her mood state
has improved so dramatically in such a short period of time.

During the evaluation Mary oscillated wildly between depression
and anger. In the former mood, she is self-critical and self-denigrat-
ing, blaming herself for the breakdown in her marriage. In the latter
she is angry and accusatory, ascribing most of the family's problems
to John's relentless ambition and demanding, critical attitudes toward her and the children. When in this mood, she portrays herself
as an unwitting victim of his rage and attack, largely unable to do
anything to rectify or even partially ameliorate the situation.

Some measure of rationalization is present in Mary's assertion that
no one could satisfy John, as a spouse generally, and as a sexual
partner in particular; therefore she gave up on her role as a marital
partner. This same tendency to rationalize is manifest when she talks
of John Jr.'s dependence on her. Mary defends her propensity for
picking up after him, indulging him, and intervening in his disputes
with his father, teachers, siblings, and peers by explaining that Johnny
needs extra love and care to compensate for a lack of fatherly love.
Angrily she protests that if she did not love him, no one would. However, when confronted with the potentially harmful effects on John
Jr. of her overly protective attitude and behavior, Mary begins to cry
and in a tearful tone of voice says she fears that she has damaged

her son by turning him into a baby. Shifting the object of her anger to herself, Mary says that because she needed love so badly, she selfishly spoiled Johnny.

Direct Discussion Mary recalls the early years of her marriage as being idyllic. As she speaks of those years, there is almost a light in her eyes. Although she initially says that she does not know how the marriage soured, later in the discussion Mary asserts that both she and her husband failed; John's relentless ambition and her overwhelming need for security doomed the relationship. Marital disruption was inevitable unless one of them "gave in." She believed that the competitive urge was too much a part of John's personality and her security needs were too ingrained in her character to permit such a compromise. She did not know if she could ever surmount them.

As the evaluation proceeded, the evaluator asked Mary about her drinking. She believed that John was making too much of it and was worried that somehow John would exploit it as a means of winning custody. Delegating the responsibility for her drinking to John, she described at great length the manner in which John had facilitated her drinking by encouraging her to drink, only to refer to her later as a drunk. With great shame, Mary acknowledged that she probably was a mild alcoholic and said that she was attending Alcoholics Anonymous (A.A.) at Dr. Nagle's suggestion. It was her hope that she would be able to gain sustained control over her drinking. At this point she had been sober for about three months.

Mary described her suspicions of John's infidelity in a rambling monologue that seemed pregnant with the sort of exhaustion peculiar to those who have too long endured great anxiety. The evaluator then asked Mary about John's allegation that she had lost sexual interest in him long before his philandering began. Grudgingly, Mary admitted that he might have felt deprived but contended that no one could have satisfied him. She predicted that John would embark on a lifelong quest of one sexual conquest after another. His inability to value her and her role as a mother killed any feeling she might have had for him.

Following a prolonged diatribe against John, Mary suddenly announced that she believed it was necessary to give up on her anger.

She had, at least to her own satisfaction, resolved that their relationship was over. As a consequence, they needed to go on and be the best parents they could, given all their flaws.

In a telephone conversation with Dr. Nagle it was obvious that he felt extremely anxious and was quite defensive about his professional conduct with the Longworths. Although he attempted, so far as he was able, to be fair to both parties it was clear that John was probably correct; Dr. Nagle saw him as the primary cause of Mary's problems. Dr. Nagle lauded Mary's willingness to stay with John for such an extended period of time, despite the verbal abuse he heaped upon her.

Insofar as the children were concerned, Mary feels, if anything, worse about Gail than she does about John Jr. Pointing out that she considers herself realistic, Mary believes that she has been a poor model for Gail. In some ways she thinks that she may have encouraged Gail to seek John's overzealous approval through her accomplishments by providing insufficient acceptance herself. Currently, Gail was being rude to her on a regular basis and blamed her for the divorce. Although her rudeness was consistently disciplined, Mary said she could understand how and why Gail had become so aligned with John. Moreover, she felt she had given Gail plenty of reason for her anger over the years.

Mary told the evaluator that she was seeking therapy at a local child guidance clinic for John Jr. The therapist had suggested that John Sr. become involved as well since he was a major role model and she was trying to negotiate this with her husband. As a means of doing so, she assured John that the therapy would not be a forum in which to vilify and blame him.

Mary also was insisting that Johnny would have to go to camp for a two-week period. Johnny was vigorously opposed and was protesting her decision by throwing temperamental outbursts, but she had so far held her ground. Johnny seemed to have regressed of late into even more infantile behavior than usual. Following weekend visitation with John, Johnny often did not want to go to school the next morning. Although Mary initially allowed him to stay home a few Mondays in a row, she believed it was becoming a pattern. Consequently, she became firm in her insistence that he attend school, even if he did have a headache or stomach ache.

Of the three children, Sarah was handling the separation best. She missed John and was happy to see him when he arrived for visitation. Although she generally returned home in a good mood, she frequently complained of bad dreams on Sunday nights after a visit.

Family of Origin   The younger of two children, Mary was raised in a working-class family. Her mother was clearly the more stern of the two parents. Mary's mother frequently remarked that if it were not for her discipline, Mary would have done nothing but sing while her father played the piano. From early childhood Mary was the "apple of her father's eye." Upon his return from work, the first thing he would do was seek out Mary to read or play with her.

A good student, Mary's shyness interfered with her making as many friends as she wanted. Her mother, referring to her as a "little home-girl," ascribed her desire to be a constant companion of her parents and her relative social isolation to her being like an only child since her brother was considerably older. She, therefore, did not have any-one her own age with whom she could play.

Although she avoided school activities, her comely appearance attracted John early in high school; it was not until their junior year, however, that he summoned enough courage to ask her out.

Custody Preference   It was Mary's wish to have sole custody. Clearly, however, she wanted John involved in the children's lives. She believed it important for all the children, especially Gail and John Jr. Gail was strongly tied to her father, and although Mary did not approve of John constantly pressuring Gail to achieve, she thought these achievements did contribute to the development of Gail's self-confidence. Probably John Jr. needed his father the most, if only John Sr. could appreciate some of Johnny's good points, including his sincere feelings for animals. In her opinion, while Sarah required her right now, she probably could do well eventually with either parent since she was the least torn between them.

Family Interviews

In an interview attended by John and the children Gail sat next to her father with Johnny assuming the place next to Gail. Sarah played comfortably in the dollhouse. Much to her embarrassment John spent considerable time extolling Gail's accomplishments as a student and athlete. In an attempt to interpose himself, John Jr. changed the subject to his coin collection. This prompted John to admonish him for being rude. Sarah easily turned the attention to herself by jumping on her father's lap.

On another occasion the evaluator met with Mary and the children. While John Jr. sat next to her, Gail sat across the room assuming a posture befitting her solemn mood. Sarah, again, took up a position by the dollhouse. As the interview progressed Mary told Gail that she understood her anger since she had missed basketball practice to attend the interview. She, however, considered the meeting important. Turning her attention to Johnny, Mary suggested he sit farther away on the sofa because they were crowding each other. As Gail's anger gradually dissipated, she and John playfully teased about who found it most difficult to get up in the morning. For the major part of the interview Sarah was either at the dollhouse or busied herself examining some blocks.

Longworth Children

Developmental History   Each of Mary's pregnancies was uneventful. It was Mary's opinion that if Gail had been her third child rather than her first she might have handled her differently and better. All of the children except John Jr. achieved their motor-muscular and language milestones well within normal limits. John was at the extreme low end of the range with regard to walking and talking. He walked at sixteen months, did not use words until eighteen months or sentences until nearly three years of age. It was John's contention that Johnny did not have to walk or talk because Mary carried him and gave him what he wanted if he merely gestured.

Perhaps the greatest concern for both of the young parents was John's attachment to security objects such as stuffed animals and, in particular, his security blanket, which she called his "gulrp." Until he was seven or eight, Johnny carried the threads of the blanket around while he sucked his thumb. His thumb-sucking reached a point where the dentist became concerned about its creating a dental problem. Each parent proposed opposite remedies. John suggested they put some mustard on his thumb and take the security blanket away while he slept. It was Mary's suggestion that eventually Johnny would grow out of it.

Medical History   None of the children had serious medical or surgical problems. Although John Jr. had bronchial asthma, it never became serious. Sarah had experienced repeated otitis media and tubes had been inserted several months ago.

Dr. Edgar Corcoran, the children's pediatrician, reported that he had little concern about their medical histories. John's asthma was not a serious matter. From a developmental perspective, Dr. Corcoran had been worried about John's dental condition because of his thumb sucking, but that was over three years ago and the concern no longer existed.

Education History   Upon reviewing her report cards it was apparent that throughout her school career, Gail has been an outstanding student. John, too, was making his scholastic mark, albeit, as was previously noted, with considerable effort. This, likewise, was clear from his report cards. Telephone conversations with the children's teachers confirmed these findings.

In nursery school two mornings weekly, Sarah was everyone's delight. She caught on satisfactorily, though not nearly so quickly as Gail. She lacked John's persistence but no one seemed to care. Owing to her friendly and out-going nature everyone loved her, including the other children. Both John and Mary marveled at how relaxed they were able to be with Sarah. The nursery school teachers agreed with the Longworth's opinions.

Gail Longworth

Appearance and Behavior   A bright, pretty, and enthusiastic just fifteen-year-old tenth grader, Gail speaks with considerable sadness about her parents' divorce. However, after commenting that she missed time spent together as a family, Gail changed the subject. It was apparent that Gail was often preoccupied, the object of her focus alternating between herself and her friendships.

Direct Discussion   Obviously enjoying school, Gail talks easily about the pleasure she finds in school attendance. According to Gail the work is "a breeze." The only subject she finds difficult is Latin, which her father insists she study in order to be well-rounded. About this Gail comments that perhaps, through her father's direction, she has found the necessary scholastic commitment.

Of more interest to her is the topic of her friends. After reeling off a list of at least fifteen girls and ten boys whom she considers friends, Gail begins to talk about her eighteen-year-old boy friend, who, she says with pride, is a senior and an outstanding athlete. Besides her academic and social activities, she is involved in school athletics, in which she excels, as well as the cheerleading squad, drama, and the school's service club.

Asked again about her parents' divorce, Gail replies that she cannot blame her father much because her mother is often down and negative. However, when queried further, Gail tells the evaluator that her mother is like that primarily when her father is around. When she and her mother are alone they have great fun laughing about clothes and things that happened when Gail was small. In a muted fashion, Gail expresses an interest in spending more time with her father, which she appreciates is not possible because of his schedule. Although he is sometimes "a drag" because he keeps mentioning Latin, where she is getting a B instead of her usual A, he is generally fun. They also talk about sports, in which both are interested. Whereas Johnny is "a pain" because he acts like a "baby," Gail considers Sarah cute.

Fantasy Material   Although she does not admit it, Gail seems eager to talk about her dreams. She dreams of a tall man who saves her from a wrecked automobile. Although she is unclear about the details of the dream, Gail thinks she was driving too fast accompanied by her best girlfriend in an expensive sports car.

If she could change anything in her life, Gail said she would like her parents not to divorce. It is Gail's ambition to become a lawyer.

As she contemplates this ambition, Gail says she would also like to marry and become a mother. Her best memory was her fifth birthday when her mother baked a special cake for her. Her worst memory was of her parents' fighting.

Custodial Preference   It is Gail's opinion that she would be better off with her father because he will insure that she gets better grades and therefore will have a better chance of getting into the college of her choice.

John Longworth, Jr.

Appearance and Behavior   A tall, somewhat pudgy just twelve-year-old seventh grade boy, John asks his mother as he enters the interview if she plans to remain in the waiting room. At least once during the interview he asks the evaluator if he thinks his mother is still in the waiting room. Remarkably passive, John allows the interviewer to direct the session completely. He responds to direct questions but chooses not to freely converse. His eye contact is relatively limited and he displays through his demeanor, sad face, and slow movements a mild to moderate degree of depression.

Direct Discussion   Asked who comprises his family, John replies that the group consists of his mother and two sisters. As an afterthought, he adds his father, who "doesn't live with us anymore." At the evaluator's request, John discusses the various members of his family. His father is tall, and in John's view, very strong. In response to a question about how he and his father get along, John says that he needs to improve his grades and make more friends. He says that he talks with his mother often and feels bad when she cries. Gail is all right, but she is rarely home because she spends so much time with her friends. In John's opinion, Sarah is a brat. She wants her own way and always pesters his mother to play with her.

When the subject of his parents' divorce is raised, John drops his eyes. Making it clear he doesn't want to discuss the matter, John sits in silence, then mentions that his kitten just ran away.

As far as school is concerned, John clearly finds it arduous. Worrying about his grades is only part of the problem. Sometimes his teachers are mean. It is difficult to ascertain what John means by this, but it appears that it equates with them expecting John to do what he believes himself incapable of doing.

A further problem with school is that the other kids tease him and pick on him. John does not understand why they do this, and he feels helpless to stop them. Furthermore, the school staff will not intervene on his behalf and this puzzles and saddens him. In his neighborhood the situation is similar. His parents give him conflicting advice about the problem. His dad says he should punch them, whereas his mother sometimes tells him to ignore the other kids, sometimes threatens to call the other children's parents, and sometimes explains that he must help himself with the kids.

Fantasy Material Johnny's dreams are of two types. The first dream is frightening. Wolves are attacking him. His parents are present but they only watch as Johnny flees. In the second, a monster is chasing Gail and Sarah. Johnny stabs the monster with a sword and kills it. In his Despart Fable responses Johnny demonstrates age-inappropriate sibling rivalry, a desire to be big and powerful, and fears of rejection and abandonment.

John's best memories are of riding bikes with his father during the summer. His worst memory is the day his father left home.

Custodial Preferences With considerable hesitancy, John says he would prefer to remain with his mother; she knows him. Pressed to explain what he means, John says he can talk to her about the kids and school. Besides his father is mean. The evaluator wonders why he was hesitant. John says his dad would really be upset and might be angry.

Sarah Longworth

Appearance and Behavior Appearing for the interview accompanied by her mother, Sarah, three-years and five months old, stands close to her in the waiting room. Giving the evaluator a smile, Sarah cautiously accompanies him to the interview room. Once inside she eagerly explores the play material. Her eye contact is good and once she begins to talk, she proves to have an excellent vocabularly and to be quite articulate. Her mood state is one of happiness and excitement.

Direct Discussion   It is easy to engage Sarah in a discussion of nursery school. Her teachers include Mrs. Marion and Mrs. Phillips, who she says are nice. Naming two kids whom she considers friends, Sarah giggles as the evaluator asks if Lesley is a boy or girl.

Asked to describe her family, Sarah says her mother is nice and her father is funny. Asked in what way he is funny, Sarah simply laughs. Gail is good but John cries a lot—besides, he is a bad boy.

Fantasy Material   Interested in the doll house, Sarah chooses a family consisting of a set of parents, a boy and an older girl. The father and mother argue. As a result the boy cries and the girl comforts him, saying "baby."

Asked to draw a picture of her family, Sarah draws a very large circle and four small ones. Identifying the figures, Sarah says the large circle is her father and the four small ones are her mother, her siblings, and herself. However, the circle representing her mother is a little larger than the other three. At the top of the page Sarah draws another circle, explaining that it is the sun. As she finishes the picture, Sarah stands close to the evaluator, touching his leg and leaning against him.

Custody Preference   Because of her age, the question of custody is raised a little differently with Sarah than with her sister and brother. When she is queried on what is good about being at her dad's house, Sarah says she has lots of toys. Regarding the same question about being at her mom's she comments that she sleeps by herself. Asked where she would like to live, Sarah turns the query into a game—first saying daddy's, then mommy's, then, laughing as she says it, daddy's.

Summary

One cannot dispute the affection and concern both John and Mary display for all three of their children. Nonetheless, there are particular differences between them in their parenting styles.

In order to put the parent's capacities with the children into perspective, one must understand their relationship with one another. In addition, examining multilateral family interactions affords one an appreciation of the dynamic interchange between parents and children.

At the onset of their relationship, John found in Mary the warmth and nurturance he had sought from his mother. In a sense, the escape from his ambition-driven conscience provided by Mary's acceptance was analogous to the escape from paternal rejection, which at least partly motivated his dependence upon and closeness with his mother.

John's strength and leadership were attractive to Mary in that it recreated for her the secure and invigorating environment she had felt when in her father's presence. John provided not only companionship, fun, and sexual pleasure, but security as well, and this was a major component of the romance from the beginning. Unfortunately, security was too fundamental an ingredient for each of them, throughout the life of their love. It created a focal point from which John felt the need to flee through compensatory seeking of achievement and upon which Mary relied at the expense of her own developing independence.

As John emerged into the fullness of adulthood he increasingly identified with his father's life-style as a means of acquiring the paternal acceptance he could never achieve in reality. This choice precluded any true intimacy with Mary. She felt threatened and repelled by his growing emotional distance and his withdrawal from the "mutual-security pact" of their early marriage. For his part, John interpreted her security-seeking as a characterologic weakness, reflecting his unconscious identification of her dependence with his own, which he was attempting to submerge.

The deterioration in their relationship began when John, in the process of identifying with his father, began reinterpreting Mary's dependence and nurturing character through his father's harsh perspective. This destroyed the unstable equilibrium of their relationship, which had been predicated to some extent on mutual security-seeking. The growing rejection Mary experienced generated anxiety, depression, and, at times, near panic, which reinforced her dependence and caused John to further reject her. At the same time she was experiencing abandonment, John was feeling smothered. In the absence of insight the bond was sure to break.

With each of his two older children John found an identification match. Gail was his bright, achieving and proud side, with which he vicariously identified. Gail herself prospered exceptionally well in the sunlight of her father's approval. It provided motivation and fuel for her school performance and evolving interpersonal skill. Consequently her self-image flourished; it was not a coincidence that Gail's choice of romantic figures was someone older than she. But because John's involvement in this regard was largely vicarious, Gail unconsciously picked up his neediness and felt compelled to accomplish partly to bolster her father's shaky, borrowed self-esteem.

Johnny, on the other hand, represented the dark side of his father's identity. Like his mother, whom his father rejected, John Jr. reminded his father of what he never accepted about himself—his reliance upon others. Therefore, he was naturally an object of disapproval. Despite this, Johnny nonetheless pursued his father's acceptance. While he wanted to be like his father, Johnny despaired of being able to do so. There is a healthy element in John's fantasied desire to become powerful and conquer external rivals and aggressors. But mixed with these aspirations to power are extreme fears of aggressors, who might be kids, teachers, parents, and especially fathers.

Mary became increasingly dependent, dooming herself to states of depression as she experienced episodically intense but regular feelings of rejection. Further, as a consequence of her depression, Mary sought security through regressed behaviors such as withdrawal and excessive use of alcohol. Gail became the focus of her anger for a couple of reasons. Not only had Gail replaced her as the object of her husband's affections, but also Gail's internally generated security and self-confidence became for Mary a source of envy.

Since Mary sought security from external sources, she compensated for the rejection of her husband by indulging Johnny and pandering to his early childhood side as a means of identifying with his infantile needs. An unfortunate consequence was that this identification reinforced Johnny's fixation at a security-seeking, achievement-avoiding level.

As much as Gail emulated her father and his aspirations, she was able to depersonalize, to some extent, her mother's critical attitude. There exists an emotional tie to Mary that rises above the animosity between them. To some degree one might speculate that Gail's anger with her mother is, at least in part, due to the natural, age-appropriate rivalry.

Sarah was born at a point where her parents, owing to the degree of disruption in their relationship, no longer needed to seek out as much vicarious gratification through their children. Consequently, Sarah was freed from the pathologic identifications that each parent had with the other two children.

One must be careful about how much credence to give the custody preferences of Gail or John Jr. Although Gail's dream of being rescued by a tall male figure is age appropriate, one wonders whether Gail believes her father's presence insures better self-discipline. She does think her father provides her with scholastic commitment. Certainly her belief that better grades will be assured by being with her father ascribes too much credit to him, thereby robbing her of self-esteem. Such convictions reflect the fact that Gail's accomplishments have not yielded her a fair proportion of self-confidence; too much has been siphoned off by the vicarious participation of her father. As far as Johnny's preference is concerned, one must take into account the extent to which his choice reflects a desire to avoid his father's critical attitude. His conviction that he can talk and emotionally relate to his mother is obviously healthy, but other factors such as Johnny's need for emotional growth must be considered.

Both parents have strengths and weaknesses. John Sr. is a strong and assertive leader whose support of achievement is laudable, despite the fact that it crosses the line of positive emotional support and becomes at times a high-pressure test with parental approval as the stakes.

Mary, for her part, is a warm, and generally empathic nurturing, person, providing security, affection, and encouragement at key moments, although her tendency to facilitate dependence and regression stifles growth and autonomy.

However, strong consideration must be given to two other features of Mary's personality. Her ability to acknowledge her faults and make some sincere attempt to rectify them is a considerable strength. It demonstrates a vital skill in the life of any parent. It is axiomatically assumed that every parent will possess many flaws and deficiencies and make many mistakes. Not only does a parent's ability to accept this allow that parent, during a child's minority years, to correct toward the path that leads to health and growth, but also it serves as a model for children and offers them hope that they too can forgive and be forgiven. If a father or mother is wrong and can admit or correct it, then there is hope for the most errant child.

Second, Mary's acceptance of the children's need for John allows as undiluted an opportunity as possible for Gail, John Jr., and Sarah to utilize their relationship with their father to benefit from his positive and powerful strengths. Since she values them, they have permission to do the same.

Recommendations

1. Joint custody to be vested in John and Mary Langworth with the children in primary residence with Mary. In addition, John Longworth should have reasonable visitation with the children. The actual amount of time should be worked out between the children and their parents. However, it should include no less than (a) every second weekend from Friday at 5:00 P.M. until Sunday at 6:00 P.M.; (b) a midweek visitation from 5:00 P.M. to 7:00 P.M. when Sarah is involved or 8:30 P.M. when only Gail and John Jr. are involved; and (c) alternating holidays. In addition, the children should spend at least one month during the summer with their father.

   This recommendation was made for a number of reasons. In evaluating the relative strengths and weakness of John's and Mary's personality organization, it was found that they would be approximately equally competent in rearing either of the two older children. While Sarah, a very healthy child, could handle a placement with either parent, she is still sufficiently attached to her mother to compel residential placement with Mary, other things bring equal.

   Joint legal custody will accord John an opportunity for a meaningful continued participation in decision-making regarding his children. Further, John can be a potentially positive modeling influence on Gail and John Jr.—if it is carried out from a distance. John's achievement orientation and aspirations are admirable qualities for the children to emulate. However, if he were in the same household with them as a single parent, the temptation and opportunity to bring the full weight of his overly invested influence to bear on their academic and interpersonal performance would be unlimited. At risk would be their ability to individuate into their own persons lest they be a disappointment to their father.

Notwithstanding their importance, overriding weight cannot be given to the children's preferences inasmuch as they are based more on subjective than objective factors.

All other factors being what they are, compelling consideration must be given to Mary's faculty for self-scrutinizing and her recognition of the other parent's worth. This not only allows her to be more adaptable to needed change, such as her tendency to foster John's dependence, but also facilitates the children's using the best aspects of John's personality.

In keeping with the principle of the children remaining together, if possible, it is best for all three children to remain with their mother since they represent, for each other, the unfractured nucleus of the family. They can supply one another with needed emotional support that may not be available in the same way from either parent. In addition, separating the children risks triggering feelings of disloyalty and guilt.

2. Postmarital counseling to involve John and Mary jointly. Goals to be addressed include:

John and Mary:
   a. Joint decision-making when possible.
   b. Improved communication whose aim is to mutually support one another's authority and individual decision-making
   c. Sharing of individual observations about the children's progress in school and in their peer relationships so as to facilitate mutual understanding of their current needs
   d. Development of the capacity to engage in such mutual sharing and decision-making discussions when the counseling ends

John:
   a. Development of an awareness of the positive modeling effects of his strong achievement orientation

b. Awareness of the presence of pressuring messages to perform for approval and their potential and actual harm

c. Recognition of the damage incurred through regular and harsh derogation of his parent partner

d. Help for the children to accept the court's decision

Mary:

a. Appreciation of the benefit of her warmth and nurturance, as well as of her ability to empathize with the children's feelings which enables her to better understand their behavior

b. Further recognition of the negative effect of responding to her feelings of threat with criticism of Gail

c. Further recognition of the damaging impact of promoting John's dependence and conflict avoidance

d. Learning to cope with any displaced anger the children, especially Gail, may direct at Mary if the court should agree with the evaluator's recommendations.

Afterword

Every custody evaluator, over some period of time, develops certain convictions about the relative importance of different factors. Of all the parent personality parameters, it is the author's opinion that, when young children are involved, the capacity to nurture and empathize is preeminent because it facilitates the development in children of all the other parameters of personal maturity. When nurturance and empathy are deficient, these other qualities usually develop very poorly. Obviously there is an interrelationship between a person's development in various areas of personality organization; it would be unusual for a parent to have a high-level capacity for nurturance and empathy and extremely poor impulse control.

For similar reasons the ability to self-scrutinize and value the other parent must be given great weight. They, too, cut across other parameters of parenting to influence the entire process of development. Further, if one is willing and able to understand oneself, there is no maladaptive quality that cannot be changed.

Evaluators should therefore always keep in mind that, given sufficient motivation, anyone can change. If sensing that a parent sufficiently desires to rectify dysfunctional parenting, the evaluator might make various rehabilitative recommendations designed to provide the opportunity for such change and even to promote it. For instance, legal joint custody might be recommended to promote continued decision-making and therefore greater involvement on the part of the nonresidential parent. For the same reason a richer visitation schedule might be suggested for the nonresidential parent. Or a reevaluation might be suggested several months or a year from the time of the current assessment to provide a parent the opportunity to change and thereby enjoy a greater level of involvement in the children's life. After all, the change and evolution of one's identity is the essence of healthy movement through life.

9

Healthy Separation

There are one million divorces annually and each year one million children are affected by them.[1] While it can have a crippling effect on all of the involved family members, children in particular are at high risk of developing depression and other emotional disorders. Obviously this population requires the attention of the mental health community. Such attention should focus not only on the emotional problems that emanate from the breakup, but also, in accordance with modern medicine's commitment to preventive care, on aiding parents to become co-parenting partners able to facilitate their children's maturational progress. It is hoped that this chapter will lend the reader further understanding of the psychological consequences of divorce and suggest some means of coping with and possibly avoiding its deleterious effects.

Variations in Adult Loss Reactions

To the surprise of many adults, the acrimony, enmity, and hurt that they sought to extinguish through divorce do not end with the decree. This is because relationships do not end with physical separation. With certain variations,[2] divorced parents go through a loss re-action similar to the grief reaction of death.[3] This is because, in each case, the grieving party must separate from the internalized image of a loved one.

As they develop, children incorporate images or mental representations of significant adults. These images allow them to sustain a concept of the represented person in his or her absence, providing the child with a feeling of security and well-being through the omnipresence of that figure. These are integral ingredients in the establishment of self-image.[4]

This process does not end with childhood. Those persons with whom one develops love ties will become internalized as images that furnish security and a feeling of being loved, thereby triggering an infusion of esteem.

In any divorce, there are two separations, external and internal. External separation is the actual physical division of the two involved people, whereas internal separation represents the gradual and incremental detachment from the internal image of the other person.[5] By far, internal separation is the more difficult and painful of the two.

Internal separation may be triggered when the negative balance of the relationship has been in existence for a prolonged period. Or it may be triggered by some event such as an affair, external separation, or a legal dissolution. Although it usually begins sooner than external separation, it may end later or not at all. It is clear, however, that psychological divorce will not occur until internal detachment is complete.

For an internally separate and independent person with strong positive self-regard, marital relationships tend to thrive because the tie is characterized by flexibility and the partner is not needed to feed one's security. Furthermore, criticism is tolerated without being experienced as a major wound. However, if this person's marriage should end in divorce, the loss reaction is maintained within a normal range, owing to the fact that the major sense of worth emanates from within rather than from others.

In contrast, an internally dependent, poorly separated person with deficient self-regard relies heavily upon the loved person to supply affection, approval, acceptance, and security. The more deficient this individual's self-regard turns out to be, the more unconditional the supply must be. Need gratification and dependency are experienced as love.[6]

People with deficient self-esteem often project their negative images of themselves onto those they love. Believing the other person thinks of them in the same negative way they unconsciously think of themselves, they render themselves vulnerable to feeling deprived, criticized, and rejected easily with little or no provocation. Obviously this can affect the stability of these persons' marital relationships. If, as is so often the case, these individuals' self-worth problem is accompanied by a lack of internal separation and by dependence, the loss reaction proceeds very slowly.

Custodial candidates in this emotional state may seek sole custody as a means of clinging to a vestige of the family rather than because they are primarily committed to their children's care. Sometimes they explicitly voice the hope that through a joint or shared custody arrangement there will be more contact with the estranged spouse, reflecting their aspirations for a reconciliation. At other times they are not even aware of their desire to reconcile.

Whatever the specific motivation, these adults are stuck in the first phase of the loss reaction, denial. Separation seems overwhelming. To these individuals even a fantasy tie is better than acquiescing to the terrible feelings of rejection and abandonment. In addition it appears that these parents regularly pursue acceptance and approval from the divorcing partner because their self-image projection is still intact. Naturally their sensitivity to criticism and disapproval by the former spouse remains high.

For some people psychological divorce never occurs. In fact, some divorced persons remain emotionally married for the remainder of their lives. Not only might this preclude a new romantic involvement, but also it may place a heavy burden on the children who feel responsible to fill the emotional void for their perpetually grieving parent. Only through being freed from this unspoken responsibility can the two parents as well as the involved children develop a healthy postdissolution reciprocal tie.

Caution was voiced earlier about ascribing the anger and blaming, representing a progression of the loss reaction, to a characterologic defect. Because it is a phase in a loss reaction, the anger will be time limited. And since the blame does not emanate from a flaw in personality organization, it may be diminished by acquiring insight that no one person is responsible for the total breakdown of a marriage.

Another step in the progression of a loss reaction is depression. Like anger, depression can be misleading since it can create the impression that this person is incapable of coping with parental responsibilities. But depression, like anger, must be evaluated in relation to its origin. A depression that is chronic in nature is far different from, and has more impact on children than, the acute depression of a loss reaction, which is not only normal, but once again, like anger, is generally time limited. Children understand loss reactions because they are experiencing the same thing themselves and are likely to respond positively to the depressed parent discussing his or her feelings. Finally the depression of a loss reaction must be discriminated from the uninvolvement of a nonnurturing parent. The depressed parent cares but may not be available. The uninvolved parent neither cares nor is available.

In most instances resolution of the loss reaction in the form of detachment from the estranged or former spouse and that person's image ultimately occurs. At this time the divorced person's mood state will stabilize, the self-image will generally return to close to its former level, and self-acceptance is usually as good as it formerly was.

If, either through introspection or therapy, divorced persons gain some insight about the degree to which their self-concept was placed in the hands of a spouse, a higher level of functioning can be achieved. Because the resolution of the loss reaction is accompanied by some degree of self-acceptance, the post-dissolution period is a good time to acquire this insight. In its absence, the risk is great that divorced persons will repeat the same mistakes in a similar fashion.

Loss Reactions in Children

Some couples may remain separated for many years, or may continue to live together long after they have recognized the terminal state of their marriage because they believe their children need them to do so. Although it is commonly believed that children will fare better if removed from an unhappy family life through divorce, the facts do not seem to bear this out. Whereas many adults report feeling better subsequent to their divorce, in at least one study, children and adolescents, as a group, did not seem to improve in their emotional health over the years following the divorce of their parents. Neither is there any evidence, however, to support the other position, that children living in an unhappy home will do better than those whose parents choose to divorce. Each course seems to have its complications and problems.[7] Thus one cannot argue that divorce is good for children and one certainly cannot contend that remaining in a tension-laden home is positive. Therefore, the decision to remain together or to divorce should be made on some basis that pertains to the adults, preferably whether their love and capacity for sustained investment is sufficient, but certainly not on the basis of what is good for their children. Neither alternative is good for their children.

Unlike adults, children of divorcing parents usually do not have to mourn the loss of a once loving person. While the parents generally surrender each other as love objects, they remain invested in their children, at least to some extent. Rather than lose their parents, as parents, children of divorcing parents experience a total loss of their family as they knew it and a substantial readjustment of the role of both their parents.

Anxiety and depression are commonly experienced by children of divorce, as are severe mood and behavioral fluctuations, which may range from hyperactive and aggressive behavior to withdrawal and passivity. Their scholastic performance deteriorates, social withdrawal and other peer problems germinate, and their relationships with adults are frequently characterized by rebellion, stubbornness, and imperiousness.[8]

One instance in which the loss is total and therefore the child is subject to the same unfolding of denial, anger, depression, and resolution as adults is that circumstance wherein the noncustodial parent gradually or even quickly loses interest in visitation. Generally that occurs when the visitation parent's primary tie was to the former mate or the family unit. When it is clear that the spouse or family has been lost, especially if the former mate has completed the detachment process and is no longer emotionally available, even to argue, commitment wanes.

More often, however, the detachment is not total. In this case the parent is not totally disconnected but simply highly ambivalent. Rather than abandon the child, this person disappears for an extended period of time, only to appear weeks, months, or even years later. Because this person's attachment falls at the weak end of the spectrum, a desire to see the child arises only when some memory or association stirs guilt. Promises of gifts, trips, and a commitment to return, made under internal duress, are quickly forgotten when the guilt level decreases.

The child of this parent is caught on the horns of a dilemma. Reactions of covert or overt depression of varying intensity, accompanied by disabling behavioral symptoms, are common. Some of these children create rich fantasies, some become bitter, whereas still others idealize the lost parent.[9] Since these youngsters always want to believe in parental love and interest, partly because it temporarily boosts their sense of worth, they almost always believe that the parent will return within the promised time frame.

If a parent has abandoned a child, it is painful, but at least the loss is unambiguous. The child will mourn the loss, sometimes at the price of a trauma to the self-concept, but in time the terrible emotions will pass. The ambivalent parent repeatedly opens old wounds, causing a plummeting of the child's self-regard and new depression every time there is a reappearance, followed by another disappearance. The ultimate damage to a child's self-image can be even greater than that resulting from parental abandonment, because the child has repetitive evidence that the parent's attachment is not strong enough to override the ambivalence. Each time there is a return and disappearance, the rejection is renewed.

At least as common as these situations, are those in which parents have inappropriately involved their children in the continued and problematic resolution of their own relationships. These adults, who may not have completely detached, can use visitation as a means of engaging in conflict with their former marital partner. Visitation can be used by the residential parent as a means of punishing a nonresidential parent: for spurious reasons visitation may be restricted or the parent may fail to encourage and assist the children in readying themselves for a visit. Or the nonresidential parent may punish the residential parent by returning the children late or not at all. They may be kept overnight or longer, ostensibly to provide for a longer visit but actually to get back at the former spouse.

At least theoretically, visitation is established so that children have the opportunity to visit the nonresidential parent and have the benefit of that person's parenting. As a secondary priority, visitation provides the nonresidential parent with a chance to enjoy the child's presence. Disputes over visitation often reflect the adult's conviction that the establishment of visitation arrangements should give priority to their interests and needs rather than those of the child. When this occurs, children are trapped between the adults, a pawn in their power struggle. The message is clear; what they think and feel is less important than their parents' wounded egos. Naturally their response is to some extent related to their age.

Commonly in visitation conflicts, children are called upon by one or both parents, either implicitly or explicitly, to take sides. The parental demand may be to end or to extend the visitation, as the case may be. One can imagine the tension suffered by a youngster when either or both parents are pressuring him or her to support their mutually exclusive points of view. It goes without saying that this is an extremely unhealthy situation that can only lead to further fear and insecurity in the child. For this reason, some have cautioned against leaving the door open to parent manipulation. It has been proposed that the decision regarding visitation rights be left in the hands of the custodial or residential parent.[10] This, however, would still allow the residential parent to use the child as a manipulative tool against the other parent.

This kind of situation may represent an indication for short term postdissolution counseling which, it is hoped, could allow each parent to accept, in a calm environment, what is in their child's best interest, once they recognize their misidentification with the child. If reason fails, however, it may be necessary to use the power and authority of the court to establish firm ground rules upon which visitation can operate. But this solution is also flawed insofar as courts can only legislate policies; they cannot modify human behavior.

Perhaps the most common emotional problem for children arising at the time of divorce is to become fixed in a state of denial about the loss of their family. Reconciliation hopes and fantasies are so common among children of divorced parents that one can almost consider them universal. It is a rare child indeed who does not want the family reunited. No hope or fantasy, however unrealistic, is harmful unless the child gives it credibility. It is in such instances that the youngster needs help. Distinguishing between wish fulfillment, fantasy, and probable occurrences is a major reality-testing function of the healthy personality. If, owing to a newly developing personality or the intensity of a desire, a youngster cannot do it alone, the assistance of a kind and compassionate, but honest, adult may be needed. That person can be a parent or a counselor. But if it is the latter, the counselor must have, at the very least, the tacit support of a parent—if not that person's active participation. After all, if given the choice of believing a friendly, relative stranger versus a parent to whom the child is strongly tied, who is the child likely to choose—especially if it fits the child's utmost, albeit totally unrealistic, wishes?

For children the most devastating effect of divorce is the long-term scarring of their personalities wrought by prolonged and intense emotional trauma.[11] Repeated rejection, loyalty conflicts, and the assumption of a premature sense of responsibility for coping with the feelings and problems of adults take their toll, resulting in a depleted self-confidence, insecurity about interpersonal relationships, and a proclivity for feeling guilty about emotions and events over which they have little or no control. The ramifications can be far-reaching; pursuit of achievement may be handicapped by anxiety about failure, socialization and love relationships may prove unstable owing to anticipatory rejection, and emotional commitments can be stifled by overprotection and too great a sense of responsibility. Although many children emerge from divorce relatively unencumbered by long-term damage, there continue to be far too many that carry its scars for years, if not throughout a lifetime.

Single-Parent Families

Currently, 60 percent of all divorces involve children. In 1970 2.3 million children were living with single parents, the vast majority of whom were mothers, whereas by 1982 the number was 5.1 million.[12] It is estimated that between now and the end of the twentieth century, roughly 33 percent of the children in America will experience a parental divorce before the age of 18.[13] Single parent families have some special characteristics and problems that deserve comment.

One of the advantages of the intact family is dual leadership, which, if it functions well, can distribute responsibility equitably between two people and allow both to contribute their particular strengths to the family. Each parent can offer suggestions, emotional support, and constructive criticism to the other. If their partnership is characterized by love and respect, such aid is enthusiastically received and profitably applied. In a healthy parental alliance, the partners support each other's decisions, whether or not they are in accord, and are available to fill-in when the other person is overwhelmed or, for some other reason, unable to cope.

The single-parent family is subject to the same pressures that face an intact family, along with many others that are peculiar to it. The children may be exhibiting disruptive or disturbed behavior. Unfortunately, these behavioral changes commonly occur at the same time that the single custodial parent is assuming a new role. At this point, the parent is usually still suffering from depression, which taxes the adult's empathetic capacity to its limit. Owing to these stresses children are better able to manipulate the sometimes overburdened parent. The oldest child in the family, especially if gender opposite to the single parent, is often placed or places himself or herself in the position of a parent surrogate. This is decidedly disadvantageous to development because it requires the child to assume premature and inordinate responsibility and places that youngster in the position of wielding too much power. Siblings may resent this brother or sister's new role, although their emotions may be mixed. To complicate the matter, the nonresidential parent has the opportunity to vent hostility by undermining the other adult's authority. In addition, the children may be used by one parent to gain access to the other person's life. Children who serve as conduits for messages, information, and the conveyance of continued animosity are subject to feeling aligned, disloyal, and possibly alienated.

Single-parent families also have some advantages. Children do not have nearly so great an opportunity to play one adult against the other, which most children do from time to time. Single parents learn to exercise far greater independence in decision-making and emotional self-reliance, often by necessity. Faced with rearing their children virtually alone, many people in this circumstance commit themselves to hardship and endurance. This can galvanize family loyalty and unity, spawning even greater strength than existed in the previously intact family. It needs to be clarified that children can grow up as psychologically healthy and happy in a single-parent family as in an intact family. To do so, however, all must learn to surmount anxiety and to effectively and bravely solve the many problems to which they are heir.

Notwithstanding all that has been said about the problems accompanying separations and divorce, alone or with the help of mental health professionals, family members can do much to allay, if not prevent, these and other problems although not without considerable self-awareness and effort. Problem-solving under stressful conditions is always difficult since it demands that we examine our flaws and avoidance patterns and our most vulnerable areas, which we carefully hide even from ourselves.

Regression Versus Psychological Trauma

Although loss is never comfortable, indeed is sometimes damaging, it also provides opportunities for personal growth.[14] It is entirely possible to live through a divorce with its attendant depression and emerge a stronger person.

Attempts to translate loss reactions in children into growth experiences must take into consideration the distinction between regression and psychological trauma. While this differentiation should be made for both adults and children, we are specifically referring to children here. To neglect this difference can lead one to the erroneous conclusion that loss will be invariably damaging to the child's personality and will universally interfere with future growth and development.

As a result of the loss experienced in divorce, a wide range of painful emotions is triggered: anger, fear, disappointment, and depression, as well as feelings of inadequacy, failure, and rejection. For children, these emotions will often manifest themselves through shifts in mood states, decline in self-esteem, age-inappropriate behavior, and verbal or possibly even physical aggression. Since many of these changes might simply be regressive, they will diminish and might even be extinguished when the loss reaction resolves.[15]

On the other hand, psychological trauma results in the alteration of a child's personality functioning, seemingly as a consequence of the loss. The effects of psychological trauma are long-lasting and generally do not spontaneously remit. Psychological trauma usually occurs in children who already experience emotional problems, leaving their personalities vulnerable to damage. As a consequence, the regressive response symptoms are more tenacious than is the case with children without existent emotional problems.

Some of the following symptomatic expressions may occur as the result of divorce exacerbating an already existing emotional problem.

The loss reaction accompanying divorce often triggers feelings of rejection. An already deficient self-esteem may be diminished to the point that trust relationships with adults or other children may deteriorate even further. The feelings of hopelessness and lack of self-control may be expressed in apathetic school performance, which may already be suffering from self-image depletion. Anticipating failure, minor frustration leads to surrender and self-defeat. Failure becomes a reality and self-esteem is further depleted. Depression is the natural consequence of the recurring feelings of rejection and failure.

Emotional problems may be accompanied by paired impulse control, and the child's conscience may be so poorly organized as to lead to a seemingly indiscriminate flow of direct or previously unexpressed anger in the form of verbal or physical aggression onto others—someone must be blamed for the divorce. It is common for this anger to be directed at the person with whom the youngster feels safer and more secure. The constant anger triggers guilt, which stirs more anger, sometimes in order to evoke punishment.

At other times primitive ego defenses such as projection are called into play. Because the child externalizes responsibility for the anger it seems justifiable.[16] In addition, various rationalizations may serve as the consciously accepted reasons for the anger, and so, again, it is legitimized.

If the child's personality is sufficiently impaired, wish fulfillment fantasies or irrational fears may substitute for reality-based thinking. Such fantasies might consist of extreme fabrications regarding great wealth or adventure. The irrational fears may take the form of a fixation on horror stories. Such thinking can be persistent and modification occurs only with difficulty. As one can see, tenacious regressive symptoms following the loss reaction of divorce can generally be traced to preexisting psychological problems that leave the child vulnerable to trauma. Such traumatization can result in emotional problems that, by their self-perpetuating nature, may last for an extended period of time.

Postdissolution Therapy

Families who have completed a divorce almost invariably want to bring an end to the pervasive uncomfortable emotions, scrutiny, and problem resolution. In contrast, quiescence and tranquility are sought. Additional therapy is one of the last avenues readily chosen to remedy problems. Nevertheless, participation in time-limited confrontational therapy is one of the most effective means of resolving these conflicts. This does not mean that such therapy should be aggressive. It means rather that the parties must honestly confront the issues.

Indications   Whereas there are no absolute indications for postdissolution therapy, there are some characteristics of the postdissolution family whose presence would point to that need. These would include the inability of one or both parties to assume some responsibility for the marital failure. In addition a visible lack of readiness to pursue a new life on the part of either or both parents might signal that the marriage has not emotionally ended. Insufficient willingness to take on new parenting roles, that of postdissolution co-parenting partners, might indicate the same thing. Naturally many such parents remain in an extended state of depression and psychological withdrawal.

For children the presence of continuing signs of emotional disequilibrium should prompt consideration of therapeutic intervention. This would include excessive emotionality, ongoing depression, or the intermittent breakdown of emotional stability. These may be indices of serious self-image damage. The same may be said of substantial academic deterioration or social withdrawal. Neurotic symptoms such as inordinate fears or phobias may also reflect personality dysfunction. Likewise, regressive characteristics such as the reappearance of habit patterns, like thumb sucking, that were given up some time earlier might demonstrate the same thing. Of course significant or prolonged loosening of impulse control and impaired reality testing are causes for concern. Certainly this listing of symptomatic expression is not intended to be an exhausive compendium of the caution signs, but any one or a combination of them would warrant at least an assessment of the need for therapy, possible special education assistance, or some other kind of therapeutic effort.

Therapeutic Interventions Obviously, when a need for psychotherapy involving an adult or child is triggered by a separation or divorce, the specific mode, length, and goals will be determined by the particular circumstances. There are, however, some common threads that run through many divorces. Resolving the conflicts contained in these issues will contribute substantially to making the separation healthier.

Denial A first principle must be to face reality. Neither children nor adults benefit from shunning the truth, kindly spoken. "Kindly spoken" is a key phrase, for the motive behind expressing a truth is usually a good gauge of whether that truth will be damaging or beneficial. There are certainly times when young children will not understand the truth or when the outcome of marital deterioration is too uncertain to predict. Always the timing in offering the truth is important. Then there may be times when the truth is used with children to punish the other parent. Blurting out information whose wide circulation will not be appreciated, prematurely divulging information, or enlightening children about a former spouse in the interest of retaliation is not helping; it is likely to be harmful.

Given these cautions, facing reality may be one of the most important things divorcing adults can do to prevent or heal the scars of family dissolution. Regardless of the issues of denial, the immutability of the financial settlement, the relative permanence of the custody decision, or the finality of the divorce, the family should be helped to live with what is now, not hope for what might be or long for what might have been. In order not to inflict further pain, parents often keep the door open to a brighter fantasy world with vagueness or evasiveness. This serves, not the child's interests, but only the child's wishes and fantasies. The therapist must be clear on this point; in order to alert families to the presence of denial and its potentially harmful effects, it must be repeatedly confronted.

Throughout childhood, children will benefit by their ability to face reality. Understanding the impact of immature behavior on peer acceptance, appreciating in advance the potential hazards of homework avoidance, and allowing in-school discipline to provide a reminder of the consequences of violation of school rules will require the capacity to avoid denial. Facing reality within the family sets the stage for doing so in the community.

Parent Polarization   Persistently and intractably blaming the other parent for family problems is damaging to children inasmuch as it reinforces the belief that someone must be blamed for problems. Such a position violates some basic tenets of healthy family operation. When a divorce has occurred, everyone is a victim, and there are no winners. Children should be helped to recognize the true role of each family participant in conflict situations, including their own. That can best be accomplished when the issue of blame has been discarded.

The parent who engages in blaming should be helped to assume responsibility for personal problems. Repeatedly pointing out that the polarization springs from underlying guilt and therefore a wish for exoneration may help in two ways. It can facilitate introspection and might also dramatically decrease the need to externalize problems. As a result there can be a substantial drop in the level of anger toward the other parent.

Not only will this better enable children to be objective about allocating responsibility for various family problems, including their own, but also it can serve as a prototype for future conflict resolution. From this an emotional lesson can be learned: excessive criticism of oneself or another mitigates against healthy assumption of responsibility.

Unsevered Marital Ties   When emotional ties between a divorced couple continue, reflected in bitterness, unrequited feelings of love, or jealously of new relationships, it can undermine the ability to parent. During the marriage the children might have served as conduits for the expression of their feelings for one another. Even if that was not the case before divorce, it may become so afterward. The parent harboring bitter emotions may retaliate through the children. If feelings of love continue, jealously might be stirred, and the children can become sources of information about new relationships. Or they may provide the means by which the spurned adult hangs onto a former marital partner.

Again, identifying the motive behind such retaliation and manipulation can help the parent model one of the most crucial requirements of good emotional health, the ability to internally separate. The capacity to let go of an experience or a relationship that is no longer viable will be required again and again throughout life.

Accepting Emotions By learning to live with the conflicting and terrible emotions triggered by traumatizing circumstances, events such as divorce can become growth promoting. The ability to do so contributes in a fundamental way to the effective personality functioning that is a hallmark of emotional health.

To the recently divorced couple and their children, certain emotions may be not only uncomfortable but also unacceptable. Conjuring up unpleasant memories, unresolved relationships, and repressed self-concept issues, they are resisted and experienced only with great pain. Either one of the divorced pair or any of the children may be harboring feelings of resentment, jealousy, failure, guilt, or rejection.

In psychotherapy the expression of emotions is almost invariably encouraged. The rationale for doing so is usually viewed in an interpersonal context, insofar as it may promote greater understanding in the listener. There is also, however, an internal benefit: self-validation. For adults and children, but especially the latter, expressing one's emotions authenticates one's own worth be demonstrating respect for one of the most personal aspects of the self. Further it facilitates independence and therefore pride by declaring one's self internally separate, possibly different, and certainly distinct.

Expressing certain emotions may also enable the adult, but again, especially the child, to distinguish between feelings and fact. For instance, they may come to understand that feeling rejected is not equivalent to being rejected. Expressing such feelings to a parent may result in reassurance for the wounded child.

On other occasions, however, it is necessary to learn to live with certain emotions, such as rejection or failure, because they represent a reality. For example, rejection is a normal, reality-based emotion in an instance where a parent, owing to intense security-seeking or need-gratifying qualities, chooses an infatuation with another adult over an emotional investment in the youngster. Learning to live with that emotion will foster an acceptance of the parents' weaknesses and may allow the youngster to appreciate other good parental qualities, even if they are not redeeming.

In the final analysis, accepting emotions means coping with them. Reconciling oneself to living with feelings of failure, rejection, anger, and guilt allows one to better manage stress and often to avoid self-destructive behavior. Such behavior is commonly unconsciously contrived in order to escape painful emotions. Thus, when minor misconduct occurs a youngster's overzealous and primitive conscience may trigger terrible guilt and repetitive misbehavior. The repeated misconduct provokes adult criticism and perhaps punishment, relieving the guilt. It is easier to suffer adult disapproval and even punishment by provoking it than to experience painful guilt. Learning to live with guilt would promote a healthier conscience and better self-control.

As one can see, it is not the emotions that are harmful. The harm arises from an unwillingness to accept them, which may trigger already existing psychological problems. A fundamental condition of mental health is the ability to live with unpleasant emotions. Once one becomes acclimated to them, they gradually lose their power to dominate and control. Through this means personality is strengthened. By the same means postdissolution conflict is resolved. One cannot alter the past. One can only influence the future by changing the present.

Compassion

If all the judges, lawyers, psychiatrists, and others who toil in the custody area were to achieve only perfected expertise, they would do their jobs imperfectly. To do this type of work one needs more than skill and learning; one needs empathy and compassion. To be successful it is not even sufficient to care; one must also be able to transmit the fact that one cares to those who are contesting and suffering.

We are a funny species. It is amazing what losses and hurts we will abide if we perceive them to have been necessarily and fairly imposed. Thus, for the sake of all participants, especially the children, the parent who loses the custody war (or feels that it was lost) must, if possible, be made to feel that those who ruled cared deeply. The loser is much more likely to accept the appropriateness of the loss if it has been imposed by a system perceived as caring, for caring implies effort, and effort implies a proper result.

It has not been given to the mass of us to create odes, symphonies, oils, novels, or structures. We create only when we procreate. We lack genius; we have only genitalia. Thus our children are our only truly distinctive contributions to the life of our species. To part us from our children is to abort our only creativity, threaten our function, diminish our worth, and deprive us of proximity to love reciprocated. It is a terrible experience to endure, producing sadness inevitably, agony often.

To those who do not grasp this, to those who grasp it but squelch it, to those who cannot communicate their grasp of it, we say: work elsewhere.

We believe that Victor Hugo said it better than we can:

> Oh thou who art!
> Ecclesiastes names thee the Almighty;
> Maccabees names thee Creator;
> The Epistle to the Ephesians names thee Liberty;
> Baruch names thee Immensity;
> The Psalms name thee Wisdom and Truth;
> John names thee Light;
> The Book of Kings names thee Lord;
> Exodus calls thee Providence Leviticus, Holiness;
> Esdras, Justice;
> Creation calls thee God;
> Man names thee Father;
> But Solomon names thee Compassion, and that is the
> most beautiful of all thy names.
>
> *(Les Miserable;* ch. 1)

Surely parents and children of upset deserve no less.

Notes

1. Perspective

1. Conversation with a judge of the Superior Court in Hartford, Connecticut, circa 1975, of which one of the authors has personal knowledge.
2. Conversation with a judge of the Superior Court in Hartford, Connecticut, circa 1971, of which one of the authors has personal knowledge.
3. Uncontested divorce hearing in Hartford, Connecticut, Superior Court, circa 1969. The author, Attorney Donald J. Cantor, represented the plaintiff husband.
4. The King Against DeManneville, 5 East 221, 102 Eng. Rep. 1054 (K.B. 1804).
5. Headnote to The King Against DeManneville, supra at 4.
6. Prather v. Prather, 4 Des 33, 37 (South Carolina 1809).
7. The King Against Henrietta Lavinia Greenhill, 629, 4 AD & E 624, 111 Eng. Rep. 922 (K.B. 1836).
8. 3 Sidry Equity 1743–1749 (1918). Hocheimer, Custody of Infants 2d Ed. (1891).
9. Homer H. Clark, Law of Domestic Relations 572 (1968).
10. DeManneville v. DeManneville, 10 Ves. 52, at 61–62 (1804). The case referred to in the text is mentioned in the above case generally; the parties are not named and no citation is listed.
11. Shelly v. Westbrooke, 37 Eng. Rep. 850 (Ch. 1817).
12. *Ibid.*, Supra at p. 850.
13. People ex. rel. Mercein v. Barry, 25 Wend 65 (N.Y. 1840).

14. State v. Smith, 6 Greenl. 462 (1840).

15. Rex v. Greenhill, 4 Ad & E 624, 111 Eng. Rep. 922 (K.B. 1836).

16. A. Digest of the Laws of the State of Alabama, Title 19, Chapter 1, Sec. 7.

   B. Revised Code of Laws of Illinois 1827, Sec. 3.

   C. The Laws of Las Siete Partidas of Louisiana, Partida Fourth, 1; 569, Title XIX, Law 3 (1820).

   D. 2 General Laws of Massachusetts (1824), Chapter 56, Sec. 1

   E. Rev. Code of the Laws of Mississippi (1824), Chapter 36, Sec. 7

   F. Laws of New Jersey (1821), Sec. 10

   G. 2 Revised Statutes of the State of New York (1829), Ch. 8, Title II, Arts. 2 and 3

   H. 2 Statutes of Ohio, Chapter 624, Sec. 3 (1833).

17. 2 General Laws of Massachusetts (1823), Ch. 56, Sec. 3.

18. Laws of Louisiana, 16 (c).

19. Revised Statutes of New York, 16 (g).

20. Commonwealth v. Addicks and wife, 5 Binney's Rep. 520, 521 (Pa. 1813).

21. Commonwealth v. Addicks and Lee, 2 Sieger 174, 176 (Pa. 1816).

22. Miner v. Miner, 11 Illinois 43, 49 (1819).

23. Miner v. Miner at 49–50.

24. Miner v. Miner at 50.

25. The State v. Smith, G. Greenl. 462, 468 (Me. 1840) quoting Story, J. in US v. Green 3 Mas. 482, Fed. Case No. 15,256 (Civ. R. I. 1824).

26. The People, ex. rel. E. Ordronaux vs. F. Chegaray and C. Condert, 18 Wend. 637, 642 (N. Y. Superior Court 1836).

27. The State ex. rel. Paine vs. Paine, 23 Tenn. 523, 524, 536, 537 (1843).

28. J.F.C. v. M.E., His Wife, 45 La. Rep. 135, 138 (1843).

29. State v. Stigall, 22 N.J. 286, 291 (1849).

30. South Carolina State Constitution of 1895, Section 3., "Divorces from the bonds of matrimony shall not be allowed in this State."

31. A. Digest of the Statutes of Arkansas (1894) Ch. 54, Sec. 2514.

   B. Mills Annotated Statutes Rev. Supp. 1891–1905 Vol. 3, Sec. 1567 (Colorado).

   C. General Statutes of Conn. (1888), Title 46, Ch. 167, Sec. 2811.

   D. Revised Statutes of Delaware, 1852 as amended 1893, Ch. 76, Sec. 11.

   E. Revised Statutes of Florida 1892, Title 3, Article 13, Sec. 1489.

   F. Revised Statutes of Idaho 1887, Title II, Ch. II, Sec. 2473.

   G. Revised Statutes of Illinois 1899, Ch. 40, Sec. 18.

   H. Annotated Indiana State Revision of 1894, Vol. 1, Ch. 2, Art. 37.

   I. Code of Iowa Annotated 1897, Title 16, Ch. 3, Sec. 3180.

   J. General Statutes of Kansas 1899, Ch. 80, Art. 28, Sec. 4946.

   K. Kentucky Statutes 1899, Ch. 66, Art. 2, Sec. 2123.

   L. Revised Statutes of Maine, 1884, Title V, Ch. 60, Sec. 17.

M. Public General Laws of Maryland, 1888, Vol. 1, Art. 16, Sec. 37.

N. Compiled Laws of Michigan 1897, Title X, Ch. 232, Sec. 16.

O. Annotated Code of Mississippi 1892, Ch. 35, Sec. 1565 (1159).

P. Revised Statutes of Missouri 1899, Vol. 1, Ch. 20, Sec. 2926.

Q. Montana Code Annotated 1895, Title 1, Ch. 2, Art. 4, Sec. 192.

R. Compiled Statutes of Nebraska 1899, Part I, Ch. 25, 2871 Sec. 15.

S. Compiled Laws of Nevada 1900, Ch. 504, Sec. 24.

T. Public Statutes of New Hampshire 1891, Title 24, Ch. 175, Sec. 13.

U. The Code of North Carolina 1888, Vol. 1, Ch. 35, Sec. 1570.

V. Revised Code of North Dakota 1899, Civil Code Ch. 5, Art. 3, Sec. 2760.

W. Purdon's Digest (Penn.) 1700–1903, Vol. II, Ch. XIV, Sec. 76, (Public Law 316 of 26 June, 1895).

X. General Laws of Rhode Island 1896, Title XX, Ch. 195, Sec. 14.

Y. Vermont Statutes 1894, Title 17, Ch. 132, Sec. 2698.

Z. Code of Virginia 1887, Title 28, Ch. 101, Sec. 2263.

AA. Codes and Statutes of Washington 1897, Vol. II, Title XXXI, Ch. XII, Sec. 5723.

BB. Code of West Virginia 1899, Ch. 64, Sec. 11.

CC. Revised Statutes of Wyoming 1899, Title 3, Div. 2, Sec. 2997.

32. Revised Statutes of Utah 1898, Title 29, Ch. 3, Sec. 1212. A similar but not identical provision existed in Ohio: Annotated Ohio Statutes 1900, Vol. II, Title 1, Div. 1, Ch. 3, Sec. 1.

33. Annotated Code of Tennessee 1896, Title 4, Ch. 2, Art. 1, Sec. 4251.

34. Annotated South Dakota Statutes 1899, Civil Code Div. 1, Part 3, Title 1, Art. 1, Sec. 3467 (Annulment) and same at Article 4, Sec. 3494 as to divorce custody.

35. Revised Statutes of New York 1896, Vol. 1, Sec. 10 (annulment); same at Vol. 1, Sec. 30 (divorce).

36. Public Statutes of Massachusetts 1882, Part II, Title IV, Ch. 146, Sec. 32.

37. General Statutes of New Jersey 1895, II: 1271, Sec. 27.

38. Civil Code of Louisiana 1898, Title V, Ch. 4, Art. 157.

39. Code of the State of Georgia 1895, Title Third, Ch. 1, Art. 1, Sec. 2452.

40. Boles v. Boles, 60 Montana 411, 199 P. 912 (1921).

41. Pangle v. Pangle, 134 Md. 166, 106 A. 337 (1919).

42. Statutes of California, Ch. CLVII, Sec. 246 (1900).

43. The Code of Alabama, Vol. 1, Ch. 37, Sec. 1501 (1897).
    Statutes of Minnesota, Vol. I, Ch. 62, Title 1, Sec. 4802 (1894).
    Annotated Laws of Oregon, Ch. 5, Title VII, Sec. 501, 1. (1887).
    Texas Civil Statutes, Vol. 1, Title 55, Ch. 4, Art. 2987 (1897).
    Wisconsin Statutes, Title XXIII, Ch. 109, Sec. 2362 (1898).

44. Draper v. Draper, 68 Ill. 17 (1873) (cited as authority in Annotated

Statutes of Colorado); Miller v. Miller, 38 Fla. 227 (1896); Haskell v. Haskell, 152 Mass. 16 (1890); Klein v. Klein, 47 Mich. 518 (1892); Johns v. Johns, 57 Miss. 530 (1879); Commonwealth v. Myers, 18 Pa. C.C. 385 (1896); Clutch v. Clutch, 1 N.J. Eq. 474 (1831); Cariens v. Cariens, 50 W. Va. 113 (1903; People ex. rel. Sinclair v. Sinclair, 95 NYS 861 (1905); McKim v. McKim, 12 R.I. 462 (1879); Smith v. Smith, 15 Wash. 237 (1896).

45. Alabama: Code of Alabama, 1940, Vol. 6, Title 34, Sec. 35.

Arizona: McFadden v. McFadden, 22 Ariz. 246, 196 P. 452 (1921).

Arkansas: Disheroon v. Disheroon, 211 Ark. 519 (1947) 201 S.W. 2d 17.

California Civil Code (1949) Div. 1, Pt. 3, Title 1, Ch. 2, Art. 4, Sec. 138.

Colorado: Hayes v. Hayes, 134 Colo. 315, 303 P2d 238 (1956).

Utah: Holm v. Holm, 44 Utah 242 (1914) 139 PAC 397.

Virginia: Mullen v. Mullen, 188 Va. 259 (1948) 49 SE 2d 349.

Washington: Ramsden v. Ramsden, 202 P 2d 920 (1949) 32 Wash. 603.

West Virginia: Settle v. Settle, 117 W. Va. 476 (1936) 185 SE 859.

Wisconsin: Wisconsin Statutes 1949, Title XXIII, Ch. 247, Sec. 247.24.

Wyoming: Ramsey v. Ramsey, 76 Wyo. 188, 301 P 2d 377 (1956).

46. 27B Corpus Juris Secundum 309(4) 457–459.

47. 70 ALR 3rd 262, 267.

48. Alabama: Linderman v. Linderman 49 Ala. App. 662 (1973).

Alaska: Glasgon V. G. 426 P2d 617 (Alaska 1967).

Arkansas: Weber v. Weber 256 Ark. 549 (1974).

Delaware: DuPont v. DuPont 59 Del. 206, 216 A2d 674 (1966).

District of Columbia: Minacelli v. Minacelli 296 A 2d 445 (D.C. 1972).

Idaho: Barrett v. Barrett 94 Idaho 64 (1971).

Illinois: Patton v. Armstrong 307 NE 2d 178 (1974).

Kansas: Dalton v. Dalton 214 Kan. 805 (1974).

Kentucky: Sharp v. Sharp 491 SW 2d 639 (1973).

Louisiana: Hudson v. Hudson 295 So. 2d 92 (1974).

Maryland: Cooke v. Cooke 319 A2d 841 (1974).

Mississippi: Sistrunk v. Sistrunk 245 So. 2d 845 (1971).

Missouri: Blankenship v. Blankenship 488 SW 2d 245 (Mo. 1976).

Nevada: Peavey v. Peavey 85 Nev. 571, 460 P2d 110 (1969).

New Jersey: Vannucchi v. Vannucchi 272 A2d 560 (1971).

New Mexico: Ettinger v. Ettinger 72 NM 300 (1963).

North Carolina: Griffith v. Griffith 240 NC 271 (1954).

Ohio: Baxter v. Baxter 255 NE 2d 637, affd 271, NE 2d 873 (1969).

Oregon: Deaderff v. Deaderff 467 P2d 137 (1970).

Pennsylvania: Commonwealth ex. rel. Lucas v. Kreischer 450 PA 352 (1973).

Rhode Island: Loebenberg v. Loebenberg 85 RI 115, 127 A2d 500 (1956).

South Carolina: Peay v. Peay 260 SC 108 (1973).
Tennessee: Mollish v. Mollish 494 SW 2d 370 (1972).
Texas: Erwin v. Erwin 505 SW 2d 370 (Tex. 1972).
Utah: Hyde v. Hyde 454 P2d 884 (1969).
Vermont: Lafko v. Lafko 127 Vt. 609 (1969).
Virginia: Rowlee v. Rowlee 211 Va. 689 (1971).
Washington: Lines v. Lines 451 P2d 914 (Wash. 1969).
West Virginia: Funkhouser v. Funkhouser 216 SE 2d 570 (W. Va. 1975).
Wisconsin: Koslowsky v. Koslowsky 41 Wis. 2d 275 (1968).
Wyoming: Butcher v. Butcher 363 P2d 923 (Wyo. 1961).
49. 70 ALR 3rd 278.
50. 70 ALR 3rd 279–280.
51. 70 ALR 3rd 281–282.
52. 70 ALR 3rd 282–282.
53. (1) Girl of nine: Rowe v. Rowe, 45 Ala. App. 367 (1970).
    (2) Girl of eight: Weber v. Weber, 256 Ark. 549 (1974).
    (3) Boy of nine: Rzeszotanski v. Rzeszotanski, 296 A2d 431 (1972) (Washington D.C.).
    (4) Boy of eight: Dalton v. Dalton, 214 Kan. 805 (1974).
    (5) Children of five, six, nine, and ten: Butcher v. Butcher, 363 P2d 923 (1961) (Wyo.).
    (6) Boy of twelve: Hudson v. Hudson, 295 So. 2d 92 (1974) (La.).
    (7) Girl of eleven: Moore v. Moore, 212 Va. 153 (1971).
54. John Demos, The Many Faces of Fatherhood: A Further Exploitation in American Family History (unpublished), p. 5.
55. *Ibid.*, pp. 5–6.
56. John Demos, *A Little Commonwealth* (New York: Oxford University Press, 1970), pp. 84–85.
57. Demos, *Commonwealth*, p. 97.
58. Demos, *Fatherhood*, pp. 8–10.
59. *Ibid.*, pp. 8–9.
60. *Ibid.*, p. 28.
61. Carl N. Degler, *At Odds: Women and the Family in America from the Revolution to the Present* (New York: Oxford University Press, 1980), p. 17.
62. Demos, *Commonwealth*, pp. 134–136.
63. *Ibid.*, pp. 134–135.
64. *Ibid.*, pp. 142–143.
65. Degler, *At Odds*, p. 69.
66. *Ibid.*, p. 71.
67. *Ibid.*, p. 67.
68. *Ibid.*, p. 83.
69. Betty Friedan, *The Feminine Mystique* (New York: W. W. Norton, 1963).
70. Smith v. Smith, 172 Colo. 516 (1970); Folsom v. Folsom, 228 Ga. 536

(1972); Turoff v. Turoff, 527 P2d 1275 (1974) Hawaii; Kockrow v. Kockrow, 191 Neb. 657 (1974); Erwin v. Erwin, 505 SW 2d 370 (1974) (Texas); FF v. FF, 325 NYS 2d 291 (1971).
71. Arnold v. Arnold, 95 Nevada 951 (1979). Also see supra note 47 and Peavey v. Peavey, 460 P2d 110 (1969).
72. Nichols v. Nichols 537 P2d 1190 (1975) was a case in which the Nevada Supreme Court held that it was not an abuse of discretion to leave a child with its father where both parents were fit and both loved the child but where the child had been "thriving" in his father's custody. This case did not revoke Nevada's then (1975) maternal preference, but it did dent it a bit.
73. The Nevada Statute referred to in Arnold v. Arnold specifically bars any custodial preference for a mother or father. Nevada Rev. Statutes (1979) Title 112.6, Ch. 125, Sec. 125.140. There are similar statutory provisions in the following states:
Arizona: 9 Arizona Revised Statutes Annotated, Section 25-332.D.
Colorado: Colorado Revised Statutes (1984), Section 14-10-124. (3).
Delaware: 8 Delaware Code Annotated (1974), Section 722.(b).
Florida: 5 West's Florida Statutes Annotated, Section 61.13(2)(b)1.
Indiana: Burns Indiana Statutes Annotated (1984), Section 31.1.11.5-21.
Kansas: 4A Kansas Statutes Annotated (1983), Section 60-1610(3)(B).
Kentucky: 14 Kentucky Revised Statutes (1984), Section 403.270(1).
Louisiana: 1 Louisiana Civil Code (1984), Chapter 3, Art. 146.A.(2).
Massachusetts: Annotated Laws of Massachusetts (1983), Section 31.
Missouri: 24 Verenon's Annotated Missouri Statutes (1985), Section 452.375.
Nebraska: Revised Statutes of Nebraska (1943), Reissue of 1978, Section 42-364.(2).
New Hampshire: New Hampshire Revised Statutes Annotated (1983), Section 458:17 VI.
New York: 14 McKinney's Consolidated Laws of New York Annotated (1977) Section 240.1.(4).
North Carolina: 2A General Statutes of North Carolina, Part II, (1984), Section 50-13.2(a).
North Dakota: 3A North Dakota Century Code (1983), Section 14-09-06.1.
Ohio: 4 Baldwin's Ohio Revised Code Annotated (1983), Section 3109.3.
Oregon: 1 Oregon Revised Statutes (1983), Section 107.137(3).
Vermont: Vermont Statutes Annnotated (1984) Title 15, Section 652.(c).
Virginia: 4A Code of Virginia (1983), Section 20-107.2.1.
Wisconsin: Wisconsin Statutes Annotated (1984), Section 767.24(2).
Wyoming: 5 Wyoming Statutes Annotated (1977), Section 20-2-113.(a).
    This listing of statutes does not include statutes in which there is a stated perference for joint custody, which is implicitly an elimination of

gender preference. For those statutes that state a preference or presumption in favor of joint custody, see note 25, chapter 2, infra.

2. Joint Custody

1. Conversation between Attorney Cantor and a member of the Divorced Men's Association of Connecticut after a speech by Attorney Cantor to the organization in January 1981.
2. Goldstein, Freud, and Solnit, *Beyond the Best Interests* (New York: Free Press, 1973), p. 38.
3. 16 Trial, 22 at 27 (June 1980) by Henry H. Foster and Doris Jonas Freed.
4. Homer H. Clark, *Law of Domestic Relations* (St. Paul, Minn.: West, 1968), p. 573.
5. Visitation rights are normally granted only to noncustodial parents, but courts have the authority, seldom used, to grant rights of visitation to third parties, principally grandparents. See, as example, Section 46–47, Connecticut General Statutes.
6. "Divided Custody" is a term sometimes used to describe a splitting of custody itself, i.e., custody of one child to one parent and another child to the other parent. It is not so used in this work.
7. Commonwealth ex rel. Strickland (1905) 27 Pa. Super 309.
8. 92 ALR 2d 695, at 697.
9. 92 ALR 2d 695, at 697.
10. 92 ALR 2d 695, at 697.
11. State ex rel. Larson v. Larson, 190 Minn. 489 (1934); Wallace v. Wallace, 26 SD 229 (1910); Bohls v. Bohls, 188 SW 2d 1003 (1945-Tex. Civ. App.); Settle v. Settle, 117 W. Va. 476 (1936).
12. Conlan v. Conlan, 293 SW 2d 710 (Ky. 1956).
13. Travis v. Travis, 163 Kan. 54 (1947).
14. 92 ALR 2d 695, at 726–727 citing cases in Alabama, Arizona, Arkansas, Colorado, Florida, Iowa, Kentucky, Minnesota, Missouri, Nebraska, Oklahoma, Oregon, South Dakota, Tennessee, Utah, Virginia, Washington, West Virginia.
15. Phillips v. Phillips, 153 Fla. 133 (1943); Kaehler v. Kaehler, 219 Minn. 536 (1945); Mason v. Mason, 163 Wash. 539 (1931).
16. McCann v. McCann, 167 Md. 167, 173 (1934).
17. 92 ALR 2d, at 707.
18. 92 ALR 2d, at 710.
19. 92 ALR 2d, at 713.
20. 92 ALR 2d, at 713.
21. See note, *J. Fam. Law* 8:58; Foster and Freed, "Joint Custody: A Valuable Alternative," *Trial* (1979), 15:26–31.
22. Parley, *Joint Custody: A Lawyer's Perspective*, Conn. B.J. 53:310; Ro-

man and Haddad, *The Disposable Parent* (New York: Holt, Rinehart and Winston, 1978). The same is true in the cases. See cases annotated at 92 ALR 2d 695 and *J. Fam. Law* 8:58.

23. Courts often declare that custody orders, to be modified, require a showing of a change in circumstances since the entry of those orders. But where this principle conflicts with "the best interests of the child" as perceived by the court, the change of circumstances requirement is generally ignored or very easily satisfied.

24. Some commentators consider this practical use of a joint custody order by counsel to be inherently dangerous. See Bobette Adler Levy and Carole R. Chambers, "The Folly of Joint Custody," *Family Advocate* (Spring 1981), 3(4):6.

25. The following State statues have an expressed presumption in favor of joint custody:

Alaska: Alaska Statutes, Section 25.20.100.

Connecticut: 22 Connecticut General Statutes Annotated (1984), Section 46b–52a.(b).

Florida: 5 West's Florida Statutes Annotated, Section 61.13 (2)(b) 2.

Idaho: 6 Idaho Code, Section 32-717B(4).

Iowa: 39 Iowa Code Annotated, Section 598.41.2.

Kansas: 4A Kansas Statutes Annotated (1983), Section 60-1610.(4)(A).

Louisiana: 1 Louisiana Civil Code (1984), Article 146 A. (1).

Maine: 10A Maine Revised Statutes Annotated (1984), Section 752.

Massachusetts: Annotated Laws of Massachusetts (1983), Section 31.

Michigan: Michigan Compiled Laws Section 722.26a.

Minnesota: Minnesota Statutes Annotated Section 518.17(2).

Mississippi: 20 Mississippi Code Annotated (1972), Section 93-5-24.(4).

Montana: Montana Code Annotated (1983), Section 40-4-223.

Nevada: 6 Nevada Revised Statutes, Section 125.480 3 (a).

New Hampshire: New Hampshire Revised Statutes Annotated (1983), Section 458:17 II.(a).

New Mexico: 7 New Mexico Statutes Annotated (1978), Section 40-4-9.1.A.

Pennsylvania: Pennsylvania Consolidated Statutes Annotated Title 23, Section 5303-08.

To exemplify how far the presumption in favor of joint custody may go, see Emerick v. Emerick, 5 Conn. App. 649 (1986), where the appellate court over-ruled an award of joint custody by the trial judge when neither party had requested joint custody and the parties had not agreed to it.

3. The Divorce Court

1. Amsterdam v. Amsterdam, 56 N. Y. S., 2d 19, at 22 (1945).
2. See Cantor, *Escape from Marriage* (New York: Morrow, 1971), ch. 1.

3. *Ibid.*, p. 25.
4. This does not mean that the party who wanted the divorce less could not have been the one with the better claim to custody. It means that custody was often surrendered without a battle as part of the divorce price with no inquiry into which party would be the better custodial parent.
5. See Williams v. North Carolina, 317 U.S. 287 (1942); Williams v. North Carolina, 325 U.S. 226 (1945). As to Mexican divorces, see Cantor, *Escape from Marriage,* pp. 127—139.
6. Cantor, *Escape from Marriage,* pp. 89—91 (incompatibility); pp. 91—96 (separation).
7. Bassett v. Bassett, 250 p. 2d 487, 495 (1952-New Mexico).
8. Private correspondence from Professor Henry Foster in possession of the authors.
9. Caldifornia Civil Code 4506, effective 1/1/70.
10. South Dakota was the last state to adopt "no-fault" divorce, in 1985.

4. The Custody Trial

1. The following states utilize the "best interests" test specifically:

State	Statutory Section
Alaska	25. 24. 150
Arizona	25-332
Arkansas	34-2716
California	4509
Colorado	14-10-124
Connecticut	46b-56
Delaware	13 #722
Florida	61.13
Georgia	19-9-3(a)
Hawaii	571-46
Idaho	32-717
Illinois	40-602
Indiana	31-1-11.5-21
Iowa	598.21
Kansas	60-1610
Kentucky	403-270
Louisiana	Ch. 5, Art. 157
Minnesota	518.17
Mississippi	93-5-24
Missouri	452.375
Montana	40-4-212
Nebraska	42-364
Nevada	125.140

New Hampshire	458:17
New Jersey	9:2-4
New Mexico	40-4-9
New York	Art. 10 #240
North Carolina	50- 13.2
North Dakota	14-09-06.2
Ohio	3109.04
Oklahoma	1277.1
Pennsylvania	23 #1003
South Carolina	20-3-160
Texas	14.07
Vermont	3a #652
Virginia	20-107.2
Washington	26.09.190
West Virginia	48-2-15
Wisconsin	767.24

The states that do not specifically enact this standard usually have standards that distill to the same essence. Alabama speaks of the children's "safety and well-being" (Art. 1, 30-3-1). Massachusetts refers to "the benefit of the children" (208-28). South Dakota looks to the "welfare" of the child (68 SD 1, 297 NW 689 (1940)). Tennessee refers to the "welfare and interest of the child" (36-828). In reality, all jurisdictions use the same standard—what's best for the child—whatever the verbiage employed.

2. Colley Clibber, *Woman's Wit*, Act 1 (1697).
3. Louis Kiefer, *How To Win Custody* (New York, Simon and Schuster, 1982), p. 21.
4. Wallerstein, The Child in the Divorcing Family *Judges' Journal*, 19(1):42–43. The statutes of Georgia, Ohio, Tennessee, and Texas make specific reference to the age a child shall have reached in order for the child's preferences to be brought to the Court's attention. In Georgia a child of fourteen has "the right to select the parent with whom he desires to live . . . unless the parent so selected is determined not to be a fit and proper person to have the custody of the child" (16 Code of Georgia Annotated 1984 19-9-1 Section 30-127). In Ohio there is similar language, but the child's age must be twelve and the child's choice is discretionary with the Court (4 Baldwin's Ohio Revised Code Annotated 1983 Section 3109.4). In Tennessee a child of fourteen must be heard by the Court if the child "has expressed a desire to make a . . . custody preference known to the Court." If the child is under fourteen the child's preference is considered at the discretion of the Court (6A Tennessee Code Annotated 1984 Section 36-6-102). In Texas a child of fourteen years of age or older may file a writing with the Court choosing the "managing conservator subject to the approval of the Court" (2 (Fam-

ily) Vernon's Texas Codes Annotated 1984 Section 14.07 (a)). In addition, in Montana, a child of fourteen or more is by statute given a potentially definitive role in determining whether or not a prior custody decree should be changed despite the fact that the basic custody statute does not grant such a definitive role to a child of fourteen or more when an original custody decision is made (Montana Code Annotated 1983 Section 40-4-219 (1) (d) as compared with Section 40-4-212 (2)).

5. Goldstein, Freud, and Solnit, *Beyond the Best Interests of the Child* (New York: Free Press, 1973).

6. See Pierce v. Yerkovich, 80 Mis. 2d 613, 363 N.Y.S. 2d 403 (1974).

7. We understand that Goldstein, Freud, and Solnit meant their concept of the psychological parent to be, not the sole determinant of divorce custody, but rather necessary and valuable determinant among others. However, in practical use by advocates and evaluators, it is often presented that way.

8. Decisions relating to the custody of a child, including support payments for a child and visitation rights as well, are modifiable orders that may be changed subsequently. The usual basis for a change in custody orders is a change of circumstances such that the best interests of the child require a change. In some states an effort has been made to impede frivolous motions for modification by imposing time constraints. In the following states time constraints have been imposed: Colorado, Delaware, Kentucky, Illinois, Minnesota, and Texas. See 6 Colorado Revised Statutes 1973 Section 14-10-131 (1); 8 Delaware Code Annotated 1974 Chapter 13, Section 729 (a); 14 Kentucky Revised Statutes 1984 Section 403.340 (1); Smith-Hurd Illinois Annotated Statutes Chapter 40 Section 610 (a); 31 Minnesota Statutes Annotated Section 518.18(a); 2 (Family) Vernon's Texas Codes Annotated 1984 Section 14.08(d).

In Alaska, California, Connecticut, Florida, Hawaii, Iowa, Louisiana, Minnesota, Nebraska, Nevada, and North Dakota, the Court in determining custody is to consider the child's preference if the child is deemed to have sufficient capacity to make a sound preference with no age requirement. See 5 Alaska Statutes 1983 25.24.150; Deering's California Codes Annotated Civil Section 4600; 5 West's Florida Statutes Annotated Section 61.13 (i); 7 Hawaii Revised Statutes 1983 Section 571-46(3); 1 Louisiana Civil Code 1984 Article 146 C. (2) (i); 31 Minnesota Statutes Annotated Section 518.17 1. (b); 3 Revised Statutes of Nebraska 1943 (reissue of 1978) Section 42-364 (b); 6 Nevada Revised Statutes Section 125.480 4 (a); 3A North Dakota Century Code 1983 Section 14-09-06.2.9. Connecticut General Statutes Section 46b-59; III Code of Iowa Section 598.41 3f.

In Arizona, Colorado, Delaware, Idaho, Illinois, Indiana, Kansas, Kentucky, Missouri, Montana, New Hampshire, New Mexico, Oklahoma, Utah, Washington, and Wisconsin, the wishes of the child in regard to custodial preferences are simply listed among the factors a court shall take into account. See 9 Arizona Revised Statutes Annotated Section 25-332 A. 2; 6 Colorado Revised Statutes 1983 Section 14-10-124 (b); 8 Delaware Code Annotated 1974 Section 722 (a) (2); 6 Idaho Code 1980 Section 32-717.2; Smith-Hurd Illinois Annotated Statutes 1979 Chapter 40, Section 602 (a) (2); Burn's Indiana Statutes Annotated 1984 31-1-11.5-21 (6) (d); 4A Kansas Statutes Annotated 1983 Section 60-1610 (a) (3)(B)(iii); 14 Kentucky Revised Statutes 1984 Section 403.270(1)(b); Revised Statutes of Missouri 1982 Section 452-375 1 (2); Montana Code Annotated 1983 40-4-212 (2); New Hampshire Revised Statutes Annotated 1983 Section 458:17 VI; New Mexico Statutes Annotated 1978 Section 40-4-9 A(2); Oklahoma Statutes Annotated 1984 Section 1277.1; 3 Utah Code Annotated 1983 Section 30-3-10; Revised Code of Washington Annotated 1985 26.09.190(2); Wisconsin Statutes Annotated 1984 Section 767.24 (2) (am).

The following states require that an affidavit supporting modification be submitted to the Court; in some states this requirement is in addition to the time constraint noted above: Arizona, Colorado, Delaware, Illinois, Kentucky, Montana, and Washington. See 9 Arizona Revised Statutes Annotated Section 25- 339; 6 Colorado Revised Statutes 1973 Section 14-10-132; 8 Delaware Code Annotated 1974 Chapter 13 Section 729(a); Smith-Hurd Illinois Annotated Statutes Chapter 40, Section 610 (a); 14 Kentucky Revised Statutes 1984 Section 403.350; Montana Code Annotated 1983 Section 40-4-220; Revised Code of Washington Annotated 1985 Section 26.09.270.

The following states cite in their statutes specific standards for modification of a custody order: Colorado, Ohio, Montana, and Washington. See 6 Colorado Revised Statutes 1973 Section 14-10-131; 4 Baldwin's Ohio Revised Code Annotated 1983 Section 3109.04(B)(1); Montana Code Annotated 1983, Section 40-4-219; Revised Code of Washington Annotated 1985 Section 26.09.260.

9. American Psychiatric Association Statement on the Insanity Defense, December 1982, p. 14. Though this statement is concerned about the role of psychiatrists in trials involving the defense of insanity, the views expressed clearly apply to psychiatric roles in trials generally.

10. Rubenstein, "A New Way of Handling Child Custody," *New York Times Magazine*, November 29, 1981, pp. 136, 137.

11. Stanley v. Illinois, 405 US 645 (1972).

12. Meyer v. Nebraska, 262 US 390 (1923) at 399. See *Columbia Journal of Law and Social Problems* 16 (149): 158 et seq. for a discussion of parents' right to children.

5. Other Custodial Issues

1. U.S. Constitution, Art. IV, #1.
2. See H. Foster and D. Freed, "Child Snatching and Custodial Fights," *Hastings Law Journal* (1977), 28:1011, for an excellent discussion of what was and why the Uniform Child Custody Jurisdiction Act was necessary.
3. Huey, "To Man Whose Job Is Child-Snatching, End Justifies Means," *Wall Street Journal*, March 24, 1976, p. 1.
4. UCCJA, Section 1 (comment) Crunch, Interstate Custody Litigation (1981).
5. UCCJA, Section 1 lists the nine purposes of the Act.
6. UCCJA, Section 2 (5).
7. UCCJA, Section 3 (a) (2).
8. UCCJA, Section 3 (a) (3).
9. UCCJA, Section 3 (a) (4).
10. UCCJA, Section 8 (c).
11. UCCJA, Section 8 (c).
12. Foster and Freed, "Child Snatching," p. 1016
13. Sampson, "What's Wrong with the UCCJA," *Family Advocate* 3(4):28, 30, 1981. See, however, McCahey et al., "Child Custody and Visitation Law and Practice," Vol. 1, #3.01 (3), pp. 3–14, where the authors state that the UCCJA "has been instrumental in decreasing child abductions and in many instances the refugee state, to which a child has been abducted, has referred the parties back to the state from which abducted for resolution of the custody dispute." The authors do make clear, though, that the UCCJA "has not, and cannot, completely deter parents from abducting and reabducting their children, and has not eliminated forum shopping by the disappointed parent in hopes of obtaining a more favorable custody award in another jurisdiction" (pp. 3–14).
14. P.L. 96-611 ##6–10, 94 Stat. 3568 et seq. approved Dec. 28, 1981.
15. *Ibid.*, #7(a), Findings and Purposes, 28 U.S.C. 1738A note.
16. P.L. 96-611, #9, Social Security Act ##454, 463, 42 U.S.C. ##654, 663.
17. P.L. 96-611, #10, 18 U.S.C. 1073 note, App. B, Ch. 3, McCahey et al., "Child Custody and Visitation," p. 13.
18. L. F. Leslie v. F. Constance, 110 Misc. 2d 86, 441 N.Y.S. 2d 911 (Fam. Ct. 1981) at 913.
19. McCahey et al., "Child Custody and Visitation," pp. 3–18.
20. R. B. William v. B. Cynthia, 108 Misc. 2d 920, 439 N.Y.S. 2d 265 (Fam. Ct. 1981); Mebert v. Mebert, 111 Misc. 2d 500, 444 N.Y.S. 2d 834 (Fam. Ct. 1981).
21. Miller v. Superior Court of Los Angeles County, 69 Cal. App. 3d 191, 138 Cal. Rpts. 123 (1977).
22. Woodhouse v. District Court, 587 p. 2d 1199 (Colorado 1978).

23. Delaware Code Title 11, §785: Class A Misdemeanor.
24. Maryland Anno. Code § 9-307: Misdemeanor if by relative or one assisting relative. Defense if abductor proves child was in danger and submits modification of custody action to court within ninety-six hours; more than thirty days equals felony.
25. Massachusetts Gen. Laws Ann. Ch. 265, § 26A: Misdemeanor if abduction by relative unless child put in danger or taken outside state, then a felony.
26. Nebraska Revised Statutes § 28-316: Misdemeanor unless court order of custody is violated, then felony.
27. Nevada Revised Statutes § 200.359: Misdemeanor.
28. New Jersey Statutes Ann. § 2C: 13-4: Custodial interference misdemeanor if by parent—otherwise felony. Defense if done to protect child from danger or child is fourteen or more and left consensually and without purpose to commit criminal offense with or against the child.
29. New York Penal Law §§ 135.45, 135.50: Misdemeanor unless child removed from state with intent to permanently remove the child and person is actually removed or if child exposed to risk that safety be endangered or health materially impaired.
30. South Dakota Compiled Laws Ann. § 22-19-9: Misdemeanor for first offense.
31. Virginia Code § 18.2-47: Misdemeanor if abduction by parent; otherwise felony.
32. West Virginia Code § 61-2-14: Parents exempt from prosecution for kidnapping own child, but § 61-2-14d concealment or removal of minor child from custodian or person entitled to visitation equals misdemeanor. If out of state equals felony.
33. Arizona Rev. Statutes § 13-1302: Felony unless child returned without physical injury prior to abductor's arrest; then misdemeanor.
34. Illinois Ann. Statutes Ch. 38, § 10-5—felony but return of child within twenty-four hours is defense.
35. Kentucky Revised Statutes § 509.070: Removal from state Class E felony. Class D felony unless voluntarily returned.
36. Minnesota Statutes Ann. § 609.26: Felony defense if taken to protect child. Dismissed if child returned within fourteen days.
37. Montana Revised Codes Ann. § 45-5-304—felony but no offense if child not taken from state and returned prior to arraignment; if left state must return prior to arrest of abductor.
38. 18 Penn. Cons. Statutes Ann. § 2904: Felony unless actor acted with good cause for less than twenty-four hours, then misdemeanor.
39. Texas Penal Code § 25.03: Defense if child returned within seven days.
40. See Kiefer, "Custody Meanings and Considerations," Connecticut Bar Journal (1979), 53 (4):371, 375, 376, for a discussion of the tax implications of custody.

41. Some states have solved this problem by statute. See, for example, Nevada Revised Statutes, Section 125.520 (2), which provides: "Access to records and other information pertaining to a minor child, for example, medical, dental and school records, must not be denied to a parent for the reason that the parent is not the child's custodial parent."

42. Raymond v. Raymond, 165 Conn. 735 (1974).

43. Massachusetts provides by statute that no minor child of divorced parents can be removed out of Massachusetts without the child's consent if the child be of "suitable age" or, if younger than that, without the consent of both parents unless such removal has been allowed by Court order. See Annotated Laws of Massachusetts, 1983, Chapter 208, Section 30. In Alaska a specific cause of action is granted to one entitled to rights of visitation but willfully denied them by a custodian at the rate of $200 "for each failure of the custodian, willfully and without just excuse, to permit visitation with the child for substantially the length of time and substantially in the same manner as specified in the court order." See 5 Alaska Statutes, 1983, Section 25.24.300.

44. Raymond v. Raymond, 165 Conn. 735, at 741–742 (1974). New York, however, provides otherwise by statute in regard to prospective payments only. N.Y. Domestic Relations Law, Section 241.

45. As of 1983, only Arizona, Nebraska, Vermont, Wyoming, and the District of Columbia did not provide for grandparental rights of visitation; they have since done so.

46. Minnesota Statutes Annotated, § 257-002 Subd. 2 (but visitation rights must not "interfere with the parent child relationship").

47. Virginia Code Annotated, § 20-107.2.

48. Utah Code Annotated, § 30-3-5. In North Carolina "any . . . relative . . ." may seek custody. North Carolina General Statutes § 50-13.1.

49. See the discussion, infra, of the Connecticut Statutes.

50. See, again, the discussion, infra, of the Connecticut Statutes. Note that in this discussion we refer to Manter v. Manter, 185 Conn. 502 (1981), in which the Superior Court ruled that a father who had given his children in adoption to their mother's subsequent husband was not an "interested third party" under the applicable statute to seek rights of custody and/or visitation. We cannot know how many comparably broad statutes may in the future be similarly restricted by judicial interpretation, and thus we caution against assuming that such general statutory language means what it seems to say. Also there is the matter of potential judicial bias against nonparents even when their rights are indisputable.

51. See California Civil Code, Title 5, Sec. 4600: "Before the court makes any order awarding custody to a person or persons other than a parent, without the consent of the parents, it shall make a finding that an award

of custody to a parent could be determined to the child and the award to a nonparent is required to serve the best interests of the child. . . ." In South Dakota it was held that a parent had to be an unfit parent before custody could be awarded to grandparents over such a parent's objection: Langerman v. Langerman, 321 NW 2d 532 (1982).

52. See as examples the "passive" Connecticut Statutes CGSA, Title 46, Section 46b-56, and the "active" statute CGSA, Title 46, Section 46b-57. These are discussed infra.

53. Connecticut General Statutes Annotated, Title 46, Section 46b-56. The power of the Court to grant custodial rights to a nonparent under this Statute has been interpreted to require that the parental parties must have proper notice that a nonparental candidate for custodial rights exists and thus be able at trial to prepare to object to such candidacy. Cappetta v. Cappetta, 196 Conn. 10 (1985).

54. Connecticut General Statutes Annotated, Title 46, Section 46b-57.

55. Connecticut General Statutes Annotated, Title 46, Section 46b-59.

56. Manter v. Manter, 185 Conn. 502 (1981). We point out that Attorney Cantor represented the intervenor in Manter v. Manter. The reader should know this in deciding whether our approach to this case is fair or not.

57. Manter, at p. 508.

58. We stress that the Connecticut law set forth respecting Sections 46b-56, 46b-57, and 46b-59 is based upon our interpretations only. No case law exists to serve as a basis except Manter v. Manter. In a private conversation with Attorney Cantor in the fall of 1984, Judge Francis X. Hennessey, then Chief Administrative Judge of the Family Division of the Connecticut Superior Court, took a different view of the three statutes in question.

59. Nevada Revised Statutes, Section 125.500.

60. See *Columbia Journal of Law and Social Problems* (1980), 16:149 and the concurring opinion of J. Parsky, in Manter v. Manter, 185 Conn. at 509 (1981). See also McCahey et al., "Child Custody and Visitation," 2:11-5—11-7, where "parental preference" state decisions are listed. See Meyer v. State of Nebraska, 262 U.S. 399, 43 S. Ct. 626, 67 L. Ed. 1045 (1923), wherein the Supreme Court defined "liberty" in the Fourteenth Amendment to also mean "the right of the individual . . . to marry, establish a home and bring up children. . . ." and Bennett v. Jeffreys, 40 N.Y. 2d 543 at 549 (1976), wherein the highest court of New York stated:

Intervention of the State in the right and responsibility of a natural parent to custody of her or his child is warranted if there is first a judicial finding of surrender, abandonment, unfitness, persistent neglect, unfortunate or involuntary extended disruption of custody, or other equivalent but rare extraordinary circumstances which would drastically affect the welfare of the child. It is only on such a premise that the courts may then proceed to inquire into the best interest of the child and to order a custodial disposition on that ground.

61. See *Columbia Journal of Law and Social Problems* (1980), 16:149.
62. We mention here that we do not distinguish among heterosexual, transsexual, disabled, and homosexual parents or nonparents as applicants for custody and/or visitation. We also note a growing, laudable tendency not to disable persons as custodians simply because of their sexual preference. See also Christian v. Randall 516 2d 132 (1973—Colorado) (transsexual); and Hunter and Polikoff, "Custody Rights of Lesbian Mothers: Legal Theory and Litigation Strategy," *Buffalo Law Review* (1976), 25:691.
63. Alabama, Alaska, Arizona, Arkansas, California, Colorado, Connecticut, Delaware, District of Columbia, Florida, Hawaii, Idaho, Kentucky, Maine, Maryland, Michigan, Mississippi, Nebraska, Nevada, New Hampshire, New York, Ohio, Oklahoma, Oregon, Rhode Island, South Carolina, South Dakota, Tennessee, Texas, Utah, Vermont, Virginia, Washington, West Virginia, and Wyoming.
64. Georgia—Georgia Code § 19-9-1 (c); Notice for any changes in residence.
    Illinois—Smith-Hurd Illinois Statutes, Chapter 40–41, Marriage and Dissolution; Posting of reasonable security to guarantee compliance with the removal order. Need permission from court.
    Indiana—Burns Indiana Statutes Annotated Title 31-1-11.5-20 (b)(2); Notice for outside the state or one-hundred miles.
    Iowa—Code of Iowa Dissolution of Marriage § 598.21 8 f.; Grounds for modification of joint custody.
    Kansas—Kansas Civil Procedure § 60-1620 (c); Written notice to other parent not less than twenty-one days before move for any change in residence or for removing more than ninety days may be grounds for modification.
    Louisiana—Louisiana Civil Code Annotated C.C. Art. 146 K. Separation and Divorce; Grounds for modification of joint custody.
    Massachusetts—Annotated Laws of Massachusetts C. 208 § 30; Consent of child of suitable age, consent of other parent or court order. Security may be required.
    Minnesota—Minnesota Statutes, 1982, Chapters 480 to 648, Para. 518.175; Consent of parent or court order unless purpose of move is to interfere with visitation rights.
    Missouri—Missouri Revised Statutes, Title 30 § 452.377; Court order for more than ninety days.
    Montana—Montana Code Annotated § 40-4-219 (f) Modification; Grounds for Modification.
    New Jersey—New Jersey Statutes Annotated, Title 9-11 § 9:2-2; Removal from jurisdiction, need consent of child or parent or court order.
    New Mexico—New Mexico Statutes Annotated § 40-4-9.1 (4)(a); Either party shall give thirty days' notice of change of address in city or state.

North Carolina—General Statutes of North Carolina § 50-13.2 (c); Order to remove, but must have security (bond).

North Dakota—North Dakota Century Code § 14-09-07; Court order unless visitation rights not exercised for one year.

Pennsylvania—Pennsylvania Consolidated Statutes Annotated; 23 Pa. C.S.A. § 5308; Grounds for review of custody order.

Wisconsin—West's Wisconsin Statutes Annotated § 767.245; Court order after notice given to parent with visitation rights and after a hearing to remove child more than ninety days.

65. Georgia Code § 19-9-1 (c); Child Custody Proceedings.
66. Ill. Rev. Stat. Chp. 40, § 609.
67. Tandy v. Tandy, 42 Ill. App. 3d 87, 355 N.E. 2d 585 (1976).
68. Gray v. Gray, 57 Ill. App. 3d 1, 372 N.E. 2d 909 (1978).
69. Hickey v. Hickey, 31 Ill. App. 3d 257, 333 N.E. 2d 271 (1975).
70. Quirin v. Quirin, 50 Ill. App. 3d 785, 365 N.E. 2d 226 (1977).
71. Gray v. Gray, *supra* note 68 at 3.
72. Burns Indiana Statutes Annotated Title 31 § 31-1-11.5-20 (b)(2).
73. Code of Iowa § 598.21 8. (f); Dissolution of Marriage.
74. Kansas Civil Procedure § 60-1620 (c).
75. Louisiana Civil Code Annotated C.C. Art. 146 K.; Separation and Divorce.
76. N.J. Stat. Ann. § 9:2-2.
77. Mass. Gen. Laws Ann. Ch. 208, § 30.
78. Minn. Stat. 1982 Ch. 480 to 648, § 518.175.
79. Missouri Rev. Stat. Title 30 § 452.377.
80. Montana Code Annotated § 40-4-219 (1) (f).
81. New Mexico Stat. Ann. § 40-4-9.1 J. (4)(a).
82. General Statutes of North Carolina § 50-13.2 (c).
83. North Dakota Century Code § 14-09-07.
84. Pennsylvania Consolidated Statutes Annotated 23 Pa. C.S.A. § 5308.
85. West's Wisconsin Statutes Annotated § 767.245.
86. Minn. Stat. § 518.175 (3).
87. D'Onofrio v. D'Onofrio, 144 N.J. Super 200, 365 A. 2d 27 (Ch. Div.), aff'd 144 N.J. Super 352, 265 A. 2d 716 (1976).
88. Hale v. Hale, 429 N.E. 2d 340 (1981).
89. Yannas v. Frondistou-Yannas, 395 Mass. 704, 481 N.E. 2d 1153 (1985).
90. Weiss v. Weiss, 52 N.Y. 2d 170, 428 N.E. 2d 377 (1981).
91. 13 *FLR* 1360 (1987).
92. One commentator has written:

By requiring exceptional circumstances to justify a move New York courts often immobilize parents who are unhappy in their present locations. As a result of their parents' unhappiness, the children suffer as well. Because of their daily contact, children are affected by the mental attitude of their parents. . . . Consequently, the best interests of the children are often neglected.

38 *University of Florida Law Review* 177, at 127 (1986).
93. Some states have notice provisions, but they differ substantially from the type we recommend. Kansas, for instance, requires notice only from a custodial parent wishing to remove a child from the state either to change residence or for more than ninety days. "The notice is to be given less than twenty-one days prior. . . ." § 60-1620(a).
94. Minn. Stat. § 518.175 (3).

6. A Developmental Model for Parent Evaluation

1. Bowlby, John, "Focusing on a Figure," *Attachment and Loss,* vol. 1: *Attachment* (New York: Basic Books, 1969), pp. 307–309.
2. Anna Freud and Dorothy J. Burlingham, *Infants Without Families,* (New York: International University Press, 1947), pp. 53–64.
3. Technically speaking, the parent qualities described are ego states. In other words, they are integral parts of the psychic vehicle that is governed by, respectively: the level of internalized object relations; the degree of internal and external separations; instinct drive control, both sexual and aggressive; the consistency and definition of ego boundaries; and the degree to which the identity has crystallized into an integrated whole.
4. Therese Benedek, "Parenthood as a Developmental Phase: A Contribution to the Libido Theory," *Journal of the American Psychoanalytical Association* (1959), 7(3):389–417.
5. D. W. Winnicott, *Playing and Reality* (London: Tavistock, 1971), pp. 10–11 and *The Maturational Process and the Facilitating Environment.* (New York: International Universities Press, 1965), pp. 144–149.
6. Winnicott, *Playing and Reality,* p. 10.
7. Christine Olden, "On Adult Empathy with Children," in *The Psychoanalytic Study of the Child* (New York: International Universities Press, 1953), 8:111–126.
8. Brandt Steele, "Psychodynamic Factors in Child Abuse," in C. Henry Kempe and Ray E. Helfer, eds., *The Battered Child,* 3d ed. (Chicago and London: University of Chicago Press, 1980), pp. 49–77; Schaffer, H. R. and Emerson, P. E., "The Development of Social Attachments in Infancy," Monograph of the Society for Research in Child Development, 29 (3):1–77.
9. Heinz Hartmann, cited by Gertrude Blanck and Rubin Blanck, in *Object Relations* (New York: Columbia University Press, 1968), p. 68.
10. Enduring feelings of self-worth, which are the basis for valuing oneself and the capacity to truly value others, are governed by a dual and interlocking pathway roughly correlating to what has been referred to as healthy secondary narcissism and internalized object relatedness re-

spectively. Gertrude Blanck and Rubin Blanck, *Ego Psychology II*: Psychoanalytic Developmental Psychology (New York: Columbia University Press, 1979), pp. 50–63.

11. Placing a child's interest before one's own should not be confused with martyrdom. By acquiescing to children's demands without regard to the need for or even the wisdom of gratifying such wishes, the parent seeks to relieve guilt. While the behavioral or material concessions thus ceded to the child may or may not prove detrimental to his or her well-being, the transaction itself certainly is. The relationship engendered by martyrdom is nakedly contractual. It simultaneously places the child in a position of inappropriate influence over the parents' mood state and burdens that child with the psychological debt which is always implicit in such transactions.

12. "DSM III-R Disorders Usually First Evident in Infancy, Childhood, or Adolescence: Reactive Attachment Disorder of Infancy or Early Childhood (313.89)," in *Diagnostic and Statistical Manual of Mental Disorders* (Washington, D.C.: American Psychiatric Association, 1987, pp. 91–93.

13. Technically, this is narcissistic deficiency. Blanck and Blanck, *Ego Psychology II*: Psychoanalytic Developmental Psychology, pp. 50–63. The self-representation is insufficiently cathected (invested) with value to lead to an adequate measure of self-regard. Because cathexis of the self and object representations occur simultaneously and are both products of emotional investment on the part of a principal attachment figure, regard for oneself will be roughly equivalent to emotional investment in others.

14. Often the impression that victimization has occurred is so great as to create the belief that one is the target of malevolent forces. It suggests a conviction of negative self-importance arising out of a sense of absolute inadequacy and impotence. This person feels marked, as if by an evil omen. The conviction is a variation on the theme of martyrdom.

15. That is, progress toward healthy secondary narcissism and satisfactory object relatedness has been made. Healthy secondary narcissism is that level of self-value that allows for a steady flow of self-worth. Satisfactory internalized object relatedness imply a progressive separation of the self-representation from the object representation with cathexis of both self and object representations with value (*Ibid.*, pp. 50–63).

16. In other words, neither has the self-representation been sufficiently endowed with value nor has object constancy been achieved. If they had been, the level of narcissistic investment would be adequate and therefore, a steady flow of worth would emanate from within. Blanck and Blanck, "The Contributions of Edith Jacobson," in *Ego Psychology: Theory and Practice* (New York and London: Columbia University Press, 1974), pp. 61–73. Thus, one's capacity to value oneself and others would

be sufficient to tolerate others demands without acquiescing even when they are acting in a rejecting fashion.

17. "DSM III-R Disorders"; pp. 91–93. Elizabeth Elmer, "Failure to Thrive: Role of the Mother," *The American Academy of Pediatrics* (1960), 25(4):717–725; Joseph Fischoff, Charles F. Whitten, and Marvin G. Pettit, "A Psychiatric Study of Mothers of Infants with Growth Failure Secondary to Maternal Deprivation," *The Journal of Pediatrics* (1971), 79(2):209–215.

18. Michael Rutter, "Maternal Deprivation Considered," *Journal of Psychosomatic Research* (1972), 16:241–250.

19. Responsiveness to the baby's crying or other signals, and the amount and nature of interaction between mother and baby have been identified as parent qualities which most intensify the child's tie to the parent. M. D. S. Ainsworth cited by John Bowlby, *Attachment and Loss*, 1:315–316.

20. It has been assumed that mothers are exclusively the principal attachment figures for infants and small children. This is understandable in light of the overwhelmingly dominant role played by women as primary caretakers in our society for the past two-hundred years. But society is changing. Because of the high percentage of working mothers and a relatively greater interest in child rearing on the part of men, there is more impetus toward joint parenting than has heretofore been present.

Recently researchers have begun to investigate the role of the father in child development and its current status in the family. Charles Lamb, for example, questions the older view that the mother-infant relationship is the prototype for all later love relations. Quoting Shaffer, Lamb suggests that "whether a child's first relationship is in any way the prototype of all future relationships, we do not as yet know: The clinical material bearing on this point is hardly convincing. If the trend of fathers becoming primary or equal caretakers continues, they may come to rival mothers as principal attachment figures." Michael Lamb, *The Role of the Father in Child Development* (New York: Wiley, 1976), pp. 2–3.

Kotelchuck elaborates on this theme, discussing the early conviction that infants are naturally "monotropically matricentric" in orientation; that is, that the child will orient himself toward one and only one person, i.e., the child is monotropic; and that person will tend to be the mother, i.e., the child is matricentric. In his studies of child-parent preferences, Kotelchuck gathered data which contradicts the earlier assumption, discovering that "depending on the measure chosen, approximately 55% of 12- to 21-month-old children show maternal preferences, 20% [show] joint preferences and 25 percent show paternal preferences. In addition, 70 percent of the infants were attached to their fathers." These data correlate well with the findings of Schaffer and Emerson's

(1964) maternal interview study. They estimated that 80 percent of 18-month-old infants are attached to their fathers, that 51 percent of the 18-month-old infants show maternal preferences, 19 percent show paternal preferences, and 16 percent show joint preference. Milton Kotelchuck, "The Infants Relationship to the Father: Experimental Evidence," in Lamb, ed., *The Role of the Father in Child Development*, pp. 2–3. See also Medford Spiro, *Children of the Kibbutz* (Cambridge: Harvard University Press, 1958); N. Pelled cited by John Bowlby, in *Attachment and Loss*, pp. 316–317.

21. Martin Greenberg, *The Birth of a Father* (New York: Avon Books, 1986), pp. 83–94.

22. It is generally accepted that infants may be safely separated from biological parents during the first week of life for adoptive placements. Carl Dors and Helen Dors, in *If You Adopt a Child* (New York: Holt, 1957), p. 78. However, the proposition that mother-infant contact and interaction during the first few hours after delivery significantly affect mothering behavior and development has been substantially supported. John H. Kennell, Mary Anne Trause, and Marshall H. Klaus, "Evidence for a Sensitive Period in the Human Mother," in Saul I. Harrison and John F. McDermott, Jr., eds., *New Directions in Childhood Psychopathology*, vol. 1: *Developmental Considerations* (New York: International Universities Press, 1980), 1:1–11. At what point regression and damage to the developing personality might be inflicted by separation from a principal attachment figure cannot be determined with certainty. Although it was formerly believed that infants could be transferred from an original foster home to an adoptive home without experiencing visible emotional duress at six months of age the fact that attachment has progressed substantially by that point in time and along with it, the crucial separation between self and other, as well as other developmental tasks, casts some doubt on the wisdom of transferring infants at the latter part of this age group from the care of an unrivaled principal attachment figure. Margaret Mahler, *On Human Symbiosis and the Vicissitudes of Individuation*, vol. 1: *Infantile Psychosis* (New York: International Universities Press, 1968), pp. 12–13.

23. Between six and eight months, attachment rapidly intensifies, reflected in the unfolding of stranger anxiety; i.e., the fear of strangers, occurring at six months. Around the tenth month, separation anxiety representing a fear of parting from a principal or even subsidiary attachment figure occurs. Melvin Lewis, *Clinical Aspects of Child Development*, 2d ed. (Philadelphia: Lea and Febiger., 1982), pp. 16–32. During this period, and for the next few months, separations trigger depressions of a sometimes profound nature. Rene Spitz, *The Psychoanalytic Study of the Child* (New York: International Universities Press, 1946), 2:313–342. This being the height of the child's sensitive stage of attachment to the principal attachment figure, the greatest vulnerability to regression, or even

damage if separated from an unrivaled attachment figure, will occur then, and probably for some time afterward.

24. By the third birthday, a child engaged in play can accept a mother's temporary absence, and by the fourth birthday the knowledge that the mother is readily available will be very reassuring. Bowlby, p. 356. While this means that at least short-term separation can be handled, the capacity to cope with a residential change or to leave a parent to whom he or she is predominantly attached will in all likelihood be less.

25. This does not, however, apply to the long-time caretaker who supposes that such service merits special consideration. This parent may have motives that are not primarily driven by and may not even coincide with the best interest of the child.

26. According to Heinz Hartmann, object constancy represents the capacity to intrinsically value others for themselves independent of one's state of need (see note 11). This reflects the endpoint of internalized object relations. Heinz Hartmann, *Object Relations*, p. 68.

27. Judith S. Wallerstein and Joan Berlin Kelly, "The Implications of the Findings," in *Surviving the Breakup* (New York: Basic Books, 1980), pp. 307–308; Richard Gardner, "The Final Recommendation," in *Family Evaluation in Child Custody Litigation* (Cresskill, NJ: Creative Therapeutics, 1982), pp. 230–231; Group for Advancement of Psychiatry (1980), cited in Gardner, "The Final Recommendation," pp. 230, 231.

28. Wallerstein and Kelly, "Implications," pp. 307, 308. A parent's inability to share the child's time and attention often arises from a security-seeking mechanism. The parent who is security seeking relies excessively on the child to provide love, affection, and a sense of well-being. As a result that person will not tolerate potential competition with the other parent.

29. Separation is a process by which the child distances oneself from the principal attachment figure and draws a boundary between oneself and this attachment figure, both physically and emotionally, i.e., externally and internally. Margaret S. Mahler, *On Human Symbiosis and the Vicissitudes of Individuation*, vol I: Infantile Psychosis (New York: International Universities Press, 1968), pp. 7–31.

30. Pine and Furer describe the process "Separation and Individuation" as two complementary developments: the one consisting of a child's emergence from a symbiotic fusion with the mother and the other consisting of those achievements marking the child's assumption of his or her own individual characteristics. Fred Pine and Manuel Furer, "Studies of the Separation-Individuation Phase," in *The Psychoanalytic Study of the Child* (New York: International University Press, 1963) 18:325–328. While separation is proceeding concurrently with individuation, the toddler is evolving a sense of self through an emotional investment in those characteristics that will identify the child as unique.

31. Infants begin life in a fused state with their principal attachment figures. As time progresses, they separate and develop increased independence. To investigate new places and activities at an increasing distance from their parents, children must have "permission" to be physically separate. Developing locomotion and motor coordination skills without significant anxiety requires the option of testing the skill with the knowledge that parental intervention is available when needed (Mahler, *Symbiosis*, pp. 7–31). Likewise, sphincter mastery requires sufficient security and independence be accorded the child that repeated attempts and failures do not imperil adult approval. For the dependency promoting parent this is a difficult assignment. Fear prevents that person from offering any measure of independence. This fear arises from a conviction that granting too much independence (which may mean any at all) will result in the child's failure, injury or even something worse. Thus, independence is hampered or actively prevented: hovering and restriction are substituted. A cycle of mounting parental ambivalence ensues; agonizing over potential errors, decisions regarding granting greater freedoms are often avoided or deferred until the toddlers rebellion can no longer be tolerated. Ironically, in this instance, the child often assumes control, rendering the adult powerless.

32. Lynn Hoffman, "Enmeshment and the Too Richly Cross-Joined System," *Family Process* (December 1975), 14 (4):457–468.

33. Likewise, the child's internal separation is characterized by struggle. The courage and resolve to pursue independent thinking often falters en route to the goal. This is especially true when there is an internalized parental object that warns of danger and predicts failure. Blanck and Blanck, Ego Psychology II: Psychoanalytic Developmental Psychology, pp. 50–63.

34. Projection is the removal of an unacceptable wish or impulse from one's own inner world and ascribing ownership of it to someone else, thereby relieving one's personality tension. Because it is an unconscious operation, the person sincerely believes that the feelings are coming from the environment rather than oneself. Charles Brenner, *An Elementary Textbook of Psychoanalysis* Garden City: Doubleday Anchor, 1957, 4: pp. 101–103.

35. In this regard the so-called permissive parent and the parent who seeks to control the child's thought processes have much in common. Both subscribe to the notion that right action springs from right thinking. Once a child arrives at the proper mental philosophy, they believe that the youngster's actions will as a matter of course be correct. But this is putting the cart before the horse.

Society never (or rarely) proscribes ideas or thought processes: society proscribes behaviors. The task of individuating requires that one develop an internal philosophy, the result of which allows one to peacefully (though not necessarily without conflict and confrontation), inhabit civilized society. The autonomous parent defines a set of acceptable behaviors (values) as the "solution set" for the philosophical problem. The child then develops a philosophy which is prescriptive only to the extent that behaviors consequent to the philosophy must belong to the "solution set" of acceptable values. As the youth gains insight and maturity, increasing ability to expand or modify his or her own value system occurs by assigning relative priority to the importance of particular values and by conglomerating old values to create new ones. This is vastly different than allowing the youngster to create personal values to suit immediate exigencies.

36. Judith S. Wallerstein and Joan Berlin Kelly, *Surviving the Breakup*, pp. 306–307.

37. This entails an acquired readiness on the part of the parent to supply whatever emotional care is required by the infant, toddler, or older child at any time and a desire to playfully share the youngster's explorations and adventures. The availability facilitates imitation and identification. Margaret Mahler, "Thoughts About Development and Individuation," *The Psychoanalytic Study of the Child* (New York: International Universities Press, 1963), 18:315–318.

38. It should not be surprising that an association exists between physical abuse, substance abuse (especially alcohol), and sexual abuse. They are impulse disorders, and anyone prone to difficulty in controlling one aspect of instinctual behavior is likely to find all aspects of instinctual drive difficult to control. Deficient self-esteem, poor identity integration, social isolation and chaotic families of origin where emotional and physical abuse were common all characterize the personalities and background of physical and sexual abusers alike. Sexual abusers, like physical abusers, were themselves likely to have been victims of sexual abuse, especially incest. There is, in addition, a greater than normal incidence of criminal behavior in the family of origin of the physical abuser. Brandt Steele, "Psychodynamic Factors in Child Abuse," p. 73; Simon Kreindler and Harvey Armstrong, "The Abused Child and the Family," in Paul D. Steinhauer and Rae-Grant Quentin, eds., *Psychological Crises for Child and Family* (n.p., n.d.), 4:546–549; Richard Galdston "Disorders of Early Parenthood: Neglect, Deprivation, Exploitation and the Abuse of Little Children," in Joseph D. Noshpitz, ed., *Basic Handbook of Child Psychiatry* (New York: Basic Books, 1979), 2:589–591.

A strong correlation also exists between alcoholism and incest. It has been reported that alcohol abuse was a significant problem in 50 percent of the homes of known incest victims. It has also been estimated that 60–80 percent of alcoholic women were once incest victims, and that 26 percent of children in alcoholic homes were victims of incest. Claudia Black, *It Will Never Happen To Me* (Denver: M.A.C. Printing and Publications Division, 1981), pp. 137–142.

39. *Ibid.*, p. 14; Brandt Steele, pp. 57–59.

40. Denial, which may afflict every family member, often enables the abusive behavior to continue unabated. A family member, other than the abuser, who facilitates this is sometimes referred to as an "enabler," particularly in the argot of alcoholism research and treatment. Almost every family situation in which impulse disturbance exists, of whatever type, contains an enabler. Without consciously recognizing it, enablers permit or even encourage impulse-ridden behaviors, either because they obtain some subsidiary gratification from the continuation of the abuse, or because their dependence on the impulse-ridden parent is so great that they refuse to confront the aberrancy of the abusive person's behavior. Black, *It Will Never Happen To Me*, pp. 33–37; Irving, Kaufman, Alice L. Peck, and Consuelo Tagiuri, "The Family Constellation and Overt Incestuous Relations between Father and Daughter," *American Journal of Orthopsychiatry* 24:266–279; Brandt, Steele, pp. 49–85.

41. Rationalization, a complementary defense to denial (Black, pp. 33–37), is a conscious attempt by a person to make an action appear reasonable when it is, in fact, motivated by some unconscious irrational or illogical impulse. Ludwig Eidelberg, Ed.-in-Chief, *Encyclopedia of Psychoanalysis* (New York and London: The Free Press. 1968). pp. 364–365.

42. It is not coincidental that abusing parents were themselves abused. Victims of emotional deprivation, they lack empathy, weakening their attachment to their children. As a result, they pay slight attention to the children's needs and lack regard for them as persons with a right to bodily protection. Abusing parents, raised in an atmosphere where they were abused or neglected, grow up with a self-perception of badness and unacceptability with an accompanying self-esteem deficiency. As it was their heritage, so shall it be that of their children. Steele, "Psychodynamic Factors," pp. 50–58.

43. Linda Tschirhart Sanford, *The Silent Children* (Garden City, N.Y.: Anchor Press/Doubleday, 1980), pp. 90–115. Steele, "Psychodynamic Factor," pp. 48–61; Galdston, "Disorders of Early Parenthood," p. 589; Kreindler and Armstrong, "The Abused Child," p. 548.

44. J. D. Gray, C. A. Cutler, J. G. Dean, and C. H. Kempe, cited by Steele, "Psychodynamic Factors," p. 55; Black, *It Will Never Happen To Me*, pp. 77–78; Kreindler and Armstrong, "The Abused Child," p. 548; S. Wasserman, "The Parent of the Abused Child," *Children* (1967), 14:175–179.

45. In his description of the second psychosocial stage of development, the stage of autonomy vs. shame and doubt, Erik Erikson explores this facet of the development of impulse control. According to Erikson, freedom of self-expression, independence, and a steadfast belief in the good will and pride of his parents will result in a child's acquisition of autonomy. If the child does not acquire a sense of autonomy, he feels shame and doubt. "Shame" or the feeling of embarrassment over his exposed in-

adequacy will be aroused if the child has poor impulse control or is unable to become self-sufficient. "Doubt" or the belief that he will never be able to achieve autonomy occurs when the toddler suffers from a crisis in confidence and despairs of ever being able to control himself. Erik Erikson, *Childhood and Society* New York: Norton, 1963, pp. 251–255.

46. Galdston, "Disorders of Early Parenthood," pp. 588–589.
47. Harold Martin, "The Child and His Development," in C. H. Kempe, and Ray E. Helfer, eds., *Helping the Battered Child and his Family* (Philadelphia and Toronto: Lippincott 1972), pp. 103–108.
48. Elissa P. Benedek, and Diane H. Schetky, "Problems in Validating Allegations of Sexual Abuse. Part 2: Clinical Evaluation," *Journal of the American Academy of Child and Adolescent Psychiatry* (1987), 26(6):916–921.
49. Adele Mayer, *Sexual Abuse: Causes Consequences and Treatment of Incestuous and Pedophilic Acts* (Holmes Beach, Fla.: Learning Publications, 1985, pp. 53–65; Lora Heims Tessman, and Irving Kaufman, "Variations on a Theme of Incest," in Otto Pollak and Alfred S. Friedman, eds., *Family Dynamics and Female Sexual Delinquency*. (Palo Alto, Calif.: Science and Behavior Books, 1969), pp. 138–150.
50. Susan M. Fisher, "Encopresis," in Noshpitz, ed., *Basic Handbook of Child Psychiatry*, 2:556–568.
51. Galdston, "Disorders of Early Parenthood," pp. 588–590; Brandt Steele, "Psychodynamic Factors," pp. 58–64.
52. E. J. Merrill, cited by John J. Spinetta, and David Rigler, "The Child-Abusing Parent: A Psychological Review," *Psychological Bulletin* (1972), 77(4):300; A. Nicholas Groth, "The Incest Offender," in Suzanne M. Sgroi, ed., *Handbook of Clinical Intervention in Child Sexual Abuse* (Lexington, Mass. and Toronto: Lexington Books, Heath, 1982), pp. 215–239; Mary Edna Helfer, and Ray E. Helfer, *The Battered Child* (Chicago and London: University of Chicago Press, 1980), pp. 117–127.
53. "DSM III-R Disruptive Behavior Disorders: Conduct disorder; Group, Solitary Aggressive, and Undifferentiated Types (312.20–312.90)," *Diagnostic and Statistical Manual of Mental Disorders*, 3d ed., (Washington, D.C.: American Psychiatric Association, 1987), pp. 53–56; Richard L. Jenkins, "Classification of Behavior Problems of Children," *American Journal of Psychiatry* (1969), 125:1032–1039; Richard L. Jenkins, "Diagnostic Classification in Child Psychiatry," *American Journal of Psychiatry* (1970), 127(5):680–681.
54. Elissa P. Benedek, and Diane H. Schetky, "Problems in Validating Allegations of Sexual Abuse. Part 1: Factors Affecting Perception and Recall of Events," *Journal of the American Academy of Child and Adolescent Psychiatry* (1987), 26(6):912–915.
55. Lenore C. Terr, "The Child as a Witness," in Diane Schetky, and Elissa

Benedek, eds., Child Psychiatry and the Law. (New York: Brunner/Mazel, 1980), pp. 207–221.

56. The part of the internal world that generates wishes and impulses is termed id, and the discriminating self is called ego. The ego mediates between the world of the mind and external reality; it is the interpreter of reality. Charles Brenner, *An Elementary Textbook of Psychoanalysis* (New York: International University Press, 1955), pp. 41–67.

57. "DSM III-R Schizophrenia (295.2X–295.6X)," in *Diagnostic and Statistical Manual of Mental Disorders*, pp. 187–198.

58. "DSM III-R Mood Disorders: Bipolar Disorder (296.6X–296.5X), and Major Depression (296.2X–296x3X)," in *Diagnostic and Statistical Manual of Mental Disorders*, pp. 225–230.

59. This process becomes institutionalized in a marriage. Before marriage, one's betrothed is seen as kind and caring. The intimacy of marriage triggers the projection process, which gets imbedded in the relationship; so deeply at times, that even long after a divorce, the parent who is hypersensitive cannot tolerate talking with, much less the presence of, the supposedly critical former spouse without feeling overwhelmed by a sense of defensiveness and anger.

60. In addition, the type of faulty communication pattern employed may be related to the child's symptom pattern. Psychotic parents utilize the most extensive and florid egocentric patterns of thinking. Although the parents recognize that children, because of their relative ignorance, require a greater degree of referential communication than adults, they seem to lack the ability to utilize this understanding in developing a communication style appropriate to their child's developmental needs. Michael Chandler, Jr., Stephen Greenspan, and Carl Arenboim, "Assessment and Training of Role-Taking and Referential Communication Skills in Institutionalized Emotionally Disturbed Children," *Developmental Psychology* (1972), 10(4):546–553; Bertram Cohen, and Joseph Camhi, "Schizophrenic Performance in a Word-Communication Task," *Journal of Abnormal Psychology* (1967), 72(3):240–246; Michael J. Chandler Jr., "Role Taking, Referential Communication, and Egocentric Intrusions in Mother-Child Interactions of Children Vulnerable to Risk of Parental Psychosis," pp. 347–357, (n.j., n.d.). See also Melvin Lewis, *Clinical Aspects of Child Development*, 2d ed. (Philadelphia: Lea and Febiger, 1982), pp. 152–153.

61. *Ibid.*, p. 41.

62. To understand the impact of parental distortion on young children's ability to assess reality, one must appreciate the developmental sequences leading to adequate reality testing. Reality-based thinking occurs only after long and arduous efforts. Children who are less than six years of age may assign life to any object in the world. As time progresses, the child limits this belief to things that move, and finally to things that move spontaneously. The conviction that inanimate things

have life may continue as late as ten years of age. E. J. Anthony, "The Significance of Jean Piaget for Child Psychiatry," (n.p., n.d.), p. 27. This belief, which Piaget called "Animism," allows that any or all inanimate objects may experience emotion and may therefore represent life. J. Piaget, cited by Melvin Lewis, in *Clinical Aspects of Child Development* (Philadelphia: Lea and Febiger, 1973), pp. 40–41, Egocentrism is defined by Piaget as a child's belief that no point of view other than the child's own is possible. In contrast to "psychological egocentrism," which derives from emotional self-centeredness, cognitive egocentrism implies that the border between the self and the surrounding world is not yet fixed. At this age, the child perceives a fluid interface between reality and fantasy. Inasmuch as a self-concept is not yet clearly developed, the youngster cannot definitively differentiate between a self-perception and a perception of the world. J. Piaget, cited by Melvin Lewis in *Clinical Aspects of Child Development*, pp. 39–40, The boy or girl possesses a similarly limited ability to distinguish between his or her own thoughts and the thoughts of others. Cognitive egocentrism in the first year of life is absolute and constant but becomes relative and transient as the child goes through the preoperational period.

63. For the very young child the parent is the surrounding world. A major task of parents during the child's infancy and toddlerhood is to facilitate objective thinking in their youngster. As the infant gradually becomes aware not only of the mother's separateness but also of his or her helplessness, the fear of potential abandonment grows. A transitional object such as a teddy bear or security blanket can serve as a temporary, illusory substitute for the mother who, in her separateness, seems to threaten abandonment or loss. The belief in the illusion that the security object does not simply simulate a mother, but actually represents her, fortifies the baby's courage, allowing a survival of the reality of separate existence. D. W. Winnicott, in his book, *Mother and Child,* describes the mother anchored in "what is" rather than in "what is imagined," as willing to provide her baby an illusion as a safeguard against anxiety and fear of abandonment. D. W. Winnicott, *Mother and Child,* (New York: Basic Books, 1957), pp. 136–137. As the separation process progresses, the parent is charged with gradually reducing the infant's dependence on illusionary beliefs. The secure parent will regulate the use of transitional objects such as security blankets, allowing their use only at times of peak separation anxiety like bedtime. By insuring well-timed and smoothly progressive separation and autonomy, and by teaching the child how to measure emotional significance of various life events, a parent can promote the baby's developing ability to test reality.

64. Karl Jaspers, cited by E. James Anthony, "The Influence of Maternal Psychosis on Children: Folie á Deux," in James E. Anthony, and Therese Benedek, eds., *Parenthood: Its Psychology and Psychopathology* (Boston: Little Brown, 1970), pp. 589–590.

65. J. Spiegel, cited by E. James Anthony, "The Influence of Maternal Psychosis in Children: Fole á Deux," in Anthony Benedek, eds., *Parenthood: Its Psychology and Psychopathology*, p. 582.

66. Anthony discusses the child's conflict in dealing with a parent who possesses impaired reality testing. It centers on the opposing choices of reality and a relationship with a significant adult. To accept reality the child must renounce his or her parent, and in so doing, risk rejection. What choice is there but to embrace the parent's irrational thinking and abandon reality? James E. Anthony, "The Influence of Maternal Psychosis in Children," pp. 571–595.

67. Wallerstein and Berlin Kelly, "The Implications of the Findings," pp. 314–315.

68. John Money, Joan G. Hampson, and John L. Hampson, "Imprinting and the Establishment of Gender Role," *A.M.A. Archives of Neurology and Psychiatry* (March 1957), 77:333–336.

69. "DSM III-R Pervasive Development Disorder: Autistic Disorder (299.00)," in *Diagnostic and Statistical Manual of Mental Disorders*, pp. 33–39.

70. In his discussion of personality development, Erikson described the epigenetic principle. In essence it meant that anything which grows has a "ground plan." Out of the ground plan the parts emerge. Each part has its time of special ascendancy and growth occurs until all parts have risen to form a functioning whole. As children progress, one of the major sources of growth or elaboration of the ground plan is selective identification with significant and admired persons. Erik Erikson, *Identity Youth and Crisis* (New York: Norton, 1968), pp. 92–96.

71. By the end of adolescence all of the "senses of self," the various attributes that characterize youth, which have accumulated throughout childhood crystallize into a total "sense of self." This "sense of self" may be fragmented or it may be well integrated and consolidated: its consolidation depends in large part on whether the adolescent during various childhood developmental stages evolved senses of self that were consistent and compatible. This aggregation represents the young adult's new self-concept. It encompasses among other components, occupational, moral and sexual aspects of self. This mature identity readies the teenager to execute aspirations for fulfilling sexual relationships and a comfortable and cherished sexual identity, meaningful systems of belief, and a successful pursuit of achievement that will fit the teenager's personality style.

    Erik Erikson refers to identify formation as arising "from the selective repudiation and mutual assimilation of childhood identifications and their absorption in a new configuration." It was accrued from the confluence of the individual's natural endowment and developmental opportunity. Identity is an integrated whole which is greater than the sum of childhood indentification: children, given the proper developmental environment, have the nucleus of a separate identity early in life. Ibid. pp. 155–165.

72. As separation progresses, the infant begins to incorporate images of parents into his or her personality. By the third year, the child becomes capable of true ego identification; the unconscious adoption of those traits, beliefs, values and identity characteristics of another and the incorporated object of the other that compel emulation. Margaret S. Mahler, Fred Pine, and Anni Bergman, "The Fourth Subphase: Consolidation of Individuality and the Beginnings of Emotional Object Constancy," in *The Psychological Birth of the Human Infant* (New York: Basic Books, 1975), pp. 116–120. Ego identification only becomes possible when the young child is able to view himself or herself as sufficiently separate from the adult model, externally and internally, that parental characteristics can be distinguished as distinct from his or her own personality traits.

The development of self-concept begins during the first several months of life, as soon as separation from the principal attachment figure has begun. At the same time that parental images are being incorporated, the child is beginning to evolve a concept of self. This nascent self-image is a "place" where the child, at first indiscriminately, stores images and habitual patterns taken from principal and subsidiary attachment figures. Eventually its presence allows a transfer of the level of trust and confidence existing in adult relationships to experiences with other children.

73. A. Mavis Hetherington, "A Developmental Study of the Effects of Sex of the Dominant Parent on Sex-Role Preference, Identification, and Imitation in Children," *The Journal of Personality and Social Psychology* (1965), (2):188–194.

74. As pointed out by Nancy Chodorow, girls identify with their mothers due to their more personal relationship with them. Whereas boys, because of the "absent father" state of our society, identify more with a cultural role model. Nancy Chodorow, *The Reproduction of Mothering* (Berkeley, Los Angeles, London: University of California Press, 1978), pp. 173–177. Therefore, one can understand why their identification is influenced to a greater extent by the presence of dominance in the family.

75. As children move through latency and into adolescence, they give up a substantial degree of dependence while, at the same time, they are acquiring organizational and competitive skills.

Organization skills enable them to concentrate, to complete the academic tasks they have initiated and to become productive students. Erik Erikson, "Growth and Crises of the Healthy Personality," *Psychological Issues: Identity and the Life Cycle* (New York: International Universities Press), 1:82–88. Competitive skills help them learn to accept winning and losing graciously, to take turns, and to tolerate failure and rejection anxiety. These all contribute to an enhanced achievement orientation and can foster greater self-confidence by providing vehicles for greater socialization. Throughout this developmental phase and on through adolescence parental support is a crucial ingredient in successful progression.

76. It has been found that children who are scholastic achievers strongly identify with their same-sex parent. Their self-perceptions as measured by a checklist of adjectives were very similar to the self-perceptions of their same-sex parent. Underachievers, on the other hand, had self-perceptions very different from the self-perceptions of their same-sex parent: underachieving boys were not even similar in self-perceptions to their fathers. And finally, mothers and fathers of achieving girls tend to be in greater agreement about their perceptions of their daughters than are parents of underachieving girls. Thus, the self-perception of the child is a significant index of the identification process. If a child's achievement level correlates with an identification with a same-sex parent, and if this correlation is fortified by the existence of similar self-images in parents and high-achieving children, then one might conclude that identification with the same-sex parent serves as motivation for academic success. Perhaps this identification provides the child with a sense of continuity and self-acceptance that in turn sparks academic aspirations. C. Merville Shaw, and Donald L. White, "The Relationship Between Child-Parent Identification and Academic Underachievement," *Journal of Clinical Psychology* (1965), 21(1):10–13.

It has been demonstrated that parents who possess high level academic self-expectations and similar expectations for their children and who discuss issues with their children influence their children by fostering achievement orientation. Norma Kent and D. R. Davis, cited by Marjorie Honzik, "Environmental Correlates of Mental Growth: Prediction from the Family Setting at 21 Months," *Child Development* (1967), 38(2):360–361; Jerome Kagen, and Marian Freeman, "Relation of Childhood Intelligence, Maternal Behaviors, and Social Class to Behavior During Adolescence," *Child Development* (1963), 34:902–911. Crucial to this process is the presence of nurturance and friendliness on the part of parents to each other and to their children. Of particular note is the importance of paternal nurturance and warmth to the intellectual functioning of boys. H. A. Moss, and J. Kagen, cited by Marjorie Honzik, "Environmental Correlates of Mental Growth," pp. 353–359; Norma Radin, "Observed Paternal Behaviors as Antecedents of Intellectual Functioning in Young Boys, *Developmental Psychology* (1973), 8(3):372–376; Norma Radin, "Father-Child Interaction and the Intellectual Functioning of Four-Year-Old Boys," *Developmental Psychology* (1972), 6(2):357–361; Bonnie E. Jordan, Norma Radin, and Ann Epstein, "Paternal Behavior and Intellectual Functioning in Preschool Boys and Girls," *Developmental Psychology* (1975), 11(3):407–

408. As important as the same-sexed parent is to the cognitive development of children, one must keep in mind that the opposite-sex parent has some influence as well. Elizabeth Bing, "Effect of Child-Rearing Practices on Development of Differential Cognitive Abilities," *Child Development* (1963), 34:631–648.

The absence of the same-sexed parent, physically or emotionally, could inhibit intellectual striving. Indeed in a study of the correlation between availability of fathers and the academic performance of third-grade boys, Blanchard and Biller concluded that those boys whose fathers were present and involved achieved significantly more than boys whose fathers left when the child was an average of nine months old, boys whose fathers left when the child was an average of five years and four months old, and those boys whose fathers were present but unavailable. Early age father-absent boys suffered the most in the classroom, while the later age father-absent boys and the low availability father-present boys suffered to approximately the same degree. The younger the child when the absence occurs, the greater will be the effect. Robert W. Blanchard and Henry B. Biller, "Father Availability and Academic Performance Among Third-Grade Boys," *Developmental Psychology* (1969), 4(3):301–305. However, if the remaining parent is nurturing and supportive of educational pursuit, the deterioration of scholastic performance can certainly be decreased if not reversed.

It should be noted that father-absence impacts girls substantially at a sensitive developmental period as well. F. Landy, B. G. Rosenberg, and B. Sutton-Smith, "The Effect of Limited Father-Absence on Cognitive Development," *Child Development* (1969), 40-941–944.

The encouragement of independence and autonomy and treating the child in an egalitarian fashion also promoted achievement in children whereas domination and autocratic parenting stifled exploration and intellectual interests. M. L. Goldschmid, cited by Norma Radin, "Observed Paternal Behaviors as Antecedents of Intellectual Functioning in Young Boys," p. 375; Charles E. Bowerman, and Glen E. Elder, Jr., "Variations in Adolescent Perceptions of Family Power Structure," *American Sociological Review* (1964), 29:551–567.

As one might expect, maternal overprotection and excessive control dampens adaptive thinking while active involvement on the part of fathers and a moderate amount of control suport intellectual adaptability. Ruth B. Dyk, and Herman A. Witkin, "Family Experiences Related to the Development of Differentiation in Children," *Child Development* (1965), 36:52; Thomas V. Busse, "Child Rearing Antecedents of Flexible Thinking," *Developmental Psychology* (1969), 1:585–591.

In summary one can say that the most positive atmosphere for the development of academic achievement in children is one in which they have an opportunity to identify with a same-sexed parent, or even an opposite-sexed parent, who possesses a good self-image in the area of achievement, who is warm and nurturing, encourages the child to become autonomous in a healthy fashion, and who is ultimately available to that child.

77. Erik Erikson, *Psychological Issues: Identity and the Life Cycle* (New York: International Universities Press, 1959), 1:129–132.

78. At different stages of the child's development, the healthy parent may use different disciplinary methods, according to the appropriate application of the "good-enough" parenting principle. These might include power techniques such as physical punishment and material deprivation as well as nonpower assertive techniques such as "love-withdrawal" and "induction." It should be remembered that while power assertive techniques return the parent-child system to equilibrium, its impact on the child's self-control occurs primarily through intimidation. Martin L. Hoffman, and Herbert D. Saltzstein, "Parent Discipline and the Child's Moral Development," *Journal of Personality and Social Psychology* (1967), 5(1):45–57. At times, power assertive discipline may only partly be motivated toward helping the child develop socially responsible behaviors. A primary aim might be to allow the adult to rapidly dissipate anger. When this is true, it, in turn, encourages the child to express his or her own anger. Joan McCord, William McCord, and Alan Howard, "Family Interaction as Antecedent to the Direction of Male Aggressiveness," *Journal of Abnormal and Social Psychology* (1962), 66(3):239–242.

In contrast "love-withdrawal" or parental disapproval will often facilitate healthy guilt production through intensifying the child's efforts to identify with the parent in order to insure the parent's love. R. R. Sears, E. E. Maccoby, and H. Levin, cited by Hoffman and Saltzstein, "Parent Discipline and the Child's Moral Development," pp. 45–57. When utilizing love-withdrawal, sometimes the discipline is terminated when the child engages in a corrective action such as confession or reparation. W. F. Hill, cited by Hoffman and Saltzstein, "Parent Discipline and the Child's Moral Development," pp. 45–57.

It must be stressed that "love-withdrawal" or parental disapproval will be effective in the development of conscience formation in children primarily when it represents a combination of warmth and affection coupled with the willingness to apply discipline when needed in the same parent. Robert W. Moulton, Paul G. Liberty, Jr., Eugene Burnstein, and Nathan Altucher, "Patterning of Parental Affection and Disciplinary Dominance as a Determinant of Guilt and Sex Typing," *Journal of Personality and Social Psychology* (1966), 4(4):356–363. Actually "love-withdrawal" implies that a loving parent has become angry; therefore, it may appear to a young child that love has been withdrawn. In addition conscience development is highly contingent upon an identification with parents, and for boys, in particular, perhaps the availability of a father figure. Stephanie P. Weisproth, "Moral Judgment, Sex, and

Parental Identification in Adults," *Developmental Psychology* (1970), 2(3):396–402; Martin L. Hoffman, "Father Absence and Conscience Formation," *Developmental Psychology* (1971), 4(3):400–406. Naturally, as is the case in other areas of development, the presence of a healthy mother figure in a single parent family can promote more than adequate conscience development.

Thus, the parent, who brings a limited degree of anger and frustration to situations where the child engages in repeated misconduct, can lead the youngster to take the situation more seriously. In this instance it is crucial that the parent reprimand the boy or girl by focusing on the child's behavior rather than his or her character. The statement "what you did was wrong" tells the youngster that the act was wrong but simultaneously implies that the child is acceptable. This is in contrast to calling the child a "bad boy" or "bad girl," which personalizes the wrongful character of the act and implies that such a child is incapable of being good. Limited and controlled expressions of adult anger are to be distinguished not only from uncontrolled venting of anger but also from "guilt tripping." This is a manipulative act wherein an adult imposes obedience through a threatened loss of love or acceptance. The enormity of the threat is of such magnitude that it leads to suppression of self-scrutiny: The child learns nothing but fear from the episode.

79. Perhaps the most sophisticated form of discipline involves the technique of induction. This constitutes enlightening the child as to the effect of misbehavior on others, particularly upon those who may have been victimized by his or her acts. Through this means the parent elicits and encourages the growth of the child's empathy. Its use implies that the youngster already has the capacity to experience some form of empathy and can appreciate the wrongfulness of certain misconduct. Hoffman and Saltzstein, "Parent Discipline and the Child's Moral Development," pp. 45–57.

80. In his discussion of morality, Kohlberg describes three levels: Preconventional, Conventional, and Post-Conventional morality. The individual functioning with preconventional morality has a sense of good and bad but interprets the designation in terms of unpleasant or pleasurable consequences: punishment, reward, or exchange of favors. At the conventional level, a person realizes that the maintenance of family, group, or national standards are valuable in their own right regardless of immediate consequences. Post-conventional ethical functioning contains all-encompassing principals of justice, human rights, equality, and respect for human beings as individual persons. Lawrence Kohlberg, "The Development of Children's Orientation Toward a Moral Order: I. Sequence in the Development of Moral Thought," *Vita Humana* (1963), 6:11–33.

81. A sound identity is also a growing identity. Throughout our lives, self-concept change is both possible and desirable. As we advance from one

phase of adulthood to another, we face new tasks which require new views of ourselves. If, for example, one moves from adolescence into young adulthood, taking on the responsibility of parenthood, it is important to see oneself as a leader and not simply as a group participant. Erik Erikson, "Psychological Issues: Identity and Life Cycle," *Growth Crises of the Healthy Personality*, 1:95–100.

82. Wallerstein and Kelly, "The Implications of the Findings," pp. 307–308 in *Surviving the Breakup*.

83. Richard Green. "The Best Interest of the Child with a Lesbian Mother," *Bulletin of the AAPL* (1982), 10(1):7–15.

84. Boys and girls both begin life fused with a principal attachment figure who is that infant's first love object: in almost all instances that person is the mother. She is likewise the major source of early identification. As time progresses and separation occurs, according to psychoanalytic theory boys sustain their mothers as their object of love but switch to their fathers as objects of identification, presuming development is normal. Girls do just the opposite.

Robert Stoller offers this point of view regarding the development of sexual identity in children. Both boys and girls begin life in an intimate merger with their mother, to the point where the child doesn't know where the mother ends and where he or she begins. Continuing, Stoller points out that, contrary to Freudian assumption, gender identity in boys doesn't begin with heretosexuality or "the triumph of the penis."

Freud had posited that boys started life heretosexual whereas girls must overcome primary homosexuality. As Stoller views the matter, in order to make the step toward identification with the father, the boy must first separate his identity from that of his mother: this leaves his masculinity vulnerable.

This may begin to account for the fact that men are overtly perverse far more often than are women and are so (relatively) sensitive to threats to their manhood. The sensitivity may drive from the marked intimacy between mother and infant which, even if minimal, leaves behind a trace of uncertainty that one's masculine identity is intact. This suggests that masculinity in males may not be quite as absolute and stable a state as Freud suggested, putting his theory of development of masculinity and feminity in doubt.

If a male infant has too intimate a relationship with his mother, her body, and psyche, and if she tried to maintain that intimacy indefinitely in an ambiance devoid of trauma or frustration, he will fail to separate from her body and psyche in the manner boys usually do. As a result, he is feminine from the start. The less these factors are present, the less feminine he will be. In what is called normal masculinity, these factors should be minimal. If there is no intimacy between mother and infant, there are risks of "excessive masculinity," the so-called phallic char-

acter. Robert J. Stoller, "Disorders of Masculinity and Feminity," in *The Basic Handbook of Child Psychiatry*, 2:542–546.
Regardless of how sexual identity begins, by two and one-half to four years of age, the basic structure of gender identity has developed. However, sexual identity will continue to evolve throughout childhood and adolescence. Gender identity is only one of its components. Defined it represents that part of the identity concerned with masculinity and femininity. It is conceptualized as the intricate balance of masculinity and feminity in children, and at least initially, it is based on the assignment to a given sex according to anatomical distinctions. Christoph M. Heinicke, "Development from Two and One-half to Four Years," in *The Basic Handbook of Child Psychiatry*, 1:172–173. Other components of sexual identity include role and preference. Gender-role behavior refers to the dimorphic behaviors considered masculine or feminine; whereas sexual preference or sexual partner orientation dictates the selection of a particular gender or both genders as preferred sexual objects. Richard Green, "Sexual Identity of 37 Children Raised by Homosexual or Transsexual Parents." Am. J. Psychiatry (1978), 135(6):692–697.

85. Richard Green, "Atypical Sex-role Behavior," in *The Basic Handbook of Child Psychiatry*, 2:535–536. Johanna H. Milic, and Douglas P. Crowne, "Recalled Parent-Child Relations and Need for Approval of Homosexual and Heterosexual Men," *Archives of Sexual Behavior* (1986), 15(3):243–245.
86. Richard Green, "Atypical" pp. 530–533. R. Green, W. Roberts, K. Williams, M. Goodman, and A. Mixon, "Specific Cross-Gender Behavior in Boyhood and Later Homosexual Orientation" *British Journal of Psychiatry* (1987), 151:84–88.
87. Robert J. Stoller, "Etiological Factors in Female Transsexualism: A First Approximation," *Archives of Sexual Behavior* (1972), 2(1):47–64.
88. Martha Kirkpatrick, Catherine Smith, and Ron Roy, "Lesbian Mothers and their Children: A Comparative Survey," *American Journal of Orthopsychiatry* (1981), 51(3):545–551; Beverly, Hoeffer, "Children's Acquisition of Sex-Role Behavior in Lesbian-Mother Families, *American Journal of Orthopsychiatry* (July 1981), 51(3):536–544; David J. Kleber, Robert J. Howell, and Alta Lura Tibbits-Kleber, "The Impact of Parental Homosexuality in Child Custody Cases: A Review of the Literature," *Bulletin of the American Academy of Psychiatry and Law* (1986), 14(1):81–87.
89. F. W. Bozett Gay Fathers: Evolution of the gay-father Identity *Am. J. Orthopsychiatry* (1981), 51:552–559.
90. Richard Green "Best Interests," pp. 7–15.
91. Kleber, Howell, and Tibbets-Kleber, pp. 81–87.
92. Richard Gardner, "Interviews with the Parents," in *Family Evaluation*

in Child Custody Litigation, pp. 137–143, (Cresskill, N.J.: Creative Therapeutics, 1982).

7. Child Evaluation

1. Richard L. Cohen and Joseph D. Noshpitz, eds., *Basic Handbook of Child Psychiatry* (New York: Basic Books, 1979), 1:547–551.
2. Cohen, "Examination of the Infant and Toddler," pp. 509–529.
3. Richard Gardner, *Family Evaluation in Child Custody Litigation,* (Cresskill, N.J.: Creative Therapeutics, 1982).
4. Richard Cohen, "Note on Speicial Considerations in Evaluation of a Child in Connection with Court Proceedings," in Joseph D. Noshpitz, ed., *Basic Handbook of Child Psychiatry,* 1:654–655.
5. J. D. Goodman, and J. Sours, *The Child Mental Status Examination* (New York: Basic Books, 1967), n.p.; Richard L. Cohen, "The Clinical Examination," in Joseph D. Noshpitz, ed., *Basic Handbook of Child Psychiatry* (New York: Basic Books, 1979), 1:505–508; Joseph, Marcus, "Examination of the Infant and Toddler," in Noshpitz, ed., *Basic Handbook of Child Psychiatry,* 1:509–529; Richard L. Cohen, "Examination of the Preschool and School-Age Child," in Noshpitz, ed., *Basic Handbook of Child Psychiatry,* 1:529–547; Richard L. Cohen, "Special Considerations in the Examination of Adolescents," in Noshpitz, ed., *Basic Handbook of Child Psychiatry,* 1:547–550; James E. Simmons, *Psychiatric Examination of Children,* 2d ed. (Philadelphia: Lea and Febiger, 1974); Stanley I. Greenspan, *The Clinical Interview of the Child* (New York: McGraw-Hill, 1981);
6. "DSM III-R Attention-deficit Hyperactivity Disorder (314.01)," *Diagnostic and Statistical Manual of Mental Disorders,* 3d ed., rev. (Washington, D.C.: American Psychiatric Association, 1987), pp. 50–53.
7. "DSM III-R Developmental Articulation Disorder (315.39)," *Diagnostic and Statistical Manual of Mental Disorders,* 3d ed., rev. (Washington, D.C.: American Psychiatric Association, 1987), pp. 44–45.
8. James Simmons, p. 37.
9. Elissa P. Benedek, and Diane H. Schetky, "Problems in Validating Allegations of Sexual Abuse. Part 1: Factors Affecting Perception and Recall of Events." *The Journal of the American Academy of Child and Adolescent Psychiatry* (1987), 26(6):912–915.
10. Melvin Lewis, "Cognitive Development," *Clinical Aspects of Child Development,* 2d ed. (Philadelphia: Lea and Febiger, 1982), pp. 35–41.
11. Cohen, "The Clinical Examination," p. 505.
12. Richard Gardner, "Evaluation of the Children," in *Family Evaluation in Child Custody Litigation* (Cresskill, N.J.: Creative Therapeutics, 1982), pp. 156–158.

13. Cohen, "Examination of the Preschool and School-Age Child," pp. 543–544.
14. Gardner, pp. 181–194.
15. Cohen, "Examination of the Preschool and School-Age Child," p. 540.
16. Joseph Goldstein, Anna Freud, and Albert J. Solnit, "On the Least Detrimental Alternative," in *Beyond the Best Interests of the Child,* (New York: Free Press, 1973), p. 53
17. Richard Cohen "Examination of the Infant and Toddler," pp. 509–529.
18. John Bowlby, "A Control Systems Approach to Attachment Behavior," in *Attachment and Loss,* (New York: Basic Books, 1969), 1:235–262.
19. Richard Gardner, *Family Evaluation,* pp. 143–146.
20. Albert J. Solnit, "Psychosexual Development: Three to Five Years," in Joseph D. Noshpitz, ed., *Basic Handbook of Child Psychiatry* (New York: Basic Books, 1979), 1:180–182; Albert J. Solnit, Justin D. Call, and Carl B. Feinstein, "Psychosexual Development: Five to Ten Years," in *Basic Handbook of Child Psychiatry,* 1:184–186.
21. Goldstein, Freud, and Solnit, pp. 17–20.
22. Anna Freud, "Identification with the Aggressor," in *The Ego and the Mechanisms of Defense* (New York: International Universities Press, 1946), pp. 117–131.
23. C. Janet Newman and Jeffrey S. Schwam, "The Fatherless Child" in Noshpitz, ed., *Basic Handbook of Child Psychiatry,* (New York: Basic Books, 1979), 1:368.
24. Simmons, pp. 46–47.
25. Gardner, pp. 171–175.
26. Judith S. Wallerstein and Joan Berlin Kelly, "The Implication of the Findings," *Surviving the Breakup: How Children and Parents Cope with Divorce* (New York: Basic Books, 1980), pp. 314–315.
27. Goldstein, Freud, and Solnit, pp. 17–22.

9. Healthy Separation

1. Monthly Vital Statistics Report (DHHS) Pub. 33-11. Washington, D.C. Government Printing Office. National Center for Health Statistics Publication of 1985.
2. C. Janet Newman, and Jeffrey S. Schwam, "The Fatherless Child," in Joseph D. Noshpitz, ed., *Basic Handbook of Child Psychiatry* (New York: Basic Books, 1979), pp. 361–363.
3. Sigmund Freud, "Mourning and Melancholia," in *Collected Papers.* Vol. IV, (London: Hogarth Press and Institute of Psycho-Analysis, 1953), 4:152–170.
4. Gertrude Blanck, and Rubin Blanck, "Normal Narcissism," in *Ego Psy-*

chology II (New York: Columbia University Press, 1979), pp. 50—63.

5. Freud, "Mourning and Melancholia," pp. 152—170.

6. Actually, love is characterized by a state of affection, warmth, and romance that emanates from a person who has reached the level of maturity wherein a steady and stable emotional commitment to another can be sustained because of a high level of self-worth and self-value therefore the emotional investment can be empathetic and based on the other's intrinsic worth and not on how much the other person is satisfying the needs of the first person. Heinz Hartmann, cited by Gertrude Blanck and Rubin Blanck, "Marriage and Personal Development" in *Object Relations* (New York: Columbia University Press, 1968), p. 68.

7. Wallerstein and Kelly, "The Implications of the Findings," *Surviving the Breakup,* pp. 306—307.

8. Wallerstein and Kelly, "How the Children Responded," in *Surviving the Breakup: How Children and Parents Cope with Divorce* (New York: Basic Books, 1980), pp. 55—95.

9. Wallerstein and Kelly, "Father-Child Relationships at Five Years," *Surviving the Breakup,* p. 248.

10. Joseph Goldstein, Anna Freud, and Albert J. Solnit, "On Continuity, a Child's Sense of Time, and the Limits of Both Law and Prediction," *Beyond the Best Interests of the Child* (New York: Free Press, 1973), p. 38.

11. Wallerstein and Kelly. "Children and Adolescents: The Outcome at Five Years," *Surviving the Breakup,* pp. 206—234.

12. Select Committee on Children Youth and Families or the United States House of Representatives. *U.S. Children and their families: Parent Conditions and Recent Trends.*

13. Paul C. Glick, "Children of Divorced Parents in Demographic Perspective," *Journal of Social Issues.* (1979) 35:112—125.

14. Wallerstein and Kelly, *Surviving the Breakup,* pp. 215—224.

15. *Ibid.,* pp. 209—210.

16. Anna Freud, "Identification with the Aggressor," in *The Ego and the Mechanisms of Defense,* (New York: International Universities Press, 1946), pp. 128—129.

Index